PRAISE FOR

Memories
THE AUTOBIOGRAPHY OF
RALPH EMERY

"THE INSIDE SCOOP ON SUCH STARS AS JOHNNY CASH, DOLLY PARTON, TEX RITTER, AND LORETTA LYNN. . . . Mr. Emery, who comes across as folksy, humble, and downright likeable, led a life that would have been perfect fodder for one of the songs he once played as the voice of country radio."
—*The New York Times Book Review*

"*MEMORIES* IS ENTERTAINING . . . INSIGHTFUL . . . CONVERSATIONAL . . . RICH IN ANECDOTES . . . A REAL STORY."
—*Wichita Eagle*

"I don't think there's anybody in country music that Ralph doesn't know. . . . You'll feel like you know these folks and Ralph himself after you read this book."
—Randy Travis

"*MEMORIES* IS A FASCINATING ADDITION TO COUNTRY MUSIC HISTORY."
—*Billboard*

A Literary Guild Alternate Selection

"Nashville's top talker takes a chance on truth. . . . The revelations in *MEMORIES* are surprising. . . . "

—*Chicago Tribune*

"A lot of people saw me for the first time on the *Ralph Emery Show*. He helped me at a time when I needed it the most. I haven't forgotten that. Thanks, Ralph!"

—Dolly Parton

"You don't have to be booked on his show [*Nashville Now*] to get on—you can just drop by . . . that's the wonderful thing about Ralph's appeal. . . . He's been helping entertainers build their careers that way for years."

—Kenny Rogers

". . . the most honest book . . . ever written by a country music personality."

—Jimmy Dean

"Ralph Emery has made a great contribution to American life."

—President George Bush

"No man in America has affected country music more. . . . Ralph Emery was the first person to bring dignity and education to country music radio. . . . He is one of country music's best-kept secrets."

—Johnny Cash

"A THOROUGHLY ENGAGING AND DE-LIGHTFULLY CANDID AUTOBIOGRAPHY.
. . . Emery is an insider, and his unvarnished takes on, among others, Patsy Cline, Hank Williams, Jr., Johnny Cash, Dolly Parton, and Keith Whitley are fresh and interesting. Emery's chapter on Merle Haggard . . . is worth the price of the book. . . . A fine outing for students of American lives and lovers of country music alike."

—*Kirkus Reviews*

"There is no greater authority in country music. Some of my fondest reminiscences have been with my dear friend Ralph Emery."

—Chet Atkins

"DREAMS CAN COME TRUE, AND RALPH EMERY IS LIVING PROOF. . . . *MEMORIES* is a down-home, easygoing autobiography. . . . a comfortable memoir. . . ."

—*Library Journal*

Most Pocket Books are available at special quantity discounts for bulk purchases for sales promotions, premiums or fund raising. Special books or book excerpts can also be created to fit specific needs.

For details write the office of the Vice President of Special Markets, Pocket Books, 1230 Avenue of the Americas, New York, New York 10020.

Memories

THE AUTOBIOGRAPHY OF
RALPH EMERY

*The moving
true story of
a country
music legend.*

WITH **TOM CARTER**

POCKET BOOKS

New York   London   Toronto   Sydney   Tokyo   Singapore

The sale of this book without its cover is unauthorized. If you purchased
this book without a cover, you should be aware that it was reported to
the publisher as "unsold and destroyed." Neither the author nor the publisher has received payment for the sale of this "stripped book."

POCKET BOOKS, a division of Simon & Schuster Inc.
1230 Avenue of the Americas, New York, NY 10020

Copyright © 1991, 1992 by Ralph Emery

Published by arrangement with Macmillan Publishing Company

All rights reserved, including the right to reproduce
this book or portions thereof in any form whatsoever.
For information address: Macmillan Publishing Company
866 Third Avenue, New York, NY 10022

ISBN: 0-671-79157-5

First Pocket Books printing November 1992

10 9 8 7 6 5 4 3 2 1

POCKET and colophon are registered trademarks of
Simon & Schuster Inc.

Cover photo by Jim Hagan

Printed in the U.S.A.

To Joy,
the wind beneath my wings.

Acknowledgments

I would like to thank Tom Carter, who believed in this book when I didn't.

I would like to thank the ladies in my office, Terry Schaefer, Angie Wallace, and Teresa Shelly, who spent countless hours transcribing the tape-recorded notes for this book.

I would like to thank my wife, Joy, who was a great help in editing parts of the book and was also a wonderful source of information. Her memory for dates and places is incredible.

A note of gratitude to Frances Preston, president of BMI, for the story about Roy Acuff/Tex Ritter at the CMA board meeting in Palm Springs, California.

I would like to thank Bud Wendell, president and CEO, Opryland USA, Inc., and all the people connected with the Nashville Network, WSM Radio, WSM Television (which later became WSMV Television under the direction of Mike Kettenring) for placing me in a position to meet and work with so many of the people that you are going to read about in this book.

Also, thanks to my mother, who persevered through many hard times in her early life, and who finally found happiness with Paul Everette, to whom she has been married for the past forty years. I would also like to thank my mother for providing me with my baby book, which I had never seen, and subsequently giving me a new source of information through her carefully kept records.

I am also appreciative of the information about the Fuqua and Emery families provided by my aunt Lorraine Cusick.

A book like this would be impossible without the contributions of the many people that I work with on a daily basis. Therefore, I would like to tip my hat to the cast and crew of both *Nashville Now* and *The Ralph Emery Show*, plus the countless entertainers, musicians, writers, producers, and directors with whom I have had the pleasure of working over the past forty years.

Finally, for their encouragement, a note of appreciation to Jerry Whitehurst, the musical director of *Nashville Now*, and to Gwen Ankenbauer and Anita Hostettler, my nightly hairdresser and makeup artist.

—Ralph Emery

Thanks to my good friend Merle Haggard for his sensitive lyrics for "Every Fool Has a Rainbow," quoted on page 194.

—RE

Foreword

I have participated in many television shows that were laced with delays but this one was ridiculous. I had been asked to record a new opening for a prime-time program for the Nashville Network, but the engineer who was to record me had no tape for his machine. Videotaping was scheduled to begin in ten minutes in the Grand Ole Opry House, where seventy-five celebrities were waiting. The cast was billed as the largest ever assembled in country music history.

Meanwhile, the engineer kept fumbling.

It was February 1990, and the show had been plagued with preproduction glitches. Barbara Mandrell, its executive producer, had asked me to appear in October 1989 and had brought it up again the following December in Aspen, Colorado, during an annual ski outing involving her family and mine.

Barbara is one of the most effective people I've ever met so I suspected nothing as she dotted every "i" and crossed every "t," planning the program. Less than a month before the production date, she grew dissatisfied with one part of the script and asked me to rewrite it. I spent a Sunday afternoon in my office rummaging through old photograph albums and doing other research for a laborious rewrite that would never be used.

A week later, my annoyance at the engineer's apparent incompetence inside the "edit bay" was about to explode when the show's producer entered the sound booth.

"Ralph, we don't have time for you to do this segment now," he said. "We need to start the show, since there are a lot of stars waiting. Do you suppose you could come back tomorrow afternoon and record the opening?"

"Sure," I said, mildly annoyed, and went out into the Grand Ole Opry House to act as emcee.

The house lights fell, the videotape rolled, and Johnny Cash kicked into an adaptation of "Get Rhythm." He blew his lines and taping was resumed twice. Barbara tried to do a number, messed it up, and the cameras were again rerolled.

The opening songs were completed, I walked to stage right, read my lines, and was about to exit. I had to prepare for other duties that night relating to an "All-Star Salute to Country Music."

Just then on stage, Cash gripped my arm.

"You're not going anywhere," he whispered.

"What's going on with this crazy show?" I thought to myself. "I'm not supposed to still be on stage, that's not in the script."

I surmised that the schedule was tight, as they often are on variety shows, and guessed that Cash, Barbara, and I were going to abandon the script and ad lib the opening. That was fine with me. But there was no pause in production and the cameras kept mysteriously rolling.

Barbara eased to the front of the stage and announced, "Ladies and gentlemen, Ralph thinks this is an 'All-Star Salute to Country Music.' But tonight, this is the 'All-Star Salute to Ralph Emery!' "

Everyone in the auditorium rose. I nearly fell to my knees.

For the next several hours, the golden names of country music sang while forty years' worth of films and photographs of celebrities with Ralph Emery were projected on a giant screen. There were even videotaped congratulations from President George Bush.

I was overwhelmed by it all, sitting in an easy chair that had been wheeled to center stage. There had been one other time in my life when I sat alone before thousands of people in the center of the stage of the Mother Church of Country Music. That was in 1972, inside the old Grand Ole Opry House in downtown Nashville where I held my last production of WSM's all-night show, the program that became a staple of American broadcasting and catapulted me to everything wonderful that has since happened in my career.

In February 1990 I had gone to unusual lengths to prepare for a show whose title had been a ruse. I even attended a "mock" rehearsal two days before the production date. I never knew the secret until it was publicly announced, although it had been common knowledge in the country music industry for weeks. Many fans even had been let in on the charade.

I saw my wife, Joy, in the audience, next to my eldest son, Steve, who was supposed to be in Boston. My mother, and Mike and Kit, my two other sons, and my grandkids were also on hand.

I was filled to overflowing with emotion when the surprise was sprung, and it happened a second time when Barbara sat on my lap and sang. She had worked tirelessly to put the tribute together for a program that would eventually air across North America for two hours on the Nashville Network.

There were artists in that cast who commanded seventy-five thousand dollars per show. They stayed, free of charge, until 2:00 A.M. to videotape the tribute. I am eternally grateful.

Watching the show unfold as thousands in the live audience did the same, my mind was a mixture of free-association emotions. I couldn't help thinking how my career was the American dream come true. I had been born fifty-six miles west of Nashville in modest beginnings amid paternal deficiencies. I never played an instrument, wrote a song, or sang in any serious way. Yet I have had a show business career that has lasted forty years and twice taken me to the White House, as well as to the premiere show rooms of Las Vegas, and given me my own network television show offered to 55 million households.

The career happened without a background in dramatics and flew in the face of some serious inferiority complexes I had.

The first time I ever heard country music was on a battery-operated radio inside one of my grandparents' houses in McEwen, Tennessee. No one in that largely impoverished farming community shortly after the depression could have predicted that country music would rise to international popularity or that I'd go along for the ride.

It's been a glorious career that, I hope, will continue indefinitely. If it ends tomorrow, well, I've already lived ten lifetimes in one. I've forgotten more memories than many men make.

And in the words of my late friend, Marty Robbins, "Some Memories Just Won't Die." Some memories that will never die for me nearly killed me in their making. At times, this book was exceedingly difficult to write. At other times, this life has been difficult to live.

Come with me now into the world of my memories.

Memories

...1...

T HE STAGGERING DRUNK THREATENED TO USE HIS FISTS
and I eased slowly out of his range. He was furious because
I'd suggested he'd consumed too much.

"Get away from me," he said, and belted down more
liquor. He renewed his aggression and I thought at least
one of his blows would connect. I was angry and I wanted
to knock this obnoxious foe on his butt.

But I couldn't bring myself to hit my dad.

When I was twenty-two, I returned to my hometown of
McEwen, Tennessee, to attend my grandmother Emery's
funeral. I tried to fetch my dad from a tavern the night
before his mother was laid to rest.

"Let's go, Dad," I said. "Tomorrow is your mother's
funeral, and you want to be in good shape."

"Get away from me!" he bellowed.

The more I persisted, the more he threw fists.

I walked out of the tavern, and said to hell with him.
Miraculously, he showed up at her funeral, where he didn't
drink during the entire service.

My earliest recollections have to do with his boozing.
The first is the uncontrollable spinning of colors. I can recall the vivid hues that filled my toy box, and their motion
when I fell headlong into the container.

I was pushed by my dad, who was falling on me. My eyes trained on my toy box, whose whirling shades were rising rapidly from the floor to smack me in the face.

I was three and that was the only time my dad's drunkenness nearly killed me. It was not the only time it broke my heart.

My mother and I had followed my father to Akron, Ohio, where he had gone to work with his brothers in the rubber factories. Most boys that young see their fathers as their whole world. For a split second, the weight of that world almost physically collapsed on my twenty-five pounds. I darted away, escaping what would have been his pin.

I would, throughout my childhood, carry the psychological load of not having a dad, just a biological father. I think it would have been easier not knowing who he was. Instead, I lived with what he did, and didn't do.

He did drink to excess. He didn't—I feel—care about me.

As a small child in Akron, I walked with adults and kept my eyes on the sidewalk, searching for Beechnut tobacco packages that bore the trademarked emblem of a rising sun. I had often seen my father scoop tobacco from those colorful containers and I just assumed that he was the only man in the world who chewed Beechnut. My search for the packages was, I guess, an indirect search for my father.

"My daddy's been here!" I'd exclaim, when I saw one of the pouches.

The fact that the containers didn't always belong to him never dawned on me.

Adults quickly changed the subject whenever I begged to go find my daddy. They would steer me off the Beechnut trail. They didn't want to discuss then what I rarely discuss now.

My father, at twenty-eight, was a hopeless alcoholic.

It pains me to say that, but I have to be as honest about the negative aspects of my life as I am about the positive.

My dad has never remembered one Christmas or a birthday of mine. He has missed 114 times.

He would disappear, often for as long as seven years, then mysteriously reappear for a few days, only to vanish again for the better part of another decade. When I was old enough to understand what was meant by a "town drunk," I understood that one of those folks was my dad.

I had no brothers or sisters. I was lonely and didn't know it. I later realized this truth and wondered if I would ever know anything but endless solitude. My mother had an early nervous disorder that eventually caused her complete breakdown. My father was no more than a drunken ghost, always intoxicated and invisible to me. I won't mince words. The relationship with him was so sparse that love never developed. I have no feeling for him today.

Following the Akron years, I lived much of my childhood in Nashville. When I was four, my parents divorced and I moved to McEwen to live with my grandparents. My mother was working in Nashville and had no time to take care of me. At the age of seven, I was returned the fifty-six miles to Nashville where my mother was a waitress. I commuted to McEwen on weekends and during summer vacations, for alternate stays with my maternal and paternal grandparents. After I turned seven, my address and body were usually in Nashville. Until I became a teenager, my heart was in McEwen. There I had grandparents and a country boy's life, wholesome and free. In Nashville, I was alone for hours while my mother hustled for tips in hotel coffee shops. She realized that this work was a dead end and enrolled in secretarial school and eventually worked for a plumbing company.

In retrospect, I don't know why my parents ever married. Both were high-strung, and then there was my father's drinking. My maternal grandmother Fuqua was against the courtship and forbade it. The Emery boys had reputations as being tough and unruly, but my mother didn't listen to her mother. One day my mother came home with her boyfriend in tow. She previously had sneaked out to meet him. On this day, in 1932, she brought him home and told Grandma Fuqua that she would grow to like him. She told her he wasn't really a bad man. She then told her she had married him the previous night.

Grandmother's wails followed the announcement, but they were not as piercing as my mother's subsequent cries during her tumultuous marriage to my alcoholic father.

Before he began to roam, he was often arrested. I'd overhear my uncles discuss having to get him out of jail. I'd hear them talk about how much they disliked their own kin, calling him obnoxious. The word cut me deeply.

By the time I was ready for school I realized that everyone in tiny McEwen knew who and what my dad was, and they knew I was his son. I was embarrassed—and ashamed that I was embarrassed about my own dad. Even then, I began to block him out.

There were nights in my Fuqua grandparents' house when the aroma of honeysuckle drifted through screened windows to lullabies of buzzing June bugs. Everything was as natural as it was tranquil. Across town, at my Emery grandparents' house, nature's spell was often broken with the thud of uncertain footsteps on the wooden porch.

My grandmother Emery bolted from bed to turn on the light. Loud and slurred rantings came from the after-dark intruder at her door. She hoped that it was my dad and that he was safe.

He always was.

My grandmother would coddle him, helping him to a bedroom and out of his clothes. The nightly scenario happened far from my own peaceful bed, and I pulled the covers over my head more for shelter than warmth.

"Why does Daddy drink?" I'd whisper beneath the linens. Then I'd roll over and wish that he was like other dads.

But he never was.

His disappearances lasted well into my adulthood. I kidded myself, thinking that time in the military during World War II had made him a better man. I'd heard adults say things like "the Army has been good for him" and "the Army is the only place he ever amounted to anything."

MEMORIES

.I was overly optimistic the day I met him at the McEwen bus station following his military discharge. Actually, there were three of us who met him: his buddy, a bottle—and me.

One was left behind.

My dad got off the bus and got into the liquor. His homecoming, which I had envisioned as special, was just another routine drunk for him. He and his pal went off somewhere for days. I went to my grandparents' house and stared at walls for what seemed like weeks.

After I had begun my broadcast career, a lawyer friend called to say my dad was in jail. "And," he added, "he can't take care of himself anymore. It's time we got him off the street."

My dad never remarried after my mother divorced him in 1937. He gave his whole life to the bottle and the bottle gave destitution to him. Today he lives in a nursing home in Smyrna, Tennessee.

I don't see him, as his mind is gone, and he doesn't know me.

He gets some kind of military pension or government stipend and it is sent to my office. I've never looked at the checks. My secretary applies the funds directly to the cost of his care.

My dad is up in years and low on health. I don't know when he'll leave this world. In a way, I'm no more than a stranger to him. At times, he doesn't remember me at all. Other times, he only remembers my childhood. I think that after forty years of drinking, the alcohol has atrophied his brain.

Some years ago, he was admitted to a rest facility. He was settled for the first time in years. It was a beginning.

I didn't find out he was there until after he was out. I might have gone to see him. Hospital officials said they evicted the old man for rules violations after catching him with an open, and empty, bottle of whiskey.

...2...

IN THE 1930S AND 1940S, EVERY BARBER SHOP IN AMERICA seemingly had them: picture calendars portraying country boyhood. Each page depicted an outdoor scene of a tow-headed lad with bare feet, bib overalls, and big freckles. Month after month the kid carried a giant bass and a cane pole, or was awe-stricken because his beagle wouldn't budge from a hollow log into which it had chased a rabbit.

You could look at those renderings and hear the dog's excited barks, or smell the fish. The scenes, drawn from pretelevision America, were as innocent as a southern childhood.

They were my upbringing come to life in McEwen, Tennessee, where no one ever locked his doors when I was a boy.

The 1980 census recorded McEwen's population at 1,390. The figure was 635 when I was born in 1933. The numbers reflected the people inside the city limits. I lived with both sets of grandparents but mostly at my maternal grandparents' house on Little Hurricane Creek, seven miles from the tiny town. (To this day, locals pronounce it "Harrican"). Let there be no mistake, I lived in the country!

We had cold water that was "running" only because we pumped it out of the ground. Like everyone in the vicinity, we had a cellar and an outdoor toilet. The house was suffocating in summertime. There was no such thing as air-conditioning, but we didn't miss what we'd never had. After living there for years, my grandparents sold the house and two hundred acres for five thousand dollars in 1945.

I was born in the Fuqua house, delivered by Dr. J. A. Suggs. The New Hope Methodist Church was nearby. The church and my birthing house are still standing, although the church is abandoned. Another family now lives in the house. Later in my childhood, when I commuted to McEwen, my grandparents and I lived inside the city limits. But there were always ties with the rural lifestyle. Only six houses along Little Hurricane Creek had telephones, and they were the old hand-cranked kind. Each house had a code. Three rings were for one household, four were for another, and so forth.

Mrs. Buleah Pullen picked up her receiver no matter how many rings sounded. She eavesdropped on everyone and everyone knew it. Whenever folks had something particularly secretive to discuss, they would say, "It's time for you to stop listening now, Mrs. Buleah." That prompted a hasty "click"' on the line.

One of my fondest childhood memories has to do with those telephones and Christmas Eve in 1938. I rang one ring, the operator's code, which we called "central." I asked her to connect me with Santa Claus. She said he had gone to deliver toys to other boys and girls, but, she said, Mrs. Claus was present. She asked if I would like to speak to her. When I said I would, that kind old woman paused, then changed her voice to a higher pitch. I was enthralled, thinking I was talking to the First Lady of Christmas. The ruse didn't dawn on me until years later.

I was almost twenty-one, and long gone to Nashville, when the McEwen state highway garage was erected in the early 1950s. It was to McEwen what Rockefeller Center once was to New York City—the most spectacular piece of real estate in town. Today, the garage remains McEwen's biggest building. It casts a one-story shadow on the swaying weeds that surround it.

The hot spot of my childhood in McEwen was the movie theater, which has long since been shut down. The theater was owned by a Chief Eaglefeather and his wife, Princess Silverheels. I don't know who proclaimed them chief and princess, and I don't know to which Indian tribe they belonged.

Their motion picture house had only one movie projector. The theater was a "one-reeler." Just as the movie's plot thickened, the reel would expire. Then the house lights would be raised, and either the chief or his wife would say, "There will be a short pause while we change the reel." Such delays really didn't enhance the suspense of a movie.

Then the film would resume, the overhead lights would lower, and you'd sit there for a few minutes trying to make out the images on the screen amid the spots in your eyes.

It cost ten cents. The Indian proprietors would take their coin receipts to my postmaster grandfather and ask him to convert them into paper currency. Eventually, he noticed that every dime they deposited had smooth edges. Gone were the normally rough edges, apparently filed. We later surmised that the chief and his wife were salvaging what little silver there is on the perimeter of a dime. They were probably turning the precious metal into powder, then redeeming it for cash.

The rural South during the Franklin D. Roosevelt and Harry Truman administrations was more than a geographical locale. Its nucleus was humility and dignity wrapped inside the work ethic. Country folks were proud, but not boastful. They were fair, but not pushovers. They were God loving, and just as God fearing.

The women were always friendly but never flirtatious. The men knew how to talk without speaking.

McEwen, and its people, were a stark contrast to my other world after my mother and I moved to Nashville.

On sleepy summer days I tilled my own garden where corn grew as high as the fence and towered over the grown-ups. I swelled with joy whenever my grandmother Fuqua praised my agriculture.

I remember driving a 1937 Ford with mechanical brakes

and having to sit on a cushion to see over the dash. My knuckles whitened as I gripped the steering wheel. Its "play" was so loose, I had to turn the wheel through several revolutions to go around corners. I remember once trying to find second gear from the sloppy linkage. In "downtown" McEwen, I missed the gear and hit reverse, and the car stopped. It sat down right on Main Street. I guessed that everyone was looking at me. I had to guess. I didn't dare look up. I thought I was twelve going on twenty-one, and too mature to make such a humiliating blunder.

I was, of course, breaking the law by being behind the wheel. But my grandfather Fuqua was the postmaster. And he was my surrogate father. I loved him more than I ever loved any male until the birth of my first son, and that, of course, is an entirely different kind of love. My grandfather knew the town constable, who knew everybody and their kids. The only real, recurring crime in town was public drunkenness. Drunks were the only ones who regularly went to jail. Wherever I went, adults knew me and my folks. If I or other youngsters broke the law, or misbehaved, our guardians were notified. Nobody bothered telling the lawmen. A twelve-year-old boy driving in the countryside, with or without his grandpa, was not aberrant behavior in McEwen. The youth might be married with offspring of his own five years later. In some ways, country children grow up faster than city kids.

I know people my age in McEwen today who were there when I left in 1940. They never got out of town. Some live in the same houses that were occupied by their parents and grandparents. I remember going with my maternal grandparents to all-day singing and preaching meetings. People brought covered baskets. The men talked about crops and drought and politics and the women exchanged recipes. No one wrote anything down. There was no need. Those farm women were such excellent cooks, they made everything from scratch. The scratches were indelibly drawn in their memories.

In preparation for "dinner on the ground," the congregation would erect a horizontal fence. The men had driven fence poles into the ground and had strung fence wire from pole to pole. The rigging was left intact year round. The women then spread a tablecloth over the wire. A sumptuous and cholesterol-rich feast would follow.

Folks wailed time-proven hymns. Farmers opened songbooks with calloused hands, but held the bindings mostly out of habit. No one ever read lyrics. Having sung those Gospel standards for decades, everyone knew the words.

Farmers removed their hats and showed the white tops of their heads in sharp contrast to the sun-darkened faces beneath. Ladies wore printed cotton dresses and sported aprons when it was time to serve. They all had Sunday finery. They were more comfortable while dressed to cook for their men. When the service was over, families clustered, then ambled into the night, en route to home and another week of work with and against the soil.

I remember endless days of squinting against the sun's glare on the barrel of a .22 rifle. My grandfather taught me to shoot before I could write. I was a tireless enemy of sheet-metal signs mounted on creosote poles. I'd shoot a tin can in the gravel road, watch it jump, shoot it again, and again, all the while loving the howl of the ricocheting bullets.

The Fuqua farmhouse was a two-story structure with a porch on the front and a dinner bell in back. We rarely rang the bell. It wasn't necessary. Each of the day's three meals was almost always served at the same time every day. Country folks are regimented.

The menus would have made contemporary dietitians cringe. They were a feast of fat and cholesterol. Breakfast was bountiful, with eggs, sausage, biscuits, milk gravy, redeye gravy, milk, and sorghum molasses. Lunch was called dinner. Dinner was called supper. Each was laden with garden-grown vegetables and freshly killed meat fried in leftover lard.

My grandparents killed chickens and hogs. Farm animals were for human exploitation, a medium of sustenance and no more. McEwen farmers killed livestock as nonchalantly as they fed it. It was all just a means to an end—the animals' end.

Farmers spent the rest of the slaughtering days skinning and cutting up hogs, making lard and crackling bread.

The whole bloody ordeal was perhaps responsible for my being a picky eater today. I'm not overly fond of pork. I refuse to eat chicken. This obsession is rooted in memories of my grandmother taking a pathetic and squawking bird by its head, then twirling it like a lariat. Momentarily, she would be left holding only the chicken's head. Its body, spewing blood, minus the head, would run around the barnyard, propelled by the bird's nervous system. A chicken, newly without its head, will run all over the place, splattering everything in its path with speckles of crimson.

My grandmother's decapitated fowl would eventually quiver onto its side, emitting a final flow of blood from its lifeless body.

At that point, Grandmother Fuqua would mechanically retrieve the bird and dip it into a kettle of boiling water. The brewing liquid loosened feathers and released a foul stench. It was a filthy and fatal procedure and affects my appetite for chicken today.

Because my grandmother Fuqua was the maternal figure in my life, I called her "Mother." I called my real mother "Mama" when she came to visit me after she moved to Nashville.

There I was, four or five years old, and some insensitive folk in McEwen would ask me, "Who do you love most, your mother or grandmother?"

A question like that put tremendous stress on a preschooler who was trained to be honest but who didn't want to hurt anyone's feelings. I never answered the question. I just walked around hoping that both women knew I loved them.

Those dummies would urge young boys to fight for the adults' amusement.

"Let's you and him fight!" one would shout, and shove

two lads together. If one boy balked, grownups mocked him. They'd call him a sissy and say that he ought to play with the girls.

Those semiliterate geezers actually wanted a fight. They'd scream, yell, and exhort, "punch him in the nose," "kick him in the belly." I think their excitement was only increased if one boy maimed another. If there was blood or tears, it was a good fight, the adults would say. Then the men might break it up and say that the winner was tough and that the loser had some growing up to do. The loser left with dried blood, wet tears, and a heavy load of confusion.

With the exception of the previously mentioned situations, my foremost memory of those folks was their disciplined kindness and country benevolence. They had the work stamina of lumberjacks and the entertainment thresholds of children. They were uncomplicated people who were easily and thoroughly amused.

Hence their fascination, and my own, for the audio miracle of the day—radio.

The biggest thing in those people's lives was religion, the second biggest was family, and the third was radio. It was not a distant third.

Families today don't congregate to watch big-screen television. But in the 1930s, families who lived on the creek joined other families in circles to listen, spellbound, for hours to the static-ridden voices and sounds of battery-operated console radios. When a family got a new radio, others came in droves to see it. People responded in numbers that were surpassed only when a new baby arrived, and not always then.

Jack Armstrong, the "All-American Boy," and Jack Benny were popular, as were the festive sounds of the Grand Ole Opry. Sitting cross-legged at the base of that wood and metal contraption, my imagination was in overdrive, especially during the Joe Louis fights. I could feel the impact of every punch as the out-of-breath announcer described the battles.

The most dramatic presentations were the Fireside Chats from President Roosevelt. Adults speculated all day before each broadcast about what the president would say. Roosevelt's deep resonant voice filled the air waves, and it sounded like the voice of God to me. None of us dared to breathe as the speech of the president filtered into our heads, hearts, and home.

I remember the intimacy of the medium. I knew that Roosevelt was speaking to millions. But somehow, I felt that he was confiding only to those inside my grandpa Fuqua's house.

We weren't just radio's fans. We were disciples. I memorized the formats of the regular shows, such as the one out of Chicago that had a cow's "moo." We had cows of our own on the farm, but I was nonetheless overwhelmed by a "moo" on the radio. I would wait the entire program for that one, three-second transmission.

We'd order picture books of stars who sang on the Grand Ole Opry, then look at the photographs whenever they performed. I'd look at the Opry stars and frown, thinking they didn't look at all like they sounded.

No one could have convinced a young Ralph Emery in McEwen, Tennessee, that he would ever meet Roy Acuff, let alone work with him. Acuff was one of my grandfather Fuqua's favorite entertainers. Roy, Pee-Wee King, Jam Up and Honey, and Uncle Dave Macon were worshiped in my young mind to a degree beyond description.

If someone had told me in the 1930s and 1940s that I would be on radio myself, I would have said there's no God in Heaven. I would have said He's in my pocket. To me, that dream was too farfetched to believe.

By 1940, Nashville was again my official address. That's when I began commuting to McEwen on weekends and during summers. My maternal grandparents had moved off their farm and were leasing a house in town.

It's funny, although not always humorous, how things begin and end.

My aunt, Mary Nell, lived with my grandparents. She was ten years older than me and suffered with asthma and pleurisy. My grandmother wakened me in the middle of the night because my aunt was having an attack. I was barely packed for the drive to the Nashville hospital when the ambulance arrived. My aunt was groaning and the siren was screaming. There was a porcelain pot inside the speeding coach. I remember peeing in that thing at sixty-five miles per hour. I was thrilled to urinate in motion, with little thought for my convulsing aunt.

I didn't think beyond the moment.

Because my grandmother had to care for my aunt, she could not take me with her back to McEwen. I was left at my mother's Nashville dwelling.

The emergency departure from my grandpa and grandma Fuqua's house would prove to be permanent. The part of my childhood spent mostly under their roof ended that quickly and unexpectedly.

...3...

RELIGION WAS AS MUCH A PART OF COUNTRY LIFE IN McEwen as home cooking. Farm children naturally went to church on Sundays the way they went to school on Mondays. I was no exception.

I'm thankful for the standards of morality and personal behavior that were given to me through my childhood church. I think youngsters mostly derive their standards from role models. Yet there is an integrity whose instillation is reserved solely for the church. Youngsters who don't attend church and don't receive the fundamental teachings of the Judeo-Christian ethic are disadvantaged in a Christian and democratic society.

That notwithstanding, I have always found it curious that the Christian church asks a child to make a decision regarding the rest of his life that is ostensibly the most important decision in all of life—religious conversion.

How can a youngster, who has never actually confronted the real rigors of this world, decide what spiritual armor he will bear against them?

No one would expect an eleven-year-old to pronounce unequivocally what college he will attend, or what life's work he will enter. Those decisions, as important as they are, have only to do with life on earth.

I never experienced that kind of coercion personally as a lad in a country church. But I did see it firsthand within the rank and file of the Baptist denomination after I was a grown man. Some in the modern church put tremendous psychological, emotional, and parental pressure upon their offspring to make a decision affecting their lives for eternity.

The institution of matrimony, supposedly a lifetime commitment, rarely works these days, and it is entered into by adults. It would be ludicrous for a preadolescent to proclaim who he is going to be married to for the rest of his life. But again, adults in some churches will accept, and indeed, demand, that he make a religious decision affecting eternal life, and make it before he dies. Then they remind him that he could die tomorrow.

Jesus Christ tried to recruit converts out of reciprocal love. Some modern churches try to recruit out of self-protective fear.

Nothing founded in fear ever fulfills.

Too often, the child convert becomes an adult backslider. The teaching he adopted for solace he later abandons with guilt.

When Jesus, in the New Testament, admonished "Suffer the little children to come unto me," he meant that they should be allowed, not forced, to come unto Him. And while the organized, twentieth-century church does not physically force childhood conversions, it sometimes seeks converts through mental coercion. This is especially true in the evangelical denominations.

The greater atrocity, I feel, is that a commitment for the ages usually is sought within minutes, at the end of an impassioned, emotional service. Shouldn't there be less emotion and more reason surrounding such a momentous decision?

This is just one of the practices I have trouble with in the modern church. I am a Christian—and try to be a good one. I'm not a regular churchgoer. I love Jesus and His teachings. I abhor Man's twisting of it all.

This chapter is the closest semblance to a sermon you'll

find in this book. I've written it for two reasons. The first is that I would be remiss as an honest autobiographer if I didn't touch on my religious and spiritual convictions, particularly when they were such a big part of my early life. The second is that the type of life-changing conversion urged upon youngsters was demanded of me. I was eleven when I accepted all of it. I was a young adult when I questioned most of it.

I made my decision to accept Jesus Christ during an evening service. There were white gas lamps strewn around for light. I even remember that three of the lights had been borrowed from another church. Country churches, in those days, had little money and cooperated with other churches when in need.

I might have been thinking about my pending spiritual decision for some time. After all, I had been attending the Shiloh Church of Christ for years at the insistence of my grandma and grandpa Fuqua. Or I might have gone to the altar that night to seek salvation—and personal acceptance. I've indicated what a tremendous influence the Fuquas were in my life, and I remember that an older boy, who was a Fuqua, preceded me in answering the minister's call. Maybe I just went down because he did, or maybe I was touched by the sermon, or maybe, as they say, I "felt the call."

The congregation was singing either "Just As I Am" or "Coming Home." I remember feeling anxiety as I approached the altar. I remember feeling at peace when I arose. And everyone, friends and family alike, was proud of me. In fact, the adults reassured, congratulated, and showered love on me in the wake of that evening as they never had before.

A few days later, in a creek near a bridge, the Fuqua boy and I were baptized by immersion, just as John baptized Jesus in the Jordan River. The preacher put a handkerchief over my nose, his hand over my mouth, and my head under that flowing water.

It was dark down there. As I bent backward, I was totally dependent on his grip.

A few days later, I received another dose of the grown-ups' pride in my conversion and baptism. The little church in Shiloh had given me a certificate to commemorate my spiritual activities. I went back to Nashville to enroll in the fall semester for fifth grade and attended the Russell Street Church of Christ. I took my Shiloh certificate to the Nashville church, where the teacher read it aloud to the class and wrote my name on the blackboard.

It was really a big deal to a little kid from the country. All that adult attention and acceptance was perhaps the biggest assuagement of my insecurity I had ever had.

Our little McEwen church did not have a regular pastor. It couldn't afford one. Once a month, we had a preacher who came to McEwen from David Lipscomb College, a theological Church of Christ college in Nashville. During the fourth week of each August, the preacher would stay for a week, residing with various members of the congregation. The Church of Christ called that week "the meeting." The families the preacher stayed with were always on their best behavior, used their best dishes and utensils, and children were admonished not to burp or pass gas.

One young preacher was Ira North, who became Dr. Ira North, who founded Nashville's Madison Church of Christ, one of the largest Churches of Christ in the world.

Years later, I left the Church of Christ to become a Baptist. I did so in connection with the wishes of my first wife. I'm simultaneously saddened and annoyed when I see the verbal fighting and friction within the Baptist and Southern Baptist denominations today. At the risk of oversimplifying, I think that too many church leaders have taken their eyes off Christ, and cast them upon their own self-importance. All the haggling over leadership and denominational policy, which often results in division within the rank and file of the church, is a poor example of the love about which Christ taught and in which He lived.

Somehow, I don't think that denominational infighting is what He had in mind two thousand years ago at Calvary. If He had foreseen the atrocities that men would eventually inflict on one another in His name, I think His burden at

Golgotha would have been even greater, prompting Him to carry the cross even more slowly than He did.

There is another qualm I have about the modern church (when I say modern, I include the 1930s and 1940s indoctrination I received in McEwen). The hard-line, Protestant churches impose too many rules upon their parishioners. The contemporary term is legalism. Children are told not to smoke, not to dance, not to go to movies, not to whatever, depending on the church and its beliefs.

All that harping doesn't prevent anybody from doing anything. It just makes them feel guilty when they do. People today receive enough guilt from their doctors and diets. Church should be a sanctuary from self-disgust. Church should make one feel good—not guilty.

In my church, and in the Fuqua household, I was forbidden to smoke or steal.

I did both.

In fact, I stole some cigarettes from my grandfather, for whom I had undying love and admiration.

That all happened years before my trip to the altar, but not before I had begun attending church. I was six.

I stole his cigarettes, a pack at a time, from inside his dresser drawer. Previously, I had rolled my own with farm boys who showed me how to wrap corn silk in a brown paper bag, seal it with spit, and light it. The preparation was a rural art form. The smoking was an exercise in nausea. We smoked weeds, rabbit tobacco (also a weed), and just about anything that grew that could ignite.

Country kids are masters of self-abuse. I remember my grandma Fuqua would give me a teaspoon of coal oil (kerosene) and sugar when I had a cold. It wasn't as bad as it sounds, when administered as a single dose. But it was really nauseating after I bragged to my buddies that I could drink a whole gallon of coal oil without ever taking the container from my lips. They said I couldn't. I said, "Stand aside."

I downed what might have been a pint of coal oil. I put it away in seconds. I threw up for hours.

*　　*　　*

There was no kindergarten in McEwen. If there had been, I would have smoked and stolen my first cigarettes, and chug-a-lugged coal oil, before I was old enough to enroll.

There was one other thing I did during my sixth year. I had "sex." I didn't know it, and I certainly didn't know how to do it. But I did my best.

When I was four, I walked in on my parents while they were making love. I noticed their nudity.

There was a blacksmith shop and gristmill near my grandparents' house. That's where I took a girl for a game of "I'll show you mine if you'll show me yours."

I did and she did. I had her naked in seconds.

I'm not sure what I saw. I'm not sure I knew what to look for. But my mind raced back to the sight of my parents, horizontal with each other. I couldn't let the little girl lie on the filthy floor of that vacant blacksmith shop. So I took her to my front porch. There, lying in her tiny arms of love, I lay atop her. I don't recall if I went up and down. But I know nothing went in and out. I didn't know it was supposed to. Then, after becoming quickly bored, and wondering why any boy would want to mash a girl he liked by lying on top of her, I stood up. The girl and I put on our clothes, and probably played hopscotch or something equally mundane. Years later, I realized that my religious and disciplinary grandma Fuqua had been cleaning her house only steps away from where I had mounted the girl. Had my grandmother stepped onto her front porch and seen her naked grandson, she never would have had to worry about his going to hell. She would have beaten it out of him on the spot.

As far as childhood drinking, which isn't uncommon among farm boys, there was none of that for me. I had seen the way booze ruined my real father's life, and besides, my grandma and grandpa Fuqua forbade it—really forbade it. It wasn't in our house, and they wanted nothing to do with anybody anywhere who imbibed, socially or otherwise.

It's a curious paradox—the way religion and experimental behavior were integrated into my country childhood.

It's ironic that in the innocence of those farms and fields I was trying things at a much younger age than children were in town, where temptations flourished in a sinister setting. I've met hundreds of country people in my life—almost all of whom told me interchangeable stories about a childhood in church, cigarettes behind the barn, and the fearful, touch and go, innocent undressing of a playmate of the opposite sex.

In the country, I was miles away from an institution of higher learning. But believe me, there was education all around.

...4...

I REMEMBER HE HIT ME, BUT I CAN'T REMEMBER WHY. I was seven, and enrolled in a school with learning-disabled children—some were perhaps very mildly retarded. At times, they became inexplicably hostile. I attended that school because my mother, her second husband, and I lived there as well. I'm sure that my short walk to class did miles' worth of psychological damage to an already insecure child, unhappy and disoriented in new and unfamiliar surroundings.

My mother's husband (I never acknowledged him as "Dad") had an aunt who taught at the school. My parents probably lacked the minimal amount of funds for me to attend public school. The special school, ironically, was home to many prosperous children whose parents brought them to class in limousines. I vaguely remember the special school. I'm vague as to why I'm vague. But there I was—fresh off the protective farm where I'd never heard of mental retardation—thrust into a school among about twenty youngsters with whom I had obvious psychological differences, although the differences weren't always dramatically pronounced. I was afraid of the unfamiliar surroundings, and afraid of those inhabiting them. Because I had left McEwen in January, I was enrolled in my new school in the middle of an academic year.

I felt that in this situation I was falling hopelessly behind in my studies. I was uneasy about having to start each textbook in the middle.

I remember the school was an old, drafty, wooden frame structure. It was hot and smelly. It seemed as though a correlation existed between uncomfortable conditions and unruly behavior. The students were most aggressive on hot days. More than once, kids who were playing or studying normally would, without provocation, erupt into rage. I learned which children were easily provoked and I learned to avoid them. Their eyes would widen, and sometimes their saliva would flow. They would hit me until the teacher pulled them off.

They were too unstable to control their emotions. I could have defended myself. Remember, I had learned to fight when the ignorant men in McEwen had said, "Let's you and him fight," and provoked the farm lads into fisticuffs for the adults' amusement. But I could not bring myself to fight the boys with learning disabilities. I felt sorry for the less fortunate, and I let them pound me until the teacher's rescue.

I wondered later if they weren't intimidated by my normalcy, and if their hostility wasn't spawned because they sensed that my mind was the way they wished theirs were. My discomfort at that school and its mysteriously impaired students sometimes ignited my tears—as unrestrained as the other students' rage.

I wish I could remember more about that school. I feel as though I ought to. After all, I was more than halfway through childhood. But memories are dim, and probably for a reason. I think there have been things in my life that were so traumatic that my conscious mind suppressed them. I hadn't thought about my grade school experiences for years until I began writing this book.

But there was that first year in Nashville, with a new stepfather, new neighborhood, and a new school where I was fed and educated among the unbalanced and violent.

I'd like to remember everything that actually happened at that place. But then again, maybe I wouldn't.

My mother, stepfather, and I shared quarters that were a striking contrast to the sprawling dwellings in McEwen. I had gone from country openness to urban confinement while acquiring a strange "father" for whom I had little use. No wonder I relished life on the farm.

I hadn't been old enough to comprehend my mother's incompatibility with my biological father. By the time of her second marriage, I understood well the violent arguments she had with her [new] spouse. My blood chilled when their voices rose. In that tiny enclosure, there was no way for me to escape their battles.

In McEwen, I never had heard cross words among my loving grandparents. But my mother and stepfather, stressed out from claustrophobic surroundings and economic hardship, seemed to rattle the walls with their verbal onslaughts.

I know that nothing brings strain to a marriage, new or proven, like financial pressure. They had it, and they had me there, listening, within feet of them as they sought to thrash out their problems. I remember a particular Sunday when we went to a Mom and Pop grocery store for "dinner." Dinner turned out to be some cellophane-wrapped cakes, paid for after my mother literally counted out her pennies.

No doubt my presence was as much an irritant to my stepfather as his was to me.

I never liked him. I felt he was invading our lives. I had never heard the word "divorce" until I heard my mother was getting one. In the 1940s rural South, divorce was something that "bad" people did in big cities, as we occasionally read in newspapers. Divorce was unthinkable among decent folks, or so I was taught in that culture. The "family" was first. One didn't leave his spouse any more than one gave away his children. You can imagine my bewilderment when my mother got a divorce, although as I've indicated, I felt no sentimental attachment to my drunken, shiftless natural father.

I didn't call my new dad "Dad." I didn't call him by name. I didn't call him anything, and can only remember even speaking to him a few times. He might have been an all-right guy, but I don't think so. Anyhow, I didn't give him a chance.

At the time, I thought he did dumb things. In retrospect, I think they were dumber. Young boys need a "father figure." My new "father" was the figure of a jerk to me.

I remember he would consistently, in the dead of winter, pawn his overcoat. The scenario was predictable. My parents would fight about money and he would take it personally. Then he would play martyr. He would stomp out of the house into the darkness and snow. He would show up at daylight—shoulders shivering and sprinkled with snowflakes—minus his overcoat. A zero-degree temperature is not uncommon during a Nashville winter. This man looked pathetic, stooped and quivering in our doorway, as if he were a common transient awaiting a handout, when he was actually an able-bodied man devoid of ambition.

I felt more contempt for him than pity.

But not my mother.

Somehow, she always managed to retrieve his wrap from the pawnbroker's snare. I think if she had spent the extra time working that she spent trotting back and forth to the pawnshop, she could have earned enough to buy him a second coat. He would then have had one for home and one for the pawnshop. Isn't that funny, in an infuriating way?

I wouldn't have minded if he had frozen to death. I say that truly and unashamedly. After all, when my preferred setting was taken from me, and my mother and I moved to Nashville, my mother was all I had. I was protective, for her sake and for selfish reasons. This "stranger" upset her and that upset me. I can remember her crying into the telephone many times, begging him to come home. The guy was a dapper dresser with sartorial skill. He would posture before the mirror for hours, exit, and not return for days, during which his two dependents literally had little or no food. Under my breath, I called him a lot of things. I would have called him anything before I would have called him "Dad."

I blamed him for our poverty. Why wouldn't a child? Life, in the country, had been prosperous without him. Life, in the city, was deficient with him.

My mother and I moved many times during the few years he was our "provider." We relocated, I suspect, because we couldn't pay rent. I remember one creaky building with numerous apartments and one bathroom. It was like sharing a public restroom at home. I'd go to the bathroom, towel in hand and prepared to bathe, and the door would be locked. It seemed strange having a stranger in "my" bathtub. I'd knock several times, finally enter, and stare in disbelief at a grimy ring that lined the tub's porcelain. I'd clean up after the stranger, only to discover that he or she had failed to flush the toilet. Our rent was low but my pride was high. Sharing an unsanitary bathroom was a rude invasion of my privacy and hygiene.

It's a wonder I ever amounted to anything, given my weak male role models, men who floundered, had no drive, and lived in substandard housing only a step above a project. Besides my rock-solid grandfathers, my male role models were a drunk and a bum. My mother met her second husband when she was a waitress at the Sam Davis Hotel, where he was a doorman. It was honest but mindless work, opening people's car doors. To my knowledge, it was the most responsibility the man ever had. It probably gave him mental overload.

School should be a second home for a child. It should be a place where he feels warmth and identity. My first Nashville school was a facsimile of a mental hospital. My second school, where I finally mixed with children more like myself, became the source of security to me—for which I was unknowingly starved.

Then it burned down.

I eagerly left home one cold morning en route to the old building. I arrived to find the architectural masterpiece reduced to ashes in the snow.

We were now living, or rather existing, from meal to meal. My life was Nashville's answer to Charles Dickens's London.

My mother was wearing out fast. I think it was the beginning of a nervous breakdown that would come years later. I vividly remember the panic in her voice as she pleaded with her husband to find more than temporary, unskilled work. I felt controlled and unspoken rage when he mocked her.

He would throw back his head and break into a song, the lyrics of which went, "This is Heaven, having no work to do." He took our poverty with amusement. He would laugh, she would cry, and I'd do my silent, slow burn.

It's little wonder that I spent weekends with my grandparents on the farm in McEwen, a grass-and-timber sanctuary, just a fifty-six-mile bus ride away.

Perhaps I never gave my stepfather a fair chance. When my grandmother Fuqua told me about my mother's impending second marriage, I cried. My grandmother seemed pleased about it, and I couldn't understand why. To my young mind, the new groom seemed like an intruder. But of all the things he was, there was one thing he wasn't—an Emery. He didn't come from the same lineage with the rowdy reputation that characterized my real father, and that's why my grandparents welcomed the new husband into the family. They thought he would be a welcome change.

He wasn't much better. From the well of matrimony, my mother twice drew a nearly dry bucket.

I was probably about eight when we moved to 226 Shelby Avenue in Nashville. I went to public school, but that really was the only healthy change for me. The three of us shared one bedroom, a kitchen, and a bathroom. My mother and her new husband would whisper beneath the covers while waiting for me to fall asleep. It irritated me. I'd think, "How dare that man invade my very bedroom, my mother's bed, and then have the nerve to speak so softly that I can't hear, but so loudly I can't sleep?"

The man did nothing to garner a distrusting youngster's acceptance.

Perhaps if I'd had a pet, I would have had a love object. All I had was a replica, an old-fashioned piggybank that hid my paltry, lifelong savings. The man stole it.

He flat took the money out of the bank, and took forever any chance that I would ever accept him, a man whose only skill was vagrancy.

We moved several times during that brief marriage. Most of the time, my mother was at work and her second husband was gone. It seemed I was always at home alone. I lived the role of a "latchkey" child long before it was added to the jargon of psychologists.

A Gospel song, "Where No One Stands Alone," has a line that runs "I don't know a thing in this whole wide world that's worse than being alone." I agree. I had a taste of loneliness in childhood. I would founder on it in adolescence. I discovered that when loneliness becomes ingrained, nothing will totally alleviate it, not even the presence of others. Except for summers, my life was often nearly incessant solitude. After my mother had gone to work, I arose alone, played alone, except for a few friends in the neighborhood, and returned to a semidarkened house—alone. The solitude kept me from learning social skills during those formative years.

I became antisocial and backward. People intimidated me, particularly if they tried to talk to me, and especially if they were strangers.

They say that every adversity carries an equal blessing. And they say that good things come from hard times.

My middle years of childhood proved those adages, for I sought, more than ever, a companionship in the electronic medium that I lacked in human beings. Radio became my surrogate family.

My postinfancy imagination had been spurred by faraway radio transmissions I heard on my grandparents' farm, where radio listening was not just a family but a community event. By the age of nine, I held fond memories of love and togetherness that stemmed from the neighbors, my grandparents, and me sitting spellbound in front of a console radio.

The seeds of imagination planted when I was small began to germinate when I was nine. Radio once had been a source of magical entertainment. By then, it had become a source of necessary companionship.

"Captain Midnight," "Jack Armstrong, the All-American Boy," "Inner Sanctum," "Mister District Attorney," and others became friends that I "saw" with my ears. Contemporary readers, raised on television, may find my early immersion in radio laughable. But in 1940s America, radio was an incredibly intimate medium, and its role as a companion remains unsurpassed. There is no big-screen television, no stereophonic sound system, no compact disc component that can arrest the imagination today the way a tiny, AM radio did for me before and during the Second World War.

I was a member of a society that represented America's last decade of innocence. Innocence and imagination went hand and hand. The matchmaker was radio.

Communication is a two-way process of transmission and reception. I spent a childhood intensely on the reception side, then my entire adult life on the transmission end. The involvement with radio I had as a child was not my primary, conscious reason for entering the medium years later. But who knows the extent of the subconscious?

And who knows how vividly my subconscious was activated during those years of mesmerized listening.

My mother's second husband entered the military during World War II. He was drafted. My biological father also was dispatched to duty, so I had two men I cared little or nothing about fighting for my freedom.

The nation, I remember, fell totally in line behind the war effort. Americans put up with gasoline, meat, and other food rationing. We had drives to collect cans and newspapers. Families who had a member in the service had a star in their window—blue if he was living—gold if he'd been killed. Everybody felt the presence of that war. Even the old men in McEwen, long past their prime, would march at night in drills and ceremonies. They prepared for the call that would never come. But that innocuous marching was their version of readiness.

At school, we were supposed to collect and deposit surplus metal and paper goods from our neighborhoods. I became passionate about the drives, but on one occasion, I didn't get my stuff in on time. The teacher confronted me.

"How can you be so indifferent to this effort?" he said, in front of the entire class. "You have two fathers who are in uniform."

He didn't realize I didn't care about either one of them. If he wanted to motivate me, he should have played on my patriotism, not paternal affection.

My mother's second husband never came home on furlough during his enlistment. I always suspected that he was given his annual thirty days' leave, but that he intentionally didn't come home. In the days preceding his departure for the military, he and my mother fought bitterly, and I actually think he felt more at ease fighting the Japanese than he did battling the stress of my mother and our poverty.

My first experience with the death of a loved one came about a year before the beginning of World War II. My grandpa Emery had gone to California from McEwen for reasons I was never told. While out West, he stepped off a curb into the path of a bus. He died on the operating table. He had a daughter, my aunt Evelyn. At the very moment my grandpa Emery was fighting to sustain his life, his only daughter was trying to take hers. She took an overdose of prescription medicine and was rushed to the same Los Angeles hospital where her father fought for life. He lost his fight, but she wound up keeping the life she had tried to throw away.

A reporter for the *Los Angeles Times* recorded the story for the newspaper—a story that was sent to me more than fifty years later.

I don't remember if Aunt Evelyn went to her father's funeral, but I do remember the ceremony, and how it was preceded by men hauling my grandfather's body to his old

McEwen house. The body lay in state in an open casket in the living room. I remember feeling terror as I beheld his badly bruised face. The mortician's makeup seemed to mock my grandfather's abrasions. I didn't like all the cosmetics, an artificial veneer on the face I loved.

Mourners brought bushels of food to the house. They sat and wept aloud for two days preceding his funeral. The wake was an ordeal, and a custom, back then in the rural South. It marked the first time I had seen a dead body; it marked the first time I had seen grownups cry.

I was seven, and before the trauma of his death subsided, I would share with the nation the announcement of Pearl Harbor.

By the time my stepfather's military departure was imminent, he and my mother had long since been throwing lamps and crockery at each other. The loser she called a husband exchanged his doorman's uniform for the United States Army's. He went off to war, was discharged, and was divorced from my mother by 1947. Neither she nor I ever heard from him again.

...5...

I SPENT THE FIRST YEAR OF MY ADOLESCENCE PERFORMING the last job anybody would want. I cleaned soot and ashes from residential furnaces. I worked for forty cents an hour and obtained jobs through Youth Incorporated, a community service that found work for boys. I also washed windows and mowed grass. Thirteen is an awkward age for an American boy, too old for child's play but too young for men's work, too old to ride a bicycle but too young to drive a car.

A young boy's body is changing. He's perplexed about girls and curious about what is happening to his own anatomy. Today, youngsters talk about those normal transitions with their parents or friends. In the uptight 1940s, such discourse was taboo. Early adolescence was a confusing and traumatic time for males.

There was one thing, however, about which I was certain: I didn't like manual labor. I liked it even less when it left me filthy and tired.

So my buddy and I went door-to-door, downtown, looking for a job—any job. I got my first official job in show business when I was fourteen. I became an usher at Loew's Theater, an opulent motion picture house in downtown Nashville that looked like an opera house.

They don't build regal theaters like the Loew's anymore. They haven't in years. Young people today who walk into the compact, architectural shoeboxes that are passed off as movie establishments have no idea how elegant the predecessors were. Today's films are projected in movie houses. They used to be projected in movie theaters.

The old screens were silver vistas that spread out in a subtle semicircle for the entire width of the room. If today's minuscule screens were painted red, patrons might mistake them for exit signs.

No one would have thought of piping recorded music into one of those glamorous theaters. Musicians auditioned to play in theaters, where they were often salaried with extra benefits. Today, the modern anthem of every movie house, elevator, supermarket, and dentist's office in the country is Muzak. The old theaters were cleaned up after every showing. The crowd wasn't admitted until the place was tidy. Patrons stepped across broadloom carpet, not popcorn boxes. The walls were ornate, resplendent with gingerbread carvings that adorned the towering, arched ceilings. The atmospheric theaters looked like mini-astrodomes with a motif. They were the working man's answer to the Sistine Chapel. Going to a motion picture theater in the 1940s was more than just going to a show, it was participation in an event. For the paltry price of admission, for two to three hours, one could see the four corners of the earth through a Hollywood lens. The effect was healthy and exciting escapism. Motion picture theaters back then were America's last vestiges of everyday elegance.

I took enormous pride in my new job. My Loew's employment had significance for one reared in the work ethic. It marked the first time I officially worked as a card-carrying taxpayer. My gross earnings were ten dollars a week. Ten cents was taken through payroll deduction for federal taxes. I kept rehashing a mental inventory of what I was doing—working in uniform, indoors, in front of the big screen, and being paid with an itemized corporate check for it all.

I was so proud that it's a wonder I ever sought a higher

station in life. I wasn't even upset that the uniform dickey I wore was cardboard.

One of the most exciting nights of my life was the night I was an usher for the return performances of the most popular motion picture of all time, *Gone with the Wind*.

The blockbuster film, an epic of epics, enjoyed its first run in American theaters in 1939. It returned to Nashville in 1948. The line for admission was three blocks long and people waited three hours to get in.

I worked for three years as an usher and ticket taker. During that span, I saw my first example of sanctioned racism. When riding the bus from McEwen to Nashville, I noticed that the blacks would sit in the rear of the coach. The same was true on city buses. Their seating arrangements were expected, but not dictated.

At the theater, blacks had their own entrance and seats. Whites had premium seats on the first floor and first balcony, while the blacks took the distant upper balcony. I don't ever remember trouble in connection with the arrangement. It's just that in retrospect it's hard for me to believe that I witnessed such open and official discrimination. But that was the South of forty-five years ago.

Working in that theater did much to whet my appetite for the bright lights. I saw all the great MGM musicals starring Fred Astaire, Ginger Rogers, Gene Kelly, and Judy Garland. Al Jolson had done a live show on that stage. On weeknights, when business was slow, I would ease into a seat and watch those pictures. I cherish that I was a part of the motion picture industry before it was deglamorized by subdivisions and shopping centers, which did to movies what fast food did to civilized dining.

My job was window dressing for the overall attempt to entertain people. My reason for being there was minimal, as people could have found their own seats. So the job at Loew's was my first experience with social graces.

I also learned about the lack of graces.

As ushers, we were admonished to be on the lookout for

"seat hoppers," men who would sit next to an unescorted woman. They would intimidate her until she moved, then move to a seat next to her new one.

These guys had a method to their madness. They often walked into the theater with an overcoat, even if it was summertime. Consequently, they were pretty easy to spot. A hopper would stand in the aisle, searching the crowd for an unescorted woman, then sit down next to her. Almost scientifically, he would spread his overcoat across his lap, letting part of the garment accidentally fall across the woman's lap. Then, ever so slowly, he would run his hand along his leg and onto hers, often trying to get his palm under her dress.

Most women would silently and angrily rise to their feet and move. When they sat down in a new chair, if they were pursued by the offending man, an usher would ask him to move away from her. There were other women, I suspect, who came into the theater alone looking for a date.

The theater manager showed me how to handle, diplomatically, a situation with a seat hopper. I had been watching this guy move all over the theater in the wake of an obviously disgruntled woman.

"I think I've got one of those seat hoppers on my hands," I told the manager.

"Oh yeah," he said, "take me down there, and act like I'm a customer, and seat me right next to the guy. Remember, you have to be discreet in these things."

I took the manager to a seat behind the suspicious-looking man. I sat him down quietly and then delicately eased into the aisle and walked toward my station at the rear. I had been the master of diplomacy, as per the order of my boss, who had not taken his own advice. He grabbed the seat hopper by the back of the neck. It must have hurt the guy, as evidenced by his kicking and screaming. The boss could have evicted a bull with less distraction.

I developed another identification skill in that theater.

I had never heard the word "queer," except as it pertained to something odd or unusual. I certainly had no idea what its sexual connotations were.

Ushers at Loew's explained that I would have to watch out for the "behavior of queers." I asked them what they meant. They told me, and I thought they were making it up.

"Men being 'smoochy' with men?" I asked.

They told me that men would occasionally come inside and sit in the dark and hold hands, and that was all I wanted to hear. I could have imagined the rest, but I didn't want to. I was sure I would never encounter anyone so unusual. But then I did begin to notice that sometimes, some of the men would escort other men, as if they were a male and female couple. They held hands. One man in the couple would seem to be dominant toward the other. Sometimes, they smiled at me strangely. Often, they reeked of sweet perfume. I was sure I was seeing my first queers but I couldn't be sure.

But not for long.

One night, an effeminate man came up to me and smiled. He just stood there, grinning, looking at and through me simultaneously. I was too young to have ever seen the look of romantic love, but I knew this guy didn't look right.

"Do you want to have some fun?" he smiled.

"Do you want me to hit you between the eyes with this flashlight?" I responded.

I was told by the manager to occasionally patrol the men's room in the basement.

"Those queers like to hang out down there," he said.

And so I went, walking lightly down the carpeted stairs looking for men who were doing things that I was sure I wouldn't understand. An old man holding the hand of a young boy, and sly smiles, were about the most unusual things I encountered—until one night.

A man hid himself inside a rest room stall. With a pocket knife, he bored a hole in the wooden partition, enabling him to see into the adjacent stall. That's where I stood, using the commode.

"P-s-s-s-t, p-s-s-s-t," I heard.

"Who's there?" I said, my voice an echo inside the cavernous, old men's room.

"Hey kid," was the reply, "stick that thing through here."

I saw the hole in the wall, and an eyeball in the hole. I discovered the source of the voice. I stopped urinating instantly and involuntarily. I had used a men's room at school thousands of times, with no thought about another male looking at me. But suddenly, I realized this stranger had been looking at me. I thought instantly about all the things the other ushers had been telling me about queers. I was furious.

I bolted from my stall, zipping up as I went through the door, and confronted the guy in his stall where he hadn't even attempted to zip up or put away anything. I began yelling excitedly, and the last I saw of him was his backside, speeding up the stairs, three to four steps at once, while struggling madly with his fly. I rounded the corner into the theater lobby but he was out the door and gone. I came to a halt and scanned the foyer, looking for the back of his head. Suddenly, I noticed that everyone I looked at was already looking at me.

I just knew they knew what had happened, and, of course, they didn't. But my embarrassment was overwhelming.

The next day, I had someone repair the hole in the men's room partition.

...6...

I WAS ONE YEAR AWAY FROM MY HIGH SCHOOL GRADUATION when I left Loew's. I had my life and the world ahead of me, but I didn't look at it that way. I was a very unhappy teenager whose disenchantment bordered on depression. I became increasingly appearance-conscious and hated the way I looked. I was, in fact, ashamed. The more I looked at myself, the more I wanted to look away.

I was an unattractive young man, with crooked teeth, and what I would later call "industrial-strength acne."

I remember a Sunday afternoon when I was about seventeen and home alone. Suddenly, the solitude was strangely overpowering. I realized I was by myself because I had no one to be with. I realized I was idle because I had nothing to do. There was nothing optional about my solitude. I felt that my life was hopeless. My despondency, born in low self-esteem, became suffocating. I didn't see any reason to live, although I don't mean to imply I was suicidal. I just felt that my life was an overall exercise in futility.

I didn't have a girlfriend until I was sixteen.

My mother and I lived upstairs at 1105 Holly Street in Nashville. In an apartment downstairs lived Betty Fillmore. She became the first love of my life, and two years later, my first wife.

They say there is no love like the first love, although I certainly don't feel as though the first love is by any means superior to all that comes later. We, however, are more "impressionable" the first time around love's track. And when young, we're more sensitive, more inclined to open our hearts and let down our guard.

There is another reason I fell for Betty as hard as I did. As I approached my senior year in high school, my mother suffered a nervous breakdown. She was committed to a psychiatric facility for two months and during that period I lived with my classmate Joe Binkley and his parents. I had observed my mother's occasionally hysterical behavior for years, throwing plates and glassware at her second husband. It seemed to peak about a year before I left home. After her hospitalization, she returned to McEwen to live with her mother for several months. I felt sorry for her. Her first husband had been a drunk, her second a bum. She didn't know where either could be found. She was penniless. There had been too much stress for too many years and she snapped.

She reached a point where she could not control her emotions most of the time. I suppose I could have gone back to McEwen to live with my grandmother Fuqua. But I wanted to graduate from a familiar school system. I had been in the Nashville system since the age of seven.

I am eternally grateful to the Binkley family for taking me into their home and lives during my senior year. Mrs. Binkley fed me, housed me, and ironed my clothes for ten dollars a week.

As an unstained teenager on his first romantic outing, I was obsessed with Betty. I saw her when she wasn't there. I smelled her fragrance long after she had gone. I carried her books in school and would have walked with her to and from school, except that she rode.

Betty had contracted polio about five years before the intervention of Salk's polio vaccine. She wore a brace on her left leg and negotiated our high school campus with a cane.

Young people today have no idea how fearful the population used to be about that dreaded disease. I can remember educators urging students not to get too hot or too tired because it would increase their susceptibility to the then incurable and debilitating affliction that was most common among children and young adults.

I'd like to paint a romantic love story here about the bliss of my first romance, but the relationship turned less blissful and more realistic. We had our ups and downs, until I went away from home, and my absence made our hearts grow fonder.

We had been dating about two years, and I had gone to Paris, Tennessee, to take my first job in broadcasting. I stayed for three months, and returned to Nashville to work at WNAH in September. We had a church wedding in December.

I was earning precious little money, as was Betty, who was a comptometer operator, having been trained by the state. So Betty and I moved in with her parents. We lived in a part of their house that included a bedroom and a kitchen. Almost immediately, unhappiness began to surface. I felt dominated. I thought Betty, who probably is nothing like this today, was insensitive. I remember our first Christmas, when I had such meager funds. I bought her gifts that were inexpensive. She was disappointed, and let me know it. I was naive enough to believe that it was the thought that counted. Betty's materialistic attitude hurt me deeply, and I told her so. We argued and did so many times thereafter whenever I felt, rightly or wrongly, that she was trying to dominate me.

Betty, I later surmised, also felt bitter because the cure for polio was not discovered in time to spare her body's ravaging by the disease. Perhaps her bitterness manifested itself in hostility or domination toward me.

After six years, the end came. I moved into one room owned by two old ladies on Nashville's Eastland Avenue. Betty and I tried to reconcile and I moved back in with her, but moved out again.

The bliss I had imagined with Betty was in fact stillborn. It just never happened. Ten months after we were married,

Steve, my first son, was born. I had tremendous guilt about leaving him. I remember the little things surrounding my departure, not the least of which was the quaint house I had bought in 1955 for $10,750. I gave it up in the divorce.

I went to see Steve after the divorce, when he was five. He tried to get me to stay. Leaving him that day I cried so hard I couldn't see to drive.

"Will you come back tomorrow?" he asked, as I stepped out of the yard.

Sorrow about leaving my son, and missing him was more than I could bear. I'd lie alone in the dark, shut my eyes, and see his face. Another time, when I was visiting, he mentioned my fondness for a favorite meal. I was impressed that my little boy remembered what his daddy enjoyed. He climbed on top of a counter and began to root in a cupboard. The little guy produced a box of spaghetti.

"Here Daddy, this is what you like!" he smiled. "Won't you stay for dinner with us this time?"

Years later, Johnny Russell coincidentally wrote a song that expressed what I was feeling.

"Our marriage was a failure, Our divorce ain't working either."

I couldn't abide letting Steve down any longer. Six months after my divorce from my first wife, I married her a second time. That lasted two years. I found that one cannot live happily with a woman because of love for a child. At the end of eight years and two marriages, Betty and I called it quits forever. Shortly after the divorce, my guilt regarding Steve resurfaced. Again, there was a child's simple but openly honest quip that stuck with me forever.

Singer-songwriter Roger Miller, who had moved to Nashville from Oklahoma, called my house.

"You can't talk to Daddy," Steve said to him. "Daddy doesn't live here anymore."

Roger wrote a song based on the experience.

Betty and I are amicable today. She remarried happily years ago, and I long since wished her the best. We've only had one encounter in the thirty-three years since our divorce.

In 1981, Steve, who by then was a dentist, was driving to his office in Goodlettsville, a Nashville suburb. He lost control of his car on ice and spun into a head-on collision with a semi-tractor truck. He was rushed to a Nashville hospital and lay in intensive care, unconscious and in critical condition, for days.

He eventually regained consciousness.

There was a crease in his skull. The doctor asked me and others close to him to go to the intensive care unit to talk to Steve. The doctor hoped that the sound of our voices would stimulate something in Steve's brain that would initiate consciousness. So we talked to Steve for days.

I saw my eldest son's body dripping with tubes that carried the medicine that sustained his life. I saw him lying next to heart attack patients and others who clung to life by a thread. I put my mouth next to his ear. I whispered his name and mine. Still, he slept.

The strain on me, and on Betty, became unbearable. I had long since been doing an early morning television show in Nashville. The schedule called for me to rise at 4:30 A.M. The early hours, plus the stress from Steve's possibly fatal condition, made me a hopeless insomniac. The exhaustion took its toll. I felt as though I was losing my sanity. I had been praying, indeed begging, for God to spare my boy's life. One morning during my television show, I felt the need of support from the people who watched. I couldn't hold myself back.

I told them about my boy's accident and his failing condition.

"I want you to please pray for my son," I said, my voice breaking.

Betty later told me she resented my phrasing.

"Who do you think you are, God?" she asked me. "He's my son too."

She was taking issue with the fact that I had referred to our helpless boy as "my son," not as "our son."

Her fixation on pronouns during such a traumatic time

was, I felt, absurd. Who cared about parental billing when our son's life was on the line?

I replied that my intention was to get people to pray for our son. Her petty complaint made me remember why I had divorced her almost a quarter-century earlier.

My marriage to Betty was preceded by my high school graduation and enrollment in broadcasting school. My grandmother Fuqua came from McEwen to the graduation with my mother. The two women were the only persons who supported me at my commencement.

I made no secret that I wanted to be a broadcaster. But I kept my reason secret: I wanted to be a broadcaster simply because I wanted to be somebody. I was approaching the end of adolescence. I felt I was defined by my inferiority complex. The fight against loneliness and insecurity had been a day-to-day battle for years. I had endured more of life than I had enjoyed.

Who knows what would have happened had I had a happy childhood and adolescence? I might never have sought the acceptance that I believed a microphone afforded.

There was a famous broadcaster in the South named John Richbourg who taught at the Tennessee School of Broadcasting on West End Avenue in Nashville. Betty's uncle Eddy, who wanted engineering training, and I decided that's where we would enroll. We made the decision casually while riding in his car. I could afford to pay only part of my tuition from the eleven dollars a week earned as a stock boy at Kroger's Grocery Store.

There were broadcasting students whose tuition was financed by the government. We referred to them as earning "Rockin' Chair" money because it was obvious they were there only for the free financial ride. They had no interest in broadcasting, and consequently, John Richbourg, who knew who they were, gave them little attention.

Besides working at the school, Richbourg worked at Nashville's WLAC under the name "John R." Eventually, he attained fame that extended throughout the Southeast, particularly during the advent of rock 'n' roll.

He brought wire copy from WLAC to the school and taught us how to read the news, showing us how to let our eyes wander four words ahead of the word we were pronouncing. He taught us how to implement vocal inflections for punctuation. He would have us simulate the shift of a disc jockey. One day we would pretend to air country music, the next day popular, and so forth. He made us listen to tape recordings of ourselves. I became aware of my irritating southern accent, a twang that I knew would restrict me to the smallest of rural markets.

Instead of saying sight, I said, "s-a-a-h-t." White was "w-h-i-i-i-t-e." Night was "n-i-i-i-g-h-t." I unnecessarily put a long vowel into every syllable I spoke. My diction was slurred and mushy. So I practiced, and practiced, in school and at home, talking and tape recording myself for hours to rid my speech of its horrendous regionalism. The process went on for weeks, and my hard work paid off. I attended school from February through June of 1951 and led my class.

Station WTPR, in Paris, Tennessee, contacted John Richbourg to ask if he had a student who could fill in for a vacationing staffer. John sent me.

I worked at the Paris station for one week, then had to return to work at Kroger's Grocery Store, a real letdown for me, in the wake of what I felt had been truly important work.

In broadcasting school, I had grown accustomed to talking into microphones. But there was no one really listening except other students and my instructor. It wasn't that way at WTPR, a real station, where I was so nervous on my first day you'd have thought I was broadcasting over fifty thousand watts from New York City. I was terrified.

Announcers were told to identify themselves by their first and last names, and then add, "at WTPR, your Dixie neighbor."

My first assignment at WTPR was a fifteen-minute live newscast, difficult even for a veteran. It's an olympian task for a beginner. I sat in the station all day watching other disc jockeys and announcers and thought that when I at last got on the air, I would be asked to play records and let the record do most of the work.

I had no idea they would ask me to read live for a quarter of an hour. I finished those five days in Paris. Later, I worked at the station full time for three months. I got the job largely on my own volition, but I did have the recommendation of broadcasting school officials. They said I was recommended because of my skills. I always wondered if, in fact, what they really wanted was to be sure I had a job so that I could pay my past-due tuition.

It was during my stint at WTPR that I honed my skills as a sports announcer, a craft at which I hoped to excel. Bill Stern and Harry Wismer were premier sportscasters of the day. They were my idols. I emulated them, and fantasized about doing play-by-play baseball for the major leagues, a dream that was never fulfilled.

I should have known it was not meant to be the day I was doing a play-by-play for WTPR. I really got into the game, viewing it from behind the screen. I was so confident I could accurately call plays, I began to call pitches before the umpire did.

In my most authoritative voice, I called "ball four!"

The umpire's voice leaked into my microphone, "That was a strike!"

My next call was "o-o-o-p-s-." It was unspoken.

I learned a lot about front-line broadcasting during my ninety days of full-time employment in Paris, Tennessee. One valuable lesson was that the show must go on, no matter how damaged the equipment. I learned how to wing it.

The hottest singer in the nation in 1951 was Hank Williams. The hottest record of 1951 was his "Hey Good Lookin'." Our tiny and unimportant station was sent only one copy of a song, which we played over and over throughout the day. The record was the old-fashioned seventy-eight-revolutions-per-minute kind. Its diameter was larger than that of a lawn disc. It was made of rigid plastic more breakable than peanut brittle. And it was flammable.

I found that out when someone accidentally dropped a cigarette ash in the middle of the grooves of "Hey Good Lookin'." We had to play it frequently if we were to have a remote hope of retaining listeners. People were so enthused, they used to request the song while it was playing!

But that cigarette burn, and the resulting hole in the grooves of the record, had to be dealt with.

We played the song until the phonograph needle reached the burn. At that instant, we turned down the pot (volume control) of the turntable and physically lifted the needle over the burn onto the next usable groove. Each time we played what was to become a bona fide American standard composition, we did so with about five seconds' worth of dead silence right in the song's middle. We never explained ourselves.

Listeners all over Paris, during the broadcasting of "Hey Good Lookin'," were hitting and cussing their radios, thinking that the instruments had shorted out during their favorite song.

The DJ who came on the air before me at WTPR was a graduate from the Keegan School of Broadcasting in Memphis, where he had hopelessly woven the word "nigger" into his vocabulary. One day he was reading a news story whose text included the word "Negro." You can guess what he said. Every black in town called the station to complain.

They were still calling during my shift. I'd have a telephone receiver to my ear and the microphone before my mouth, but I pressed on.

Those were happy and terrifying days. Back then, radio stations tried to be all things to all people. Announcers were disc jockeys, newsmen, sportscasters, farm reporters, and readers of on-the-air obituaries. Musical programming, in those days, was not specialized. I played a variety of music, including country and "pop," and even Hawaiian music. These were the days before "Top 40" radio. Radio stations received "pop," hillbilly, and race records from the record companies. The race records were a prelude to rhythm and blues. In Paris, Tennessee, we didn't play them.

The Paris station was affectionately referred to by its staff as a "thousand-watt 'daytimer,'" meaning that because of its position in a crowded frequency, it only broadcast during daylight. In wintertime, the station went off the air as early as 4:30 P.M. In the summertime, we were on until 7:00 P.M.

...7...

FOUR MONTHS AFTER I SIGNED ON AT PARIS, ROMANCE pulled me back to Nashville, where I landed a job at WNAH. I was again an announcer and disc jockey, during the early morning shift. I was never an early riser and yet I always managed to draw the predawn shift at most of the six radio stations early in my career. I also learned, in those beginning days, an axiom of broadcasting: The preference of the station management takes precedence over the listener's tastes. By 1957, when I went to radio's powerhouse of the South, WSM, the public was clamoring for rock 'n' roll. But the management team didn't want to play it, and it wasn't played, no matter how intense the swelling demand. When I refer to management I know full well that management often answers to ownership, and is often one and the same.

I saw management's omnipotence firsthand in 1951 during the final game of the National League pennant race. The game has been called the most exciting in baseball history. The New York Giants had chased the Brooklyn Dodgers for the pennant lead since August 12 when they were thirteen and a half games behind. Near the end of September, they caught them. There were no playoff series back then except when teams were tied at the end of the regular season. The team that won the most games in each league won the right to compete in the World Series. During that last game, an entire season's worth of competition went down to the final batter.

One occasionally still sees reruns of the pennant-deciding home run that my listeners hoped to see that day with their ears.

The game was running late; the score was tied. Suspense was mounting. Television was not predominant in American households. People were still relying on radio for information and entertainment, and especially sports. In the early 1950s, baseball was the sport of preference in the United States. It was truly the national pastime, and on that day, the pastime bordered on passion.

At 5:30 P.M., I was scheduled to air a religious broadcast. The time slot had already been purchased. The church service was imminent, but the deciding game of the National League season was still underway. Station WNAH did not pull a large share of the listening market. I suspect that its largest audience of the year, however, was tuned in on that suspenseful Sunday.

I didn't know what to do. The listeners, I knew, wanted the baseball championship. They were glued to radios all over town. But a preacher owned the upcoming broadcast time, scheduled to begin in minutes. The clock was ticking.

I called my boss at home.

He ordered me to discontinue the ballgame and begin the religious broadcast on schedule. Although there was more listener interest in baseball, there was more money for management in religion.

In the bottom of the ninth inning, with the bases loaded and the winning run at the plate, I pulled the plug on the biggest game of the year, and perhaps the biggest of the decade. I stopped the sports world cold as surely as David stopped Goliath.

About that time, Bobby Thomson hit a home run that ended the game and garnered the pennant for the Giants. Fans around the country were ecstatic.

Red Smith, of the *New York Herald Tribune*, wrote of

the game, "Now it is done. Now the story ends, and there is no way to tell it. The art of fiction is dead. Reality has strangled invention. Only the utterly impossible, the unexpressibly fantastic, can ever be plausible again."

My listeners, who had followed the Giants all season, did not hear what some insist was the most dramatic moment in baseball. But I immediately heard from them.

Angry, profane calls clogged the switchboard. There were so many so fast, and their tone was so hostile, that I took the studio telephones off the hooks. The audience blamed me for the incident.

I was called names that I suspect weren't even applied to umpires. Meanwhile, the religious show pressed on. People wanting baseball got the Bible. A sermon about loving thy neighbor, particularly one who works in radio, would have been in order.

I saw firsthand how radio had its own Golden Rule: The man with the gold makes the rules. If a preacher, or anyone else, can pay enough to dictate programming, the programming stands. Management, then and to a great degree now, goes for cash over culture.

Live, religious broadcasting, the shows of the 1950s, were embarrassingly bad, and I don't say that as a reflection on the sincerity of their proponents. Sincerity, in fact, was about all some of those well-meaning ministers had going for them. Many were self-proclaimed preachers, minus any formal or theological training. They were far more enthusiastic than informed. Their credentials were simply that God had "called" them to preach. For some, He obviously should have called back—with a new directive.

At another station, I was the engineer running the sound board for a zealous preacher. The hysterical man of God was beating his Bible all over the studio. A miracle was needed for me to keep his voice within range of the microphone. I naturally thought he was totally consumed with his thoughts. But there was another reason for his zeal. I didn't know it at the time but the preacher had not been paying his bills to the station. I decided later that he was yelling particularly fast so as to condense his sermon to fit the time left. He had been warned to pay me first for running his sound board. That came to nine dollars. He had also been told that if he ran overtime by one second, he would be cut off the air.

When it was time for his program to end, he didn't wind down, or in any way indicate that his sermon had come to a close. There wasn't even the sustained invitation for listeners to accept Christ into their hearts. There simply was no clue that the preacher was about to finish.

"The 'Lorda' God, my time's done come and gone, here's your friend and mine, Ralph Emery!" he shouted, and was off the microphone and out the door without another syllable. There was plenty of "dead" time as I scrambled to play a record.

Another preacher, a woman, used to speak with such a dulcet delivery, she nearly lulled me to sleep each time I ran her board. She talked about Jesus only slightly above a whisper, the way people speak at funerals. She reeked of self-approval, as if she knew that Jesus delighted in her overly affectionate portrayal of Him. I found her whole presentation to be sickening and sanctimonious.

She packaged Christ as a sissy. She referred to Him as "our beloved and precious Rose of Sharon." I know Jesus was gentle, but she made Him sound like a fairy.

Here was a guy who walked all over Israel, and she made him out to be a weakling. She was unduly mushy and proper, and put a doily under her Bible. Yuk.

I once worked the board when an exuberant man of the cloth came into the studio with his wife, another woman, and a guitar with an electronic short in its amplifier. I could tell it was defective by the loud "hum" in his speaker.

I walked from the control room into the studio to exchange pleasantries, then assumed my position on my side of the glass separating the rooms. I raised the sound as they played their opening theme song, faded the volume, spoke over the music, let the theme finish, and then said, "Here again is Brother So and So."

These preachers were loud and demonstrative fundamentalists. To escape his screaming, I would simply turn off the monitor in my control room. I couldn't hear any of his yelling, although I could see through the glass his jumping and straining. Every so often, I would raise my eyes from a newspaper and watch the Gospel pantomime.

Suddenly, I heard him yelling through his sheer lung power.

"Oh-Oh-Oh-Oh!" he said, his face contorting.

"My God, he's epileptic," I thought, and jumped to my feet.

No, I decided, he's just gotten the spirit early this week.

Then I noticed his thumb. The instant he touched the steel string of his guitar and simultaneously reached for the steel microphone in front of him, he grounded himself because of the short in his amplifier.

He was jumping and shaking as 110 volts shot through his torso. His moist palm was rigidly clamped to the microphone.

The guy couldn't let go. He was a captive of voltage.

His wife raised her arm, and in karate fashion, hit his arm with all her force. The blow broke his grip from the charged microphone, but his painful yells had gone over the air.

As calmly as I could, I said, "One moment please." I imagine listeners thought he'd really gotten a dose of the Holy Ghost, as he frequently spoke "in tongues" as part of his sermon. I hoped the fellow believed in divine healing.

Bill Ormes, the station manager, called in with some yelling of his own. He, of course, wanted to know, "What in the hell is going on?"

I told him, and he laughed uproariously.

I settled Bill, as well as the preacher, who finished his sermon without ever touching the microphone again.

I was in the control room another time when a singer in a Gospel group, who weighed more than his piano stool could support, sat down, broke one of the legs, and tumbled onto the floor like a sack of fertilizer. He too howled over live radio, prompting a barrage of curious calls.

I'm not poking fun at the old religious broadcasts, merely

pointing out that in radio money talks, no matter how bad the programming. If the radio preachers could pay, they could pray, as loudly and for as long as they wanted.

Sometimes people who own radio stations will use them as a medium to further their own beliefs. That was another lesson for me at WNAH.

I suspect that WNAH was the least listened-to radio station in Nashville in 1952. There was so little public feedback, management didn't bother subscribing to a ratings service. Although I was on the air during early daylight, I felt as though my voice was floating into an abyss and frequently wondered if anyone was out there.

I did a show called *Rise and Shine* in which I was forbidden to play country music, which management thought catered to hillbillies and low-class people. I was allowed to play Gospel, and some pop music.

In an effort to bolster the listening audience, which was, after all, my job, I decided I would open my telephone lines and take requests. Everybody, I thought, likes to hear his name on the radio, and maybe this ploy would attract new listeners.

Someone called and asked for Buddy Morrow's "One Mint Julep." A mint julep, of course, is a cocktail. The song's arrangement was straightforward, and sounded nothing like the Blackwood Brothers, Stamps Quartet, or other southern Gospel quartets. Neither did it resemble the works of Sammy Kaye or Guy Lombardo, two artists we also played regularly.

"One Mint Julep" was playing live over the radio and the station owner stormed into my control room.

"Take that off!" she commanded. She grabbed the phonograph record, oblivious to the needle, which bounced heavily, several times, on the record. The ensuing noise, as it went out over the air, must have sounded like a basketball dribbling in a hollow gymnasium.

I immediately turned down the pot so the listeners couldn't hear any more of the bobbing needle.

I was embarrassed and humiliated and decided that I didn't want to work there anymore.

The spiteful woman got her way, the listener didn't get his request, and no one, in her mind, heard the devil's music.

To the credit of WNAH, it did decline to air one of the sickest examples of commercialism I ever saw. I was working at the station on January 1, 1953, when Hank Williams died. To this day, I'm still asked for personal recollections about the effect of the death of Hank Williams on the country music industry. Back in those days, fans didn't just love the stars—they worshiped them. It was unadulterated idolatry. Williams's fans wanted him to touch their children and bless their babies.

I was nineteen years old, working for the most insignificant station in town, and was really, as Tom T. Hall would say, "about as important as wallpaper."

A man sneaked into Williams's funeral in Montgomery, Alabama, and recorded the star-studded service. Ernest Tubb sang "Beyond the Sunset," Roy Acuff did "I Saw the Light," and Red Foley sang "Peace in the Valley." These three men were the country music giants of the day.

In a May 19, 1955, article by Eli Waldron in Montgomery's *The Reporter,* the funeral was called "the greatest emotional orgy in the city's history since the inauguration of Jefferson Davis."

Three thousand people jammed the municipal auditorium and twenty-five thousand reportedly were turned away. The print coverage of Williams's death, at least in the South, was exceeded only by coverage of the death of Elvis Presley almost a quarter century later.

This guy with the clandestine recording thought he would make an incredible killing off the dead. He tried to sell an audio and possibly bootlegged recording of the funeral, for broadcast, to WNAH. Station officials sent him packing, and I was proud, although I suspect an additional reason they declined was that they hated country music.

I wondered how low some people could go.

I had worked for two stations in less than a year after leaving broadcasting school, and it was now apparent that

John Richbourg hadn't told me about every occupational situation one might encounter.

I was determined to get out of WNAH. Because it wouldn't play country music, its library was swollen with unused records. A new station in nearby Franklin, Tennessee, got wind of the collection. Bill Ormes, the Franklin owner, visited WNAH to inquire about buying its unused library. When he did, I pulled him and his program director, Bob Holland, off to the side and asked for a job.

In April 1953, before WAGG in Franklin was one month old, it retained Ralph Emery as a staff announcer and disc jockey for sixty dollars a week. I learned almost as much at WAGG as I did in broadcasting school.

The only time I had ever met celebrities back at WTPR in Paris was when the Carter Family visited the little, thousand-watt station to promote a show they were doing that night at a football field. One of the Carter girls, June, grew up to become Mrs. Johnny Cash. Given the Carter Family's importance, I naturally wanted to interview them that day in Paris. But I was the junior announcer on staff, and I was not allowed to. That wasn't the only time rank was pulled on me. I discovered that radio had a seniority system and pecking order.

But things were different in Franklin. I had more broadcasting history than the month-old station did. That's the reason I got my opportunity to interview celebrities from nearby Nashville.

The first was the legendary Grand Ole Opry performer Del Wood, who died in 1988. She had just recorded a song that for years was her theme song on the Grand Ole Opry. It was called "Down Yonder" and became a standard, although she only did the song as an instrumental. The day I first met Del she was accompanied by Fred Foster, who later founded Monument Records and signed Roy Orbison and Dolly Parton.

I routinely stopped my car at the office of music publisher Fred Rose on the way to Franklin, about twenty miles from Nashville. Mr. Rose discovered the songwriting talents of Hank Williams, who had died three months earlier. Mr. Rose, with Roy Acuff, founded Acuff-Rose Publishing Company, one of the world's largest and most prestigious country music publishing houses right up to this day. The staff was helpful in sending records to our fledgling music library at WAGG and equally helpful in securing celebrity interviews. I think that if Hank Williams had lived, Mr. Rose would have put him on the air with me, even though I was a novice.

The second interview was with the late Webb Pierce, indisputably a country music force in the 1950s. The day he appeared on my show Webb was perhaps the most popular living country music singer.

Another act popular at the time was the Wilburn Brothers. Teddy Wilburn was in the service. One day, Doyle Wilburn and Webb Pierce walked into my studio and sat down before the microphone. Both men were enjoying heavy air play on the Armed Services Radio Network aimed at our fighting men in Korea.

"Look at this," I thought to myself. "I have two international stars on my show—right here in Franklin."

I suddenly felt that being in radio was unequivocally the right thing for me after all.

I was braced and prepared for the interviews. I just knew I could dazzle these dashing young stars with my poignant questions, and that I could impress Fred Rose, listening in Nashville.

I was about to get another lesson.

I had done my homework on Webb Pierce. I naturally wanted to talk about his career, but I also planned to impress Webb and the listeners with questions about his personal life.

"Now Ralph," admonished Webb's manager, Hubert Long, just before the show. "Don't mention anything on the radio about Webb's wife. In fact, don't even let folks know he's married. He's got a lot of young girls for fans, and we don't want them to know he's taken. So you just pretend he's single and available and we'll get along fine."

Eventually, I would grow to understand the importance

of a public image in show business. But at such a young age, the idea of doing a candid interview with ground rules seemed like an obvious contradiction.

Before I left Franklin, I learned yet another lesson. In my mind I suspected that I had a guardian angel. The Bible talks about God giving His angels charge over his worshipers. I believe that He has given at least one angel the responsibility of watching over me. That angel was riding with me one frosty morning en route to my early shift in Franklin. Thank God the angel wasn't mortal. He might have been killed.

I was sleepy, and my drowsiness was worsened by the hum of a loud car heater, whose purr, coupled with its warmth, put me to sleep—at the wheel—at forty-five miles per hour.

When I bolted awake, my car was running along a barbed wire fence. The vehicle kept upending and breaking off fenceposts as if they were toothpicks. The front windshield broke, and barbed wire was snapping like twine, its razor sharpness whipping and lashing in and out of my car. If just one of those wire strands had failed to break, I could have been decapitated.

Before I could stop the car, it overturned. Most of the windows were shattered, and the doors and fenders looked as though I'd lost a demolition derby. I was scratched from the barbed wire and I had bruises, but miraculously, that was the extent of my injuries.

I stood there shivering and watching my breath in the winter predawn, conscious but addled. That was the beginning of my end at WAGG; I didn't want to drive there when I was often virtually asleep in my seat. I was permanently off that station and back in Nashville within days.

The accident could have been more serious, but for some reason, I didn't think about it at the time. I didn't think of it until two days later when I was in church and began to take mental inventory of my life, which seemed to be passing rapidly in front of me. My brush with death became clear to me with the force of my jalopy striking those fenceposts.

I began to quiver and felt myself weaken. Right there in that sanctuary amid the congregation I went into shock. I left the service early. I rested and thanked God and didn't even think about getting up for two full days. I never once turned on a radio.

...8...

IN NOVEMBER 1953, RADIO STATION WSIX ANNOUNCED
that it would share its call letters with what would become
Nashville's second television station. That meant many of
WSIX's radio personnel would be moving to television,
which meant that there would be openings at WSIX radio.

I went to the program director, Jimmy Kent, and let him
know my dissatisfaction at working the early morning slot
in Franklin. I told him about my car wreck, and how they
had removed enough barbed wire from my crumpled vehicle to bind several bales of hay. I told him I wanted to get
out of Franklin. I told him I wanted to fill a vacancy at
WSIX.

He said, "Start Monday," and I bade the Franklin folks
good-bye.

WSIX was a step up for several reasons. First, WSIX
was considered a pioneer Nashville radio station. With
WSM and WLAC, it was one of Nashville's "big three."
There was no such thing as FM radio, and there were only
about six AM stations in Nashville. WSIX had been on the
air since the heyday of radio itself. WSIX was also the first
station I worked at that had more than one thousand watts
of power (it had five thousand). It was my first full-time
station and my first with a network affiliation (ABC), and

my first that subscribed to a ratings service. Its market standing with listeners was published and advertising was sold on that basis. This was my first brush with the "real thing."

Another bonus came my way, although it was a surprise. At WSIX, I was allowed to announce, for my first time, on television! It wasn't my own show, and it wasn't exactly prestigious.

It was studio wrestling.

It was the same stuff that led to the mega-industry today with celebrities such as Hulk Hogan and Junk Yard Dog, whose enthralled fans fill Madison Square Garden and support any number of cable and major network television channels. The "sport's" popularity explosion was not even a sparkle in 1954 when I made my television debut. Twenty-eight years later, I would become host of a prime-time cable show whose kind viewers would eventually vote me cable television's favorite talk show host. I would also have guest appearances on the NBC television network.

My subsequent success belies my auspicious television premiere in the dressing room of WSIX-TV in 1954. I wasn't intimidated by the visual medium, but neither was I overconfident. For the first time in my brief career, I was being asked to expand rather than abbreviate my thoughts. I was to do "play-by-play" for a sport I had never observed before and do it live.

I studied pages and pages of wrestling holds. Jack Simpson, the show's regular announcer, for whom I was substituting, showed me various postures so I would know the name for each hold. I committed them to memory, and prepared for my guest shot as thoroughly as if I were doing commentary for the Olympic Games.

This introduction to studio wrestling was perhaps my best training in keeping my wits while those around me lost theirs.

A woman got so excited once that she urinated on the studio floor. Another fan, who had been extremely vocal throughout the events, was distressed with the referee's pick of a winner. He broke a soda bottle across a bleacher, making jagged glass. He gripped the neck and charged a wrestler with the improvised dagger. There were no injuries because the fan was informed that the wrestler was stronger than he looked.

In a low and authoritative tone, Nick Gulas, the show's promoter, told the would-be assailant, "Old man, he'll kill you."

The old man sat down.

My wrestling days were also an exposure to theatrics of a kind I had never seen. Those "contestants" would scream at each other, and appear to beat upon each other, violently and without restraint. Then they would retire to mutual dressing rooms and laugh and socialize as if the previous minutes had all been a show. They had, in fact, been just that.

Much has been written about television wrestling in the 1950s not being genuine. It was. It was a genuine fake.

The Nashville bouts began after the *Lawrence Welk Show*. The dressing room was filled with the wrestlers sitting together, some arm-in-arm, watching Mr. Welk and giggling and tittering about his bubble machine.

Minutes later, those same men were pretending to bash each other inside the ring, on a floor so spongy it could have been used as a trampoline.

I'm sure I missed some of the calls. Spotting a hammerlock was easy. So was a full or half nelson. But the Australian crawl was impossible for me and I didn't hit on too many of the toeholds.

I should have been touted as a wrestling emcee, not an announcer. The former term is associated with a show, and that's exactly what wrestling was, grand entertainment.

I performed my wrestling-related duties twice, once when the regular announcer got married, and once when he had a heart attack. One didn't spawn the other.

About that same time, when I was twenty-one or twenty-two years old, I made my debut on the ABC Radio Network. A touring, in-depth news program called *America's Town Meeting of the Air* came to Nashville's David Lipscomb College, and WSIX provided an announcer to do the program's opening and closing on live radio. I got the assignment and even did a spot advertisement in the middle. I wasn't paid but I didn't really mind. I had been on a major radio network, and for a few minutes, my voice had been heard all over the United States.

In 1955 I was an announcer for a high school student who had a live music show on Saturday mornings. He would graduate and go on to David Lipscomb College (now David Lipscomb University). On the strength of my having worked with him in those early days, I would eventually get my first out-of-state job in radio and a one-hundred-dollar-a-week salary. That figure was my exact goal, about which I had often dreamed.

The star of that 1955 Saturday show, a man I did not take seriously at that time, became one of the most popular recording artists of the 1950s, alongside Elvis Presley, Ricky Nelson, and Jerry Lee Lewis.

Back then, Pat Boone was just a frightened kid, with less experience than I had.

Pat did a half-hour show called *Youth on Parade,* which called for me to announce the opening, closing, and all commercials. Between my segments of banter, Pat sang. I got the job only because I happened to be the announcer on duty at the time.

Pat Boone was as friendly and polite then as he is today. He is one celebrity I've known who has remained unaffected by fame. He was then dating the former Shirley Foley, Red Foley's daughter, and he eventually married her. They were such an innocent, vanilla couple, I used to wonder if they were intimidated by the environment of a radio station where men freely smoked, swore, and drank to excess, usually, but not always, when off the air.

The station employed a likeable, competent guy, a boozer named Joe Calloway. Joe worked with me in the mornings. He would smuggle inside his trouser leg a half-pint of whiskey. He would polish off the hooch during his shift, then throw the bottle over his shoulder and out the window. The roof of a lower building next door was covered with Joe's half-pint disposables.

One morning when I was reading the news, Joe put a skunk in the studio with me. I figured it had been deodorized, or Joe wouldn't have been able to carry it. The thing got behind a radiator, and we had a terrible time getting it out. Joe loved animals. I loved Joe.

He once bought a live cougar and had the monster delivered to his apartment. He stuck the animal in his bathroom, but didn't tell his wife. When she opened the bathroom door, the cat, it was reported, nearly ate her alive.

She divorced Joe soon after.

When Joe and his wife weren't getting along, he would come to the station and sleep in the television viewing room, usually reserved for advertising clients to see their commercials. Joe would often sleep off a drunk in that room in his underwear. Shirley Foley watched television in that room while waiting for Pat while he did his evening show. She would often behold a snoring Joe in his boxer shorts. I always wondered what that unblemished child thought about the sight.

Joe, on the other hand, was constantly complaining about *her*. He'd fume that she was just a kid, and that kids ought to be at home. He was so old, so intoxicated, and had been at the station so long that he had become cantankerous and territorial. He was annoyed because she had interrupted his sleep. I liked him a lot, and was sorry when he died a few years ago.

A cohort at WSIX tried to fool management by taking two hats to work. He would put one on the rack, to make it appear he was on the premises, on the job. His name was Mr. Smith, and he was the head of accounting.

He spent most of his workdays at a nearby pool hall. One day the station owner, Louis Draughon, figured out the ploy, and marched down to the pool room.

But he wasn't admitted.

The pool hall was inside the Elks Lodge and with all of his money Mr. Draughon, who was not a member, could not get inside. He was furious, and Mr. Smith was nearly fired.

I learned much in a short time once I became affiliated with WSIX, a real radio station. I felt, for the first time, the stress of wanting to do a job correctly. At WSIX work was not as "good ole boy" as it had been at the smaller stations. I discovered that people under pressure do unusual things to relieve it. With Joe, the release came from a bottle. With others, the relief came from humor.

I've read countless stories and seen motion pictures about chicanery in a pressure-filled newspaper city room. I suspect it was a similar pressure, or at least a similar personality type, that prompted much of the mischief that I enjoyed in radio, beginning at WSIX.

Radio staff members were intolerant of anyone they thought was phony. The career guys were accustomed to letting down their hair, and they wanted their peers to do the same. One day, a fellow joined our WSIX ranks claiming to have worked for the NBC Radio Network. We checked his story and found that he had in fact worked for the network—as a page boy.

That discovery, coupled with the guy's pompous personality, made him a prime candidate for a practical joke. The gang plotted for days. The favorite ploy was to force the victim to lose his composure while on the air.

That's what we did to this guy. Unfortunately, our timing was terrible. The joke was on us.

The announcer was reading a public service announcement. We were making faces through the studio glass. Someone dropped his pants, a standard stunt to break someone up. We were acting like fools, paying no attention to what the intended victim was saying.

His announcement went something like, "Did you know that last year 495 children were killed on the nation's highways? . . . Ha! Ha! Ha!"

He couldn't stop laughing. It was 6:15 P.M., and the telephone switchboard was closed, the only reason, I'm sure, we weren't inundated with angry calls. Otherwise, I'm sure every one of us would have been fired.

I was earning seventy-five dollars a week, participating in what at times was a perpetual party. Morale was high, as it often inexplicably is among economically oppressed people. Those were glorious days.

I did a midmorning show that was off-the-wall, free-association hilarity. I figured I needed a handle, and came up with "Roof the Goof." Man, it was silly. But it was a hit. The program was initiated to fill a thirty-minute slot and was expanded to an hour and forty-five minutes.

The late and legendary Marty Robbins, who many critics still contend was the greatest country vocalist of all time, used to visit me frequently at WSIX. His monumental hits, such as "White Sport Coat (And a Pink Carnation)," "El Paso," and "Begging to You," were still in the uncertain future. Marty was a Grand Ole Opry star at the time, looking for the big songs he eventually found. Yet, even as early as 1955, his velvet talent was heralded among fans. I ran a singer popularity contest among my listeners. I didn't break down voting into group or gender categories. I simply asked listeners to tell me the name of their favorite country music singer.

Marty won hands down. Ironically, I staged a similar contest fifteen years later, after legends such as Jim Reeves, Johnny Cash, Faron Young, Johnny Horton, Conway Twitty, George Jones, Ray Price, and others had long been on the scene. The 1970 all-time favorite (male) country singer among my listeners was again Marty Robbins.

I expanded the latter balloting to include the favorite female singer, won by Loretta Lynn, and the favorite group, won by Flatt and Scruggs. When Marty and Loretta came to my show to accept their awards on live radio, I thought it would be clever to have them sing a duet. It was the only time they ever did, and I have it on tape. But the duet almost never happened. They couldn't decide what to sing, so I suggested the obvious, and said they should do a Hank Williams song, "Your Cheatin' Heart." As it turned out, neither of them knew the standard. That was unheard-of among country stars. I was shocked. I thought everybody knew it.

Marty's career could have been launched in 1955, he felt, if his records had been played on the dean of country music radio stations, WSM. It was about four blocks up Union Street from WSIX.

Marty would visit my show, and when the microphone was turned off, he shouted and waved his fist at the window facing WSM.

"Those sons of bitches won't play my records!" he'd yell. He was especially angry at WSM's Eddie Hill, then the overnight and arguably most influential disc jockey in country music. Marty overflowed with energy and ambition, much the way Barbara Mandrell does today. He was consequently frustrated when someone wouldn't give him an outlet for that unbridled drive. He had only been in Nashville for a couple of years, and the obstacles of the entertainment business at times were too much for him.

Ferlin Husky, on the other hand, was a show business veteran. He had recorded several hit records under the name of Terry Preston on the West Coast, where he had also made many motion pictures. Ferlin did a comedy routine involving an alter ego named Simon Crum. He would come to WSIX regularly, sit in front of my microphone, and talk to fans as Ferlin, and then in the high-pitched voice of Simon, holding conversations with himself, and the people loved it.

There was a final lesson I learned at WSIX: the value of reputation for an air personality. Although my show commanded second- and sometimes first-place ratings in the market during my time slot, I had no national reputation. When WSIX was sold, the new owners imported a number of personalities who did and paid them more than they paid me. I thought this was unfair. None of the newcomers had paid his dues at WSIX. None had the immediate ratings I had. All had great track records at other Nashville stations. Eventually, I would learn the value of name, but at the time, all I felt was cheated and frustrated. So once again, I started looking. A record promotions man told me WLCS in Baton Rouge, Louisiana, needed a disc jockey. He took a tape recording of one of my WSIX shows to Baton Rouge and the station officials called me. They offered me a job, and my first chance to work outside my home state, and it marked the first time I would be paid one hundred dollars a week! I moved to Baton Rouge. The year was 1956 and Pat Boone was just about the hottest vocalist in the free world.

Before I could get my suitcase packed for the move, the Baton Rouge press broke a story with headlines the size of those announcing the end of the Second World War: Ralph Emery, former announcer for Pat Boone, was headed for Baton Rouge radio.

My nest, I felt, was already feathered. And I had yet to speak my first word inside Louisiana.

...9...

I HAD A LESS THAN STELLAR CAREER IN BATON ROUGE BE-
cause I stayed there less than a month. While there, I
quickly rented a sleeping room.

I was finally earning a three-digit salary, my goal. But
when shifts were finished, I was alone—alone to the bone.
Betty chose not to accompany me to Baton Rouge because
of mounting marital friction.

It was as if my marriage, and the birth four years earlier
of my first son, Steve, had not even happened. Weekends
were the worst, all three of them. During the week, I had
the company of the radio staff. Although I hardly knew
them, I joined the obligatory shooting of the breeze about
radio.

But then those guys went home to families, and I went
to my rented cell.

Why did I ever bother to get married, start a family, go
to school, begin a career, or anything, I wondered? I was
by myself when I began all of that and I was still alone. I
discovered that there was something worse than feeling
lonely when you were around people. That was feeling
lonely when nobody was around. The conventional word
for that is homesick. I had a terminal case.

Perhaps it was my nonexistent "home life" that forced

me to focus on my profession. It was a futile cycle wherein I lived to work and worked to live merely because I had nothing else to do. Word of my workaholic performance spread to Nashville. The program director at WMAK, a new rock 'n' roll station, called me. We had a brief conversation.

"Ralph, are you happy down there in Louisiana?" the caller asked.

"No, I'm miserable, but they're paying me one hundred dollars a week, my lifelong salary goal."

"I'll pay you $125 a week to work here," he said.

"I'll quit today," I said, but in fact gave two weeks' notice. Baton Rouge management matched the Nashville offer, but it was too little too late. I don't think I would have stayed for $150. That was thirty-five years ago, and these monetary figures represented a respectable salary, although they are less than minimum wage today.

I knew that I would get to play rock at WMAK. The new music that was a hybrid of country and Gospel was leaving both in its wake. Most disc jockeys in the nation realized that popularity was guaranteed to any air personality who played rock. I especially needed no convincing because of the personal experience I had about a year earlier with Elvis Presley. I saw firsthand how uncontrollably magnetic was the draw of Presley and his musical peers, all of whom were grinding out hit records as fast as plants in Nashville and Memphis could produce them for a rock 'n' roll–starved world.

I was still at WSIX when Ed Hines, a promotion man for RCA (with whom Presley had recently signed) called me while I was on the air. That call was a directive from Colonel Tom Parker, Presley's controversial and flamboyant manager. Parker told Hines to let me know that Presley would be leaving the RCA studio on Nashville's Seventeenth Avenue South about 2:00 P.M.

"Okay," I thought to myself, "so what?"

"Well, some of your listeners might like to know," Hines said. "Would you please announce it on the air?"

I did, and thought little about it. After all, WSIX was

not an exclusive rock 'n' roll station. Presley had only done one hit at that time for RCA, and had therefore only released one song from Nashville (his previous releases had come out of Memphis, some 220 miles west).

Before Hines hung up, he asked if I would say hello to Elvis, which I did. I don't recall the gist of our conversation, except that he seemed overly polite and humble about being able to talk to a disc jockey. I felt sorry for the kid. He was probably going to get his feelings hurt because nobody cared that he was going to be walking outside of the RCA studios. It was a weekday and people had better things to do than show up hoping to get a glimpse of a hopeful singer.

Over the telephone, I said good-bye to Presley. City authorities subsequently said hello to mayhem.

Typical of the colonel's promotional savvy, he did not let Presley leave RCA that day until three hours after his scheduled departure. Soon, the streets were hopelessly clogged with fans hoping for a peek at the soon-to-be king. Apparently someone touting Presley just "happened" to arrange for photographers to come by about the time Elvis was leaving the studios. The frenetic mob was captured on film and was reproduced by newswires throughout the country.

We in radio were later asked to monitor the crowd and provide updates about the jubilant goings-on downtown, spawned because a teenager in saddle shoes had walked from a concrete block building to an idling automobile.

The reaction was that pronounced to a gesture that insignificant. I couldn't wait to get back to Nashville to play the music. In Baton Rouge, I didn't even have a car, and had to take taxicabs everywhere. That too added to my sense of isolation.

Back in Nashville, I continued working a part-time job at Theater Recording Company, which made tape-recorded programming for drive-in movie theaters. The job provided an extra fifty dollars a week. The recordings were played through speakers attached to car windows between feature film attractions.

The enterprise employed many Nashville disc jockeys, including Bud Dancey, who is now John Dancey, of the NBC Television Network. NBC news officials made him change his first name because "Bud" didn't sound dignified.

I worked at those two jobs to make ends meet.

And I was fired by my primary employer, let go, the only time in my career, by a station that had encouraged me to quit my former job. I had been hired by owners who had sold the station shortly before I assumed my duties. The new owners hired a new program director, who fired me.

That firing was terribly traumatic. With hindsight, I think it was the best break I ever had. I would not have gone to The Nashville Network (cable television) had I not previously gone to syndicated television. I would never have moved to syndicated television had I not moved to the Cadillac of country music radio stations, WSM. And I definitely would never have gone to WSM if I hadn't been fired at WMAK.

It all began when I hired a guy to work at the Theater Recording Company (which, by now, I had purchased). I also worked with him at WMAK. He was a nighttime disc jockey, Wayne "The Brain" Hannah, and truly a visionary. He had been the first white person to pick up the race records, and saw how the white public responded overwhelmingly to the music. He saw the coming of nonblack vocalists performing black music before it was ever given the handle "rock 'n' roll."

Wayne was undeniably ahead of his time and we became good friends in that special mold reserved for people who are trying something new, and trying it together. We shared a lot of uncertainty, given the untested musical art form we were playing, and my fledgling tape recording company. That made a bond between us, which was why I was outraged and wounded when WMAK fired Wayne.

Wayne said or did something that really made management angry. There was no risk in replacing Wayne, since the world was filled with young men who wanted to play rock 'n' roll. He, in so many words, was going to be told not to let the door hit him in the rear when he walked out—for the final time. To make matters worse, his wife was pregnant.

I was told about the pending firing and was warned not to tell him. I went directly to the control room and told Wayne all I knew. I put my loyalty to my friend above that to my employer.

"Wayne, they're going to fire you," I announced. "Get a job and get it quickly. They told me, they just haven't told you, but they're about to."

With that disclosure, I learned still another valuable lesson about radio. Not every listener is in the audience.

A man in the control booth overheard my pronouncement. He was a "brown noser."

He told the bosses about my revelation to Wayne and they in turn told me to get out. Because I had tried to alert Wayne about his forthcoming firing I myself was fired.

Wayne kept his job, but only for a week. He was still reeling over my canning when he went to an announcers' meeting and called the program director a son of a bitch.

Wayne was instantly fired. The employment for which I had sacrificed mine was terminated.

I was desperate for a job—any job. The only available air job in Nashville happened to be the best job at the best country music station in the world. I had just heard about the opening, took a long shot and made the long walk to WSM in October of 1957. I walked in the doors of the biggest fifty-thousand-watt, clear-channel country station in the South. I would have just as quickly gone back to tiny Paris, Tennessee, if there had been a position there. I had nothing to lose, and everything to gain by trying for the big time. I made a bet with myself that Elvis would sing opera before WSM would let me join its roster of broadcasting legends.

The position was on the all-night shift, previously held by the nocturnal dean of country announcing, "Smilin' " Eddie Hill, who was succeeded briefly by T. Tommy Cutrer, who was, in turn, succeeded by Bill Morgan, brother to the late Grand Ole Opry star George Morgan. George was the father of contemporary singing star Lorrie Morgan. Eddie and Tommy were so established, they didn't have to sit up all night playing "hillbilly records," as they were affectionately then called in the industry. None of the other WSM announcers wanted the all-night shift either. Their refusal to work the graveyard shift was a green light for a newcomer. That was the only thing in my favor as I reached for the intangible brass ring.

A number of personalities were auditioned for a week each. Out of all the applicants I was the only one who had straight announcing and disc jockey experience, so I was hired.

I had been living on my pittance from the little drive-in tape-recording company and was almost broke when I was hired by one of the biggest radio stations in the world! I ironically took a salary cut from what I had been earning at WMAK. I began at ninety dollars a week and learned firsthand that there is no correlation between wattage and salary in the radio industry.

And there was a further twist.

The station that fired me for protecting my friend, then fired my friend, called me to replace him. I was offered Wayne Hannah's old job.

And I took it.

I accepted the job at WMAK knowing that I had been hired by WSM and would begin there in a few days. I took the job so that I could intentionally abuse the station that had abused my friend and me. I wanted revenge.

I returned to the WMAK microphone, worked the week, and told the boss to kiss my ass. I told him I didn't want to talk to him, but he could listen to me on the "power-house of the South," WSM Radio.

I started in November 1957 and worked all night during most of the next few years. From my perch, my voice would be boomed across North America. I would be named "Disc Jockey of the Year" six times by various trade organizations.

And I amassed a wealth of compelling memories drawn

from one-to-one interactions with entertainment's loftiest luminaries. I could randomly select from those WSM nights and write an entire book about almost any one of them. In six years, I had gone from a small station in Paris, Tennessee, to the premier country music broadcasting job in the world. Life was getting immeasurably sweeter.

... 10 ...

I HAD BEEN WORKING AT WSM FOR JUST ABOUT A WEEK when I attended my fifth annual disc jockey and Grand Ole Opry birthday party convention in Nashville in 1957. (It used to be held each November, the actual Opry anniversary, but was moved to October in 1965. However, it wasn't until 1968 that the actual Association awards show became a perennial prime-time ceremony on CBS-TV.) I was used to being a delegate from small stations and was astonished at how differently I was treated after I became part of WSM. I was the target of overt schmoozing from entertainment executives and celebrities alike.

The people who were giving me their business cards and best lines wouldn't have given me the time of day six years earlier in Paris, Tennessee. They seemed to know I was getting fan mail from, besides the United States, Central America and sailors floating the Atlantic Ocean hundreds of miles from the eastern seaboard.

Increasingly I became the focus of stars' favors. Was it me or my position that was being chased by show business's best and brightest? I had to surmise that it was Ralph Emery the professional, not the person, whose friendship was sought. I have a lot of acquaintances in the entertainment industry, but just a few friends. I know who belongs to which group. During my early years at WSM, I was befriended by Ferlin Husky and the late Marty Robbins. Other friendships were proven in time. But almost immediately, I sensed the warmth and humanity from those two.

I had thought that the most exciting event in my life would stand as my being hired by WSM. I was wrong. The most exciting event, up until that time, was actually settling behind the microphone, and beginning my affiliation with the greatest radio station on earth.

I was with a national broadcast force originating from my own community. The late country crooner Jim Reeves, whose satin voice has never been replaced, was doing a daily, live show that was fed by WSM to the ABC Radio Network. On Saturday nights, WSM fed the Grand Ole Opry to NBC.

Within days of joining WSM, I began receiving mail from many corners of the globe and correspondence from men in uniform.

Some of the late-night telephone calls were unusual. One call was from a prison guard in Jefferson City, Missouri. He said rain was falling on the cold gray walls, the prisoners were asleep, and he had the flu.

"Could you play me a good blues tune to make me sad?" he asked.

What did it take to bring that guy down?

One day on the Jim Reeves Show, the late David Cobb, the announcer, ab-libbed a line that should have allowed him to retire with a sultan's riches had the words been copyrighted.

The program, he said, was originating from Nashville, Tennessee, "Music City U.S.A."

Up to that point, Nashville's second name had been "the Athens of the South," which is still used. But the Athens handle today is a distant second to the Music City nickname. Contemporary phone book pages are overrun with "Music City" businesses, including a taxicab company, dry cleaners, road builders, barber shops, and scores of others.

There was even a Music City Escort Service, a front, it is said, for a prostitution service.

David Cobb did get a plaque, presented at a Vanderbilt University football game, the only recognition he ever received for his map-changing and multi-million-dollar phrase.

In 1957 I became aware of discontent among country music celebrities. I knew that not every member of the Grand Ole Opry was as fraternal as he appeared to be on stage. I was not so naive that I thought the cast was truly one big happy family, as implied in the promotional advertising. That notwithstanding, I did see the Opry as the Mother Church of Country Music. I quickly became unsettled by the friction within this secular church, as I would about division within the Baptist denomination thirty years later.

The late Jim Denny was director of the Grand Ole Opry and the Opry's Artist Service Bureau, which arranged personal appearances by Opry cast members around the nation. Rumor at the time was that an Opry entertainer didn't get ASB bookings unless he paid Jim Denny under the table.

I had no personal experience with anyone wanting me to pay closed-door commissions. I do not know if Denny ever solicited or accepted bribes. I'm only relaying rumors that were rampant among those close to the Opry.

Many Opry legends, as well as up-and-coming stars, resented Denny bitterly. Roy Acuff, long called the "king of country music," was among them. A Nashville street is named after him, as well as an auditorium at Opryland, the world-famous theme park. Comedienne Minnie Pearl was equally resentful of Denny.

The late Ernest Tubb, whose hit recording of "Walking the Floor Over You" captured the hearts of millions in the 1940s, was distressed about Denny.

Roy, Ernest and Minnie knew their way around the entertainment world in 1957 and were outraged by Denny. They were very vocal in their backstage accusations. Tubb worked himself into a psychological lather and went, pistol in hand, to the WSM studios to kill Jim Denny.

Tubb took the weapon into the lobby of the National Life and Accident Insurance Company at Seventh Avenue and Union Street and fired a shot into a door. Security guards showed me Tubb's bullet hole.

Denny was fired from the Opry, and there is, I suspect, a great deal more to the story than I know. The Opry cast became factionalized when Denny left. He took many legendary performers with him—those who believed he was innocent of wrongdoing, including Carl Smith, Webb Pierce, Jimmy Dickens, and George Morgan.

The fact that the allegations surfaced is unfortunate.

Jim Denny was a real mover and shaker who did as much as anybody to get the Grand Ole Opry on NBC Television. It had been on radio since 1939. Bill Denny, his son, is equally energetic, and is a vital force on the board of directors of the Country Music Association.

Jim Denny went on to form another talent booking service, independent of the Grand Ole Opry. Some of his acts had been Opry members who wound up competing with artists who chose to remain at the Opry, including Webb Pierce and Carl Smith.

Given the close relationship between WSM and the Opry, I felt that it would be vocationally unwise for me to play Webb Pierce and Carl Smith records back to back. I was never told that, and I certainly wasn't told to boycott any country music from my show. But my sixth sense dictated that I shouldn't unduly feature artists who were at war with the highest-rated program on my station—the Grand Ole Opry.

I had another glimpse of in-house turmoil at the Opry, which after sixty-five years on the air is currently the longest-running live radio show in the world. The turbulence had to do with the influx of rock 'n' roll. Management at WSM would not allow it to be aired. Rock 'n' roll records were not in our library. Buddy Holly once came to visit me on *Opry Star Spotlight,* my all-night show, in 1958. He was brought by the Jordanaires, with whom he had just recorded. I told him I could not play any of his records, because I had none. I apologized. He was very gracious, and we talked about country music. A year later, he was dead.

WSM is more responsible than any other station for the popularity of country music today. It was a keeper of the country music flame when other stations were consumed with the fires of rock 'n' roll. In the radio business, the key word is business. In business, the name of the game is profit. There was more profit in rock than country in the waning 1950s. The WSM listenership was down and could have been improved by playing rock 'n' roll.

But the station had been founded in 1925 largely on country and Gospel music, the anthems of the rural breadbasket South. Management did want to expand its audience but was more concerned about keeping its initial, predepression families of listeners. It wisely felt that old-timers would see to it that the station stayed an institution in their families. WSM remained a "radio relative" to many whose grandparents had grown up with the facility. In parts of the nation where loyalty is life, management knew that those folks would keep dials tuned to 650, no matter what musical trends were afloat elsewhere.

In the middle to late 1950s, country music reached an all-time popularity low, and was on its deathbed. Station WSM was a fifty-thousand-watt life support system. Had the station relinquished country air play entirely to smaller stations, the national advertisers for country music would have pulled their funds. Big sponsors rarely advertised on small stations, where you heard commercials for local markets, service stations, and the like. In my early days at WSM, major league sponsorship for country music was heard almost exclusively on the Grand Ole Opry.

Country music, as we know it today, would have to have been revived from its grave rather than its sickbed. Every young person who performs country music for a living today should be grateful to the dogmatic programming stance of WSM thirty-some years ago.

Because WSM boycotted recorded rock 'n' roll, a lot of people were astonished when the station allowed live performances of Elvis Presley and the Everly Brothers on the Grand Ole Opry. Those acts were considered country at that time. Otherwise, they would never have been heard on either the Opry or WSM.

Ira Louvin, a regular Opry performer, and his brother Charlie recorded some of the biggest country hits of the 1950s. He was outraged by the acceptance of rock 'n' roll. The Louvins had struggled for years to gain fame, but hadn't risen as meteorically as Presley and the Everlys.

I remember the time the Everlys were performing on what is now called the *Friday Night Opry*. Back then, it was broadcast from Studio C at WSM and was known as the *Friday Night Frolic*. It had a studio audience of about three hundred, some of whom might have seen Ira Louvin disgustedly hurl his mandolin backstage. He was furious because the Everly Brothers were receiving tumultuous applause. Ira tossed the instrument down a hallway about half the length of a football field.

Those weekend Grand Ole Opry shenanigans were the high points at the end of the long and sometimes lonely weeknights inside the WSM studios. Stars graced my studio regularly but not nightly. I had telephone calls from all over North America, but sometimes, especially around 4:00 A.M., the phone stopped ringing. I lived on coffee and cigarettes, waiting for my shift's end at 5:00 A.M. Confined to my chair, the most energetic thing I did was stretch.

By the time I joined WSM I had polished my broadcast style. I had abandoned the good-ole-boy, broken English delivery that had traditionally been the country music disc jockey's signature. I continued to use the diction that John Richbourg had instilled in me. I knew at the time, and am certain in retrospect, that some fans thought I was conceited or highbrow. They didn't get the dignity I was trying to implement, and wrote me off as a pseudosophisticate who was too big for his broadcast booth.

For those folks, what I lacked in down-home demeanor, I made up for with homespun honesty. Directness was as much a part of rural life then as beans and corn bread. I vowed early in my tenure that I would not do celebrity interviews that consisted of manufactured, fawning admiration. The approach annoyed some interviewees, but pleased most of the fans, who to this day appreciate the truth.

Many of the interviews, and most of the calls and letters, were from fans who were happy that we maintained a country music format. A radio powerhouse clinging to the single-minded playing of country music in the late 1950s seemed as doomed as a laundromat preferring to use washboards instead of washing machines.

But WSM would prove itself to be right.

Pressure mounted on management each time a new rock station sprang up to compete against the time-proven country giant. Then a strange thing happened, a phenomenon rooted in public taste more than radio programming. In the face of WSM's refusal to play rock, the rock stations began to play songs first heard nationally on WSM. I should add that WSM wasn't the only station to resist rock 'n' roll, just the biggest and most influential.

Sections of the population began to listen to what came to be called the "crossover" music, songs that scored high on more than one type of music survey. In 1957, Ferlin Husky had a big hit playing on WSM called "Gone." By the time it reached the number-one spot, it had begun to rise on rock and popular surveys as well. The same thing happened with songs such as Jim Reeves's "He'll Have to Go," Patsy Cline's "I Fall to Pieces," Marty Robbins's "El Paso," and Johnny Horton's "Battle of New Orleans."

Suddenly, stations that were programming Bobby Darin, Fats Domino, The Platters, Dion, The Big Bopper, Paul Anka, and various teenage heartthrobs were also airing "hillbilly singers." I still hate the term.

Every singer in Nashville wanted a crossover record because of the financial rewards of appealing to more than one set of demographics. The trend became an obsession. It lasted right up until recent times when stations became strict about categorizing genres. During the 1970s and 1980s, the crossover craze became so heated that many singers were accused by fans and critics of compromising country music.

Many artists pled guilty.

But country artists, producers, songwriters, and virtually everyone else affiliated with the industry thirty years ago were thinking more about commercialism, and less about the country craft, in the wake of this unexpected acceptance of our music by audiences at large.

Artists were "covering" each other's songs—that is, recording each other's works—to a degree that was unprecedented. If somebody had a hit, somebody else felt he could hit harder with the same song for a broader audience.

Buck Owens was a young artist from the West Coast who struck pay dirt with a song called "Under Your Spell Again." Ray Price, who was in Nashville at the time, reportedly bragged that no one would ever listen to Owens's version again after hearing Price's rendition. Billy Brown, a Florida singer, recorded "He'll Have to Go." It was played on WSM almost exclusively. Eight months later, Jim Reeves recorded his number-one version. Reeves cut the song after monitoring its success on my show.

Typical of the hit-and-miss nature of pursuing a hit song is the story behind "The Battle of New Orleans."

The song had been recorded by its author, folk singer Jimmy Driftwood. Johnny Horton, whose eventual hits included "Whispering Pines," "Honky Tonk Man," and "North to Alaska," decided he had to have "Battle of New Orleans."

Driftwood's rendition was already getting crossover recognition, and I had a theory why. Driftwood recorded his composition using the word "damn." In those days "damn" was considered profane, and profanity was nearly unprecedented on commercial radio. Young people, whose heads were being turned by crossover country records from Nashville, were, I would have bet, particularly intrigued by a record with a cussword. Defiance is often indigenous to youth.

Driftwood's version had been recorded on an album on RCA but never released as a single, despite its locomotive popularity. Horton persuaded Columbia, his label, to let him do the song as a single release. The rest, as they say, is history.

I remember Horton bringing his version to the all-night show. He had the acetate (a rough production). He wanted me to hear his cut, so I punched in a syndicated Bible show at midnight and went with Horton to another part of the building. I heard his rendition and was taken aback.

He had intentionally omitted the word "damn" that I thought was so integral to the original version's success.

"You have messed up this song," I told Horton. "It had a pioneer element that you have removed. It won't work."

That was one of many times I have been wrong predicting popularity. I was on hand the day CBS gave Horton two gold records commemorating the sale of two million copies of "The Battle of New Orleans."

Horton and I later laughed about my judgment. I learned long before WSM that a sense of humor was mandatory merely to last, much less succeed, in the chaotic world of radio.

Not long afterward, I learned how temporary is this transparent world of show business, with its fast but soon-faded thrills.

Johnny Horton became a pillar of Nashville music, although he retained a home in Louisiana. Horton soon was getting as much air play from Dick Clark on *American Bandstand* as he was from Ralph Emery on WSM.

In 1960, I was busier than ever at that year's disc jockey convention. Every current star, has-been, and hopeful wanted to be on my show, broadcast from the Andrew Jackson Hotel, and on the subsequent all-night show inside the studios.

My guest one night was Buck Owens, who had already made some waves, and would become the biggest country star in the world by 1965. We were doing a relaxed interview, all that two weary conventioneers could muster. We were gabbing about Owens's burgeoning career, about the established acts, and could have been talking about Horton, who listened to me religiously on his car radio as he traveled from show to show.

I remember vividly the time and place of the interview, and Buck Owens, because that was the hour when Horton was killed in a car wreck. People suggested that the last voice he ever heard was mine. I think about that each time I hear his voice today.

...11...

RADIO TAPS THE IMAGINATION. LISTENERS NATIONWIDE
sent letters saying they had seen a Grand Ole Opry souve-
nir book or perhaps a WSM publication and discovered I
looked nothing like they had envisioned, and made the
same point about the studio where I worked, having notions
about the surroundings from which they heard the banter
and occasional misbehavior of their favorite stars.

I remember listening to live radio programs from the lush
ballrooms of America's largest cities and hearing the announcers describing the decor. Perhaps I should have done
the same for my home inside my home inside WSM. But I
realized people were seeing the place in the mind's eye so
I decided not to elaborate. A graphic portrait might dampen
the magic that goes with late-night listening.

History was made from 1957 through 1972 in the WSM
studios.

Hank Williams recorded in Studio D in the late 1940s.
Cowboy Copas cut "Tennessee Waltz" in the same room.
The song later became the official state song of Tennessee,
and one of Patti Page's biggest hits. Those songs were produced by WSM staff engineers.

The room where I spun records with guests was not elaborate. The walls were covered with dingy acoustic tile. A

suspended ceiling contained a square pattern of holes in each tile. A clock hung before me, and a telephone was on my right side. If a guest agreed to talk to the listening fans, he had to walk around me and stand in a tight space while I continued to play records.

Most of the time, however, guests sat in chairs with a black Formica table between us.

There was a grand piano in a corner where Marty Robbins sang live many, many nights. He also played his trademark baby Martin guitar. On those nights, I would let listeners request songs of Marty. I can't imagine a star of that magnitude doing something like that today.

Marty was very shy. He would sing over the airwaves for millions, but if one person (other than myself) was in the studio, he wouldn't. There were two times during the night when my guests would leave. The first was at midnight when the syndicated Bible show was aired. The second was at 2:30 A.M. when watchmen made their rounds. One night I was returning to the studio, when I heard a distant "P-s-s-s-t, p-s-s-s-t."

Marty had been hiding behind a door to another studio waiting for my guest to leave so that he could enter the studio. Eventually, Marty did become comfortable with studio guests and as many as twenty, about all the place would hold, sat in on his sessions.

Around 1963, a famous rock star began to call me regularly on the all-night show, asking to visit, and he eventually did. Upon his arrival, he told me that he was really a country singer, despite having sold millions of rock records.

I didn't believe him.

"If I had a guitar, I'd show you," he retorted.

"I've got a guitar in the car," piped up singer Johnny Russell, who was also visiting.

"Go get it," I said, and Russell left to retrieve it.

He returned with the instrument, and I opened the microphone to my confident guest. He cut down on a George Jones song. That might have been the first time that Conway Twitty ever sang country music publicly.

Since then, he has recorded more number-one country songs than anyone else.

Many disc jockeys listened to my show. Perhaps they wanted to hear the off-the-cuff voices of the singers they were playing. I received a postcard in 1959 from Puyallup, Washington. The writer was a disc jockey and singer, and he thanked me profusely for playing his first record.

His name was Buck Owens.

The card had to do with my persistence in spinning "Under Your Spell Again" in place of Ray Price's cover version. I guess rumor of Price's unhappiness with me had spread all the way to Washington State. Price complained to Ott Devine, my boss at WSM, about my playing a song by a non-Opry artist, when the same tune had been recorded by an Opry star.

Although I was a big Ray Price fan, I told Devine that I played Owens's version because it was better, and not for any political or personal reasons. I was also a big fan of Ralph Mooney, who played the steel guitar introduction in Owens's version. The constant play on WSM "broke" the record, that is, established it nationally. As Owens continued to release songs, many recorded in California, I continued to play them. Records back then had an "A" and a "B" side. The latter was supposed to be the less commercial, or less entertaining, of the two songs. I remember receiving an Owens release in the 1960s and adamantly playing the "B" side over the "A," an established hit, "My Heart Skips a Beat." The tune was called "Together Again." I suspect I played "Together Again" because my "B" marriage was failing. Others have said I single-handedly constructed Buck Owens's career, and on April 4, 1964, "Together Again" went number one for Buck Owens.

I would never claim such a feat, but the suggestion reinforced for me the power of the position I held.

Price must have forgiven me for playing Owens's "Under Your Spell Again," since he has been a regular on my shows ever since. I guess this incident didn't slow him down much. He continued to have hits and I continued to play them. Thirty years later, Owens gave me one of his trademark red, white, and blue guitars, which is, even now, propped up in my office.

I cannot assume credit for starting the talk show format that became so popular during my radio nights at WSM. Three disc jockeys came before me and used the concept. I just did it longer.

When I inherited the microphone, the program was called *Opry Star Spotlight*. It acquired various unofficial handles, including the "all-night show." Each night, I featured one Opry entertainer and played his or her records more than anyone else's during that shift and made an extra effort to ensure that the highlighted star was my guest. To avoid favoritism, I simply worked down the official Opry lineup in alphabetical order.

People have often asked me how I was able to recruit such an impressive lineup of stars, especially from country music, when the show paid no performance fee. The answer is simple. Although television was pretty much a household commodity by the time I debuted on WSM, it was not easy for country stars to gain acceptance there. They were still thought of as hillbillies. Only two network shows that I can recall featured country music: *Red Foley's Ozark Jubilee* from Springfield, Missouri, and the *Jimmy Dean Show* from New York City.

My show on WSM was the only other regularly scheduled national talk program for country artists, almost all of whom came by whenever they had a new record.

One subject that everybody in radio and television is familiar with but few people talk about is payola, the acceptance of money or bribes by broadcasters in exchange for air play. Marty Robbins once bought me a suit as a welcoming present to WSM.

I don't feel that Robbins's gift in any way constituted anything improper. He was my longtime friend, and was such a hot recording star that I had to play his records, as

I had been for years. If he had been an artist who had offered the present with implications, I would not have accepted.

I know I wouldn't—because I once did turn down such a request.

A singer offered me cash in 1962 to play his records. He called me at home and put the deal squarely in my ear. He spoke in a whisper, gave an exact amount, and indicated that payment would be repeated for repeated playings.

I don't know if he went to other disc jockeys with his offer. I told him where he could go with mine. There was something eerie about the proposition: I felt as though our conversation was being tape-recorded.

I had reason to believe that this particular artist didn't like me. My sixth sense mysteriously told me that he was recording our conversation to use against me. I don't think that I was being paranoid. When you work around recording equipment as long as I have, you just know when the microphones are live, or the cameras are rolling.

I've been asked if I've ever been propositioned sexually to play a record. The answer is no.

The management team at WSM must have realized that payola could creep up as an issue, since their broadcasting dynasty was only blocks from record company corporate offices where millions of dollars came and went, determined largely by what WSM programmed. Management contemplated the temptation of money under the counter to ninety-dollar-a-week disc jockeys. They came up with an idea to police the employees.

Once a month during the 1960s, the entire on-air staff at WSM had to fill out a form, a disavowal of acceptance of payola. Each staffer had to sign his name.

I did wonder about the trustfulness of management; if someone was dishonest enough to accept a bribe, would he be honest enough to tattle on himself?

The payola headlines that rocked the entertainment world in the 1950s and 1960s related almost exclusively to rock 'n' roll, where the money was. As late as the early 1960s, there wasn't enough money in country music sales to justify a record company's using payola. A country artist could sell as few as thirty thousand records and have a number-one song. In rock, an artist might have to sell a million copies to capture the number-one slot.

Opry Star Spotlight was preceded by a classical music show, whose host was David Cobb. There was a news break at 10:00 P.M. and my show opened at 10:15 P.M. with Lester Flatt and Earl Scruggs's "Shuckin' the Corn," a bluegrass song with a heavy banjo part.

Listeners, lulled by symphonic strings performing Beethoven, must have been shocked when my show exploded onto the airwaves with a high, rapid twang. I envisioned radio dials spun away from WSM from sea to shining sea. But surveys showed consistently that more folks were tuning in than tuning out.

I filled in for the classical show host when he was ill. I knew little about the music. The audience was quite knowledgeable and I didn't know an overture from a sonata, so I would fake it and play only composers whose names I could pronounce.

I'd push my voice into a lower range, and read from the backs of the record albums. Thank God those were the days before cassettes with no information. I could bluff, but not as effectively as I thought I could. Many titles, composers, and contemporary maestros had foreign names and I stumbled over the pronunciations. My one advantage was in the length of the selections. I'd play an entire movement, which might last up to thirty minutes, and could hide my ignorance for most of the program.

My memories of the first two or three years behind the superpower microphone are as precious as they are sketchy, but I didn't realize until recently that some of those events were part of bona fide broadcast history.

The producers of television's *Tonight Show* would have envied the lineup I had on one night in 1959.

Jim Reeves and Marty Robbins had recorded back-to-back, number-one, crossover records. Robbins held the number-one spot during November with "El Paso." Reeves took over from Robbins a month later with "He'll Have to Go." The songs were number one and number two the night those guys graced my show, but the visit wasn't entirely gracious.

Robbins was the first to arrive and we talked for about thirty minutes, having a high old time. Then Reeves showed up. I greeted him from my chair as he came through the studio door.

"Ladies and gentlemen, it's Jim Reeves!" I said. "Come on in Jim, and sit down."

There was a pause.

"After he's finished," Reeves mumbled, motioning toward Robbins.

"What's wrong with him?" I thought to myself.

Robbins was his ebullient self, but his happy state belied his real feelings. He too had sensed Reeves's reticence. Without fanfare, one of the biggest stars in American country music history rose to his feet, dismissed himself graciously and left the studio. He left about four hours earlier than he normally did.

Reeves took Robbins's seat while it was still warm, picked up the telephone and graciously answered fans' questions most of the night. He just didn't want to talk to Robbins. I don't think it was anything personal—just professional jealousy. Jim wanted all of the attention. One star was simply unwilling to be on the air with another. That's all I can surmise, even after asking Joyce Jackson, Reeves's secretary for seven years. She had no explanation, since Reeves was a Robbins fan.

The incident was my first in what became a series of egotistical clashes. I haven't seen them as much in country music as in rock.

The open-door policy on that show swung so widely, I even accepted artists with "bucket lid" records. A "bucket lid" was a nickname for a minor recording label with little chance for a national hit. The records were pressed at budget rates inside inconspicuous plants and were about as big as a lid for a gallon bucket. They played at the usual forty-five revolutions per minute. They were "vanity records," meaning that their singers had paid to have them made.

There are too many memories about the early days to confine to one chapter, or for that matter, to this entire work.

One night Merle Haggard, Crystal Gayle, Loretta Lynn, the Wilburn Brothers, and six others were in that tiny studio on the air. Many were unexpected. That old show was a wonderful combination of informality and celebrity. Relaxation and candidness grew during the wee hours, especially for the few guests whose tongues had been loosened by alcohol. Tootsie's Orchid Lounge, a legendary watering hole for country music stars, was just a few blocks from WSM. Many nights I marked the closing of Tootsie's by the arrivals of guests to my show.

Patsy Cline was one of the happily oiled and regular visitors, a woman many critics contend was the greatest female country singer who ever lived. Patsy loved to party and didn't care who knew it.

Sometimes she was not the best of guests. She would often bring her husband, Charlie Dick, and other revelers with her. They usually were feeling no pain and inside jokes flew back and forth.

I'd ask Patsy a question, she'd whisper an answer to her friends, and the group would roar with laughter. They had a good time, but neither I nor the radio audience was included. I'm sure it annoyed the listeners. I know it bothered me.

There was an exception, however. Patsy once unexpectedly walked into the studio alone. We had a revealing and intimate conversation, just the two of us and a few million others. I wish I had recorded that evening.

Another legendary performer and partygoer was *Hee Haw* comedian Junior Samples. The man sported a bulging waist, cropped hair, and good-ole-boy face. He looked like the stereotypical good ole boy. Appearances, in his case, weren't deceiving.

He was a natural comic talent.

Junior was recruited by *Hee Haw* because he was genuine. He played the part of a mentally slow bumpkin but needed little rehearsal. There is a story about Samples's difficulty reading a cue card.

"I can't read them there lines," Samples snapped.

"Well Junior," responded an embarrassed member of the production crew, "those lines are from William Shakespeare."

"I don't care who wrote them," Junior reportedly said. "I can't read them big words so fire him!"

Junior dropped by the studio one night unexpectedly. My invited guest was the renowned Grand Ole Opry star Jimmy Dickens, who, with Ernest Tubb and Roy Acuff, was a cornerstone of country music in the 1940s and 1950s. Dickens is small in stature, and seemed engulfed by Samples's mammoth frame, approaching Dickens silently from behind. Samples raised a finger to his lips, signaling to me that he didn't want his presence made known. His other hand gripped an enormous snake, whose head protruded before Junior's bulging torso like a perpendicular lightning rod.

Dickens was chatting along at his characteristically fast pace. He is a hyperactive and often excitable little man.

Junior and the snake were in the background, and all I could think of were the millions who were listening. I wanted to blow Junior's cover but I was trying to listen to Jimmy and was afraid of antagonizing the friendly giant who had booze on his breath and a reptile in his hand. I opted to see what would happen.

Jimmy Dickens was a true professional, never at a loss for words, and he never said the wrong words—until that night.

When Dickens looked away for a second, Junior placed the reptile's tongue an inch from Dickens's face. He was eye to eye with a giant serpent.

"God damn!" was all Dickens could say. I sensed that he wanted to leap from his chair, but he was frozen with fear.

The moment Junior placed the snake next to Dickens, I hit the microphone switch. Dickens's shocked profanity was merely unexplained "dead time" over the airwaves. When I returned the audio, the audience suddenly heard hysteria.

"Junior Samples has joined Jimmy Dickens, ladies and gentlemen," I said. "And he has brought along his pet snake. I say that for those of you who are wondering just what is going on."

I have spent much of my career offering explanations for that and other evenings on that show.

...12...

In 1960 I married Skeeter Davis. She was, at that time, one of the most popular vocalists in country music, and by 1963, she was one of the most popular in all of American music. Skeeter walloped the top of the crossover surveys with the song, "The End of the World."

There are two things that can be said about the vast majority of show business marriages: They often fail, and the public and press have an insatiable curiosity about the details.

My marriage fit the bill. During the four-year union she commanded the record charts and I dominated the night on the radio. It was life inside a doomed fishbowl for both of us. What I felt when the marriage ended twenty-seven years ago has nothing to do with how I feel today. I'm sure she feels the same way.

I had given serious consideration to not discussing my marriage to Skeeter here. I didn't want to appear to harbor ill will. But I've been told that my credibility as an autobiographer will suffer if I don't address a headline-grabbing marriage that rode a roller coaster of emotions.

I hesitate to reveal much about our past together. Skeeter is not in the best of health now and she has undergone rocky times in recent years. I don't want to unduly add to her burdens. I wish her the best.

I thought about including a chapter here, with a headline reading, "Things I Enjoyed About My Marriage to Skeeter Davis."

I was going to leave the pages blank.

No one would have been hurt by the text, and the idea seemed clever.

The first time I met Skeeter was before my affiliation with WSM. I was attending a disc jockey convention for a small station. Skeeter was one-half of a red-hot act, the Davis Sisters. Skeeter's real last name wasn't Davis, and she wasn't really a sister to her singing partner, Betty Jack Davis. They had a big record called, "I've Forgot More Than You'll Ever Know About Him." Skeeter gave me an autograph and some kind of memento during an RCA Records luncheon as part of the convention, held at the Andrew Jackson Hotel.

I think that the second time I encountered her she was a guest on *Opry Star Spotlight* at WSM, round about 1958 or 1959. Her singing partner had been killed in a car wreck in August of 1953. Skeeter sang for a while with Georgia Davis, Betty Jack's sister. It didn't work out, so Skeeter went solo.

I got to know Skeeter as a friend. She came to our house regularly while I was still married to Betty. The three of us, my son, and other friends often played softball in my front yard. I was aware of her good looks, but there was nothing improper about our behavior. I was drawn to her personality and I enjoyed hearing her talk about the music business. She was very knowledgeable and taught me a great deal.

After my marriage ended, Skeeter and I remained friends. We eventually began to date. I use the word date loosely. Seeing each other regularly was all but impossible. During the week, I worked all night. On weekends, Skeeter toured as a featured vocalist with Ernest Tubb. The year was 1960.

Perhaps it was just because we had so little time together that we decided to marry six months after we began dating.

Skeeter and I drove to nearby Franklin, Kentucky, not

far from the Tennessee state line, obtained a blood test and a marriage license, and were married in a matter of hours.

We returned to Nashville, and shortly thereafter bought a two-bedroom house on three acres in Ridgetop, Tennessee, where our neighbors included Grandpa Jones, Stringbean, and eventually, Willie Nelson. I'd like to say we lived happily ever after, but we only lived happily for three years.

Then things began to unravel. Actually, they came apart at the seams.

I was learning, with difficulty, to live with Skeeter's absence while she was on tour. She was gone almost every weekend; after "The End of the World," she was also gone every weeknight and weekday, or so it seemed. Our long-distance love affair was based on the Bell Telephone System more than romance.

We came from different backgrounds. She had come from family, I had come from solitude. I wanted marriage to be the end of solitude, not its continuation. I thought my wife should be home more than she was. Perhaps I was too possessive, if wanting to see your spouse in person more often than you hear her on the radio is being possessive.

She didn't really come home that often—she just came to our house. Our limited time together was split with her relatives. I looked forward to seeing her alone. Instead, she divided herself among family, some of whom weren't among my favorite people. Many lacked ambition and appeared to take advantage of Skeeter. I wanted to get her into bed; they wanted to get into her wallet.

Sometimes she bought them groceries. Other times, she let them run a tab at the store, and paid it. She even bought a house for her mother and sister. Some family members were always hanging around for a handout. I wasn't being sarcastic when I suggested she give them her checkbook and let them take all her money. I thought that was the only way they would ever leave us alone.

"Maybe we won't have to bother with doling out your funds," I said. "We can just present it to them in a lump sum."

I didn't want to be a kept man so I paid all of our household bills. Skeeter's time and money were mostly split between the road and her family. Our expenses and her absence were mostly absorbed by me.

Her family sensed my dissatisfaction with them, and they resented it. They probably thought I was interfering. I thought some of them were leeches. Skeeter let them take advantage. She loved them, and I think she felt guilty about having more than they did.

My anger toward her family was compounded by my suspicion of a guitar player in her band. He called our house a lot during the final year of our marriage. I couldn't understand why they needed to talk so often. After all, he was with her for hours on end while they were touring. Why did he have to occupy so much of her time at home too? During a temporary separation, Skeeter moved in with her mother and sister. I discovered that the guitar player was spending a lot of time at her mother's house.

I was livid and confronted her. She denied any involvement with the man. I could see the beginning of the end of our marriage all too clearly and I began to panic. I didn't want another divorce.

I suggested that we see a counselor, the Reverend Bob Daugherty, pastor of Forest Hills Baptist Church, where we had attended services. Skeeter declined.

Meanwhile, my life as a solitary, all-night disc jockey moved into high-gear anxiety. I'd sit there smoking stale cigarettes and drinking cold coffee, wondering where my wife was, what she was doing, and with whom. I was saturated with the lyrics of love-gone-wrong songs. My imagination was running away with me, taking me places I didn't want to go. My life became a sleepless and overwrought marathon of unharnessed jealousy. I began to lose weight, along with my grip on reality.

I looked for another target to condemn, and settled on the man I suspected she was seeing. If she wouldn't stop her suspected affair, I would.

I decided to shoot him.

I was hysterical. I called the Reverend Daugherty and

Tom Binkley, my friend and attorney, who advised me to get a divorce. He thought it would alleviate the pressure and prompt an eventual reconciliation. I paced for miles in my den before their arrival. I threatened to kill Skeeter's lover, and I meant it.

Both men told me what I already knew, but had forgotten in my madness—that no woman and no situation was worth going to jail over. They reminded me of the legacy I would leave my son, Steve. Those men were instrumental in preventing me from doing something totally out of character while I was virtually out of my mind. The wonderful life I would later have would never have transpired if I had yielded to impulse that day. I'm eternally grateful to the Reverend Daugherty and Tom Binkley. I suspect I drove the pastor crazy during that bad period. I would call him in the middle of the night, during my show, to unload my feelings. I'm sure he was tempted to ask, "Can this wait?" He never did, but instead graciously provided a healing ear.

Even after Skeeter found out how upset I was about the guitarist, she continued to see him, which made it increasingly difficult for me to kid myself into believing that she cared about me.

Steve, then twelve, was very fond of Skeeter. One night I was driving him to his mother's house and told him that I was about to go through another divorce. He just sat there speechless in the darkened car. I could feel his silence as much as my guilt.

Skeeter and I were living in Brentwood, a fashionable Nashville suburb. I spent the night with her in that house on the eve of our divorce proceedings.

We did not make love.

She talked about reconciliation, but the terms were outlandish. She wanted me to live in one end of our new home, and she in the other. I thought the idea of living separately together was ridiculous, and I refused.

The next day, September 10, 1964, I left town so that Skeeter could wind up the divorce with discretion. I didn't want my presence to prompt press curiosity. Vanderbilt's football team was playing Georgia Tech the next day in

Atlanta. I went to the game, stayed through four quarters and later couldn't recall one play.

I returned to Nashville a few days later a single man. Skeeter went on a European tour for three weeks, so I stayed in the house that she retained in the settlement. When she returned I was out of our house and marriage. But she wasn't out of my mind.

I moved into a one-bedroom apartment in the Oxford House on Nashville's Twenty-first Avenue South. I took a one-year lease for space that was small by daytime and smaller by night. That's when the walls closed in.

Sleep and hunger left me, and yet I felt fatigue and the need for nutrition. My nerves were electrified, live wires. I lay in bed for hours, looking at the ceiling and seeing her face. I had never ached so badly. Life was an open wound and I thought the pain was going to kill me. Death, I felt, was only for the fortunate.

It's hard to believe now that I hurt that way then.

My sleeplessness was compounded by a rash. My skin felt on fire. The doctor diagnosed hives, and said the affliction was induced by a nervous disorder.

He had recently treated a celebrity friend of mine for psychiatric disorders. The friend was suicidal, and the doctor obviously had seen many such cases. His guard was raised against a patient's potential self-destruction. But I didn't realize how much.

"Now Ralph," he said, "you are in terrible condition. We have to treat you for depression."

He was a short, hyperactive fellow who I suspected had a nervous disorder himself. He was very excitable.

"To alleviate your depression," he continued, "you must not smoke, drink, have sex, or eat fried foods."

I said, tongue-in-cheek, "Well Doc, I might as well kill myself."

"Don't say that!" he thundered. "Don't say that!" The poor man nearly suffered a coronary himself.

When I realized how seriously he had taken me, I realized how pathetic I must have appeared.

Stress had depleted me. My defenses were down, and I contracted pneumonia. The doctor put me in the hospital.

I lay motionless on sheets saturated with sweat and self-pity. I called Skeeter to ask if she would visit me in the hospital.

She said no. I was astounded by her insensitivity. I had been married to a woman I didn't know.

After a year at Oxford House, I moved into a place on Shys Hill Road, scene of a famous Civil War battle. I had been there about two months when Skeeter surprised me with a visit. It was pleasant but awkward. I tried to force out my best behavior but contain my emotions. Wounds from her had been psychologically sewn and her presence that day tore at every stitch. As she was leaving, she handed me a note. I don't know why she chose not to speak her piece aloud. The note said that she liked my little house on a hill, and envied my privacy. The note said she needed me. It was signed "Skeeter."

That's all I needed. Twelve months after our breakup and my tumultuous recovery, I began to call her again.

But she wouldn't see me.

Then what was the intention of her spontaneous visit and note? I asked myself. I never knew the answer.

By the time of our divorce, I was working with the Grand Ole Opry, announcing more segments than any other announcer on staff. *Opry Star Spotlight,* the all-night show, was in popularity overdrive. My career was in full swing and the loop just kept getting bigger.

And I walked away from all of it.

I couldn't get my mind on my work because I couldn't get my mind off my ex-wife. More wee hours with ballads about breakups were not what I needed. I got out, ending thirteen years in radio with a two-week notice.

I was away from WSM for about fifteen months. I returned and had been back at the all-night microphone for about four years when Skeeter was signed to Mercury Records. She had been dropped by RCA. She came to the all-night show to plug her new record. I played her song.

She sat in the studio all night, talking to me and the scores of fans who called. It was still dark when we left the studio and were standing in the quiet WSM parking lot.

I remember the parking lot lights as they shone on the face that had once glowed brightly in my mind.

"Ralph," she said. "I love you more today than I ever did."

"Bullshit!" I thought to myself, and then thought some more. I assumed she was saying this hoping that I'd play her records because she was feeling the pangs of rejection by the music business and the people who used to buy her records.

I wouldn't let myself be taken in.

Love *is* blind, and blindness overlooks the obvious. In retrospect, I am confident that Skeeter was in love with Ralph Emery the disc jockey, not the person. She, I strongly suspect, was largely interested in me for what I could do for her career.

Like the lovesick fool I was, I did more for her career than anyone ever knew—until now.

I have chosen this forum for confession about the way I used to alter "record play" reports in her behalf. The reports influenced the national charting and sales of Skeeter's records. *Billboard* magazine, the Bible of the recording industry, asked the WSM disc jockeys to fill out "play lists." The lists recorded the frequency of a record's air play. The list largely determined *Billboard*'s weekly Top Ten country songs. Although there were other reporting stations, disc jockeys around the nation based their air play largely on the *Billboard* Top Ten. They were directly heeding a survey that I was indirectly influencing.

I would log Skeeter's air play on my show as number one. Then I would take the discarded reporting slips meant for the other disc jockeys and fill those out with Skeeter at the top of the list. I hasten to add that I never stole another disc jockey's report form. I took it if he threw it away. Some disc jockeys didn't care who had the number-one record. They weren't married to, and madly in love with, Skeeter Davis.

I don't know if what I did constituted a crime. I just know I didn't want anyone to know. I would go through wastebaskets looking for discarded forms. When I saw one, and saw that no one was looking, I would snatch it from its paper grave. I'd fill it out regarding record play as if it had been sent to me.

Ironically, there were members of the country music community who, during my marriage to Skeeter, complained that I played her records too much. One was Jim Reeves, although I didn't know why, since I played his records more than anybody's. He didn't know that I was reporting them as being played even more than they were.

The things we do for love.

I've already indicated my convictions about Skeeter's motives toward Ralph Emery. I'm not astonished to realize them now, only astonished that I didn't at the time.

Skeeter threw malice in my face. RCA released a new song of hers about the time of our divorce. I wondered about its title, and for whom it was intended. The record was called, "Got Along Without You Before I Met You, Gonna Get Along Without You Now."

...13...

I HAD BEEN DIVORCED THREE TIMES FROM TWO WOMEN BY
the time I was thirty-one. I was more depressed than I had
ever been, and cared less than I ever had, about my job,
myself, anything, or anyone.

As they say in the South, my give-a-shitter was broken.

Upon reflection, it's no wonder I so easily fell into the
mental and behavioral traps. I realize, however, that the
reasons for my fall are not excuses. Because of the nature
of my work, I was hearing songs regularly about the foolish-
ness of trying to drown one's sorrows in liquor.

The announcer who pulled the shift before mine on Fri-
days on WSM was the renowned Grand Ole Opry personality Grant Turner who played country records following the
Friday Night Frolic. I intended to relieve him at 11:00 P.M.
but got drunk instead on about twelve margaritas before
one shift. Grant had to work an additional seven hours to
fill in for me while I stayed out drunk with Rose Hill,
Bobby Goldsboro's secretary.

He is a kind and gentle soul who, to this day, has never
mentioned the offense. The program director, Dave
Overton, called me in.

"We've gone about as far as we can go with you," he
said. His point was well taken.

I had been in a six-year tailspin that started with booze and ended with amphetamines.

Addiction is one of the most talked-about subjects of our day. I don't want to make too much of my former situation for fear that I'll be jumping on a bandwagon. Today, everyone seems to claim to have had an addiction. Amphetamines were my drug of choice, and alcohol was second.

For a long time I didn't think I had a problem. I lived in a world where a lot of people were just like me. In that world it was normal to be abnormal.

There was no pronounced trauma for a while. But gradually, I took the liquor, and eventually pills, until all of it started taking me. I didn't take the pills and liquor at the same time, the way others in Nashville were doing. I had heard about the dangers of mixing the two. I only wanted to have a good time or escape. I didn't want to kill myself.

It would have taken me to my grave had it not been for my doctor and my wife, Joy, who helped me overcome the worst of my addictions. Today, she understates the importance of her role. I'm not sure if that's because she's modest, or because time has dimmed the memory of the severity of the situation. I did take steps to prevent her from finding out how often I was consuming the pills, concealment being a characteristic of the problem user.

I would not have abandoned substance abuse had it not been for Joy's support, spoken and unspoken. I tried unsuccessfully to quit amphetamines six times before Joy and I won.

After my divorce from Skeeter, I lived alone, except when I occasionally had a woman spend the night. Solitude bred depression; depression bred desperation. I couldn't deal with life, so I occasionally took leave of it, through alcohol. The pill intake started innocently.

I was complaining to my bandleader about fatigue from doing the all-night show. It was about 4:00 A.M. and I had another hour of radio and sixty minutes of television waiting before my night and day work was complete. There was a one-hour break between the two jobs. The last show ended at 7:00 A.M.

I went into the WSM lounge and shaved. I might have reclined.

"I'm beat, and I don't know how I'm going to get through the morning," I told the musician.

"Here, let me help you," he said.

He offered me bottled energy. It was my first experience with "uppers." I was amazed at the instant zest.

I knew nothing about the dangers of amphetamines. A lot of doctors didn't at the time. Hundreds of people in Nashville show business were gobbling amphetamines. It was an open secret and an unfunny joke.

One time my pill-providing friend called me on the all-night show and asked me to come by his house for breakfast. When I arrived, my place setting was a knife, fork, and two pills on a plate. That was the meal. It was his idea of a joke.

The most popular pill was named "Old Yeller" and you would frequently and openly hear the musicians say, "Got any Old Yellers?"

On one stage show, as a practical joke, someone stuck a yellow thumbtack into the floor near the main microphone. As each band came on, the musicians would try to pick up what they thought was a happy pill.

Roger Miller was in the Far East on a tour that began without pills. He told me he tried every source he had in Los Angeles, from where he embarked. He was walking down a street in Hong Kong or somewhere and saw an apothecary. Roger spoke pidgin Chinese, and thought he'd give the place a try.

He cornered the pharmacist and very deliberately said, "You got Simco?" Simco was a brand name for amphetamines.

"Yes, Simco," said the Asian.

"You do have Simco?!" Roger said, with mounting elation.

"Yes, Simco," the man again responded.

"Will you sell me some Simco?" Roger asked timidly, not wanting to be arrested in a foreign country.

"Yes," replied the merchant. "How many do you want?"

The postscript to that story is that Roger didn't have to worry about getting the contraband through customs, since he and a friend reportedly consumed it all while still overseas.

In America, obtaining a prescription for pills was little more than a formality. Physicians prescribed amphetamines as an aid to weight loss and as antidepressants.

A favorite Nashville physician among music personnel was Dr. Snap. Songwriters would get a prescription from him, then sit up for days writing tunes. He should have been given half the writer's credit for half of the hit songs to come out of Nashville in the 1960s and 1970s.

Given modern society's enlightenment about drugs, it may sound suspicious to contend that we, as recently as twenty-five years ago, were unaware of the down side to drugs. I never bothered to ask about the dangers, and neither did most other Nashville entertainers.

In our defense, I offer an analogy: I heard most of my life that it was healthy to eat red meat and eggs. Nutritionists urged their intake as part of basic food groups rich in protein. In the last few years, however, dietitians have cringed about red meat and eggs, due to cholesterol. But in the 1960s cholesterol was not the daily mass media subject that it is today. Neither were amphetamines.

All I knew was that taking pills gave me energy. I also took them as mood elevators. I was trying to achieve chemically what my attitude would not afford mentally. The predictable self-destruction was undertaken mostly, but not always, when I was away from the microphone. There were plenty of nights when I was "wired" on pills while talking to millions of unknowing listeners. Depression began to take its toll on my job performance. So I quit what many regarded as the most coveted job in American radio.

The sad songs, in the wake of my divorce, would hit close to home. I don't think I listened to most of them. I was emotionally numb. I tuned out the lyrics and merely played whatever the people requested.

While I was away from WSM, from late 1964 throughout 1965, I became financially strapped. My cash flow was cut by more than 50 percent, because of the absence of a paycheck and the legal expenses I incurred during the divorce from Skeeter.

I went to a New Year's Eve party at the home of Felice and Boudleaux Bryant, the legendary husband and wife songwriting team who penned so many early rock 'n' roll and country hits. A woman took me home because I was too drunk to drive. She might have had romance on her mind. I had nausea in my stomach. We hadn't dated long, and I made a distinct impression by asking her to stop the car. I threw up on the road, as well as on my shoes and cuffs. Pretty romantic.

She took me to my apartment and dumped me on my mattress. I was too drunk to see the alarm clock and asked her to set it for 5:00 A.M. It rang for fifteen minutes. I was too pickled to hear it. I woke up in the same clothes I had worn the previous calendar year, shaved, showered, changed, and hoped the television makeup would cover my condition.

I made it through the show but I'm thankful there is no videotape to remind me of it. My movements were deliberate and I sat up as straight as a poker, trying to hide my intoxication. Because it was New Year's morning, I suspect I failed to fool a lot of people.

In 1965, the first sunset of the year filtered its winter amber through my closed curtains and onto my bed where I sat with my face in my hands, crying. All I wanted was more of what I didn't need. It was a holiday and the liquor stores were closed.

My indifference to life increased. I was living in limbo.

The Commerce Union Bank sent someone to repossess my car. I didn't argue with him. I just gave him the keys.

"We don't want the car!" the man said. "Can't you find some way to make a payment?"

What he didn't know was that I couldn't find myself. He refused to take the car, and I made the next payment.

I returned to the all-night show on January 1, 1966. I was broke, and would have had to reach up to touch economic bottom. The station allowed me back because its ratings had slipped. The station gave me a raise, and I went to work with the legendary cowboy star Tex Ritter. He and I were cohosts of the *Opry Star Spotlight* for sixteen months and those days were the most enjoyable and fulfilling in radio for me.

By 1970, I was trying very hard to quit pills and the result was that I began to experience withdrawal. I could feel in my voice the lethargy that characteristically goes with. "coming down" when trying to get off amphetamines. It was my sixth attempt and it was successful. I paid a heavy price, depression induced from the absence of certain chemicals.

The disc jockey famous for his open-door policy didn't want to see anyone. I hoped no guests would come by, and took measures to ensure it. I had built my popularity as a talk show host, and now I didn't want to talk.

In 1970 the studio phone rang from downstairs. The celebrity caller wanted to be interviewed. A few years later, he would record an album with Willie Nelson, Jessi Colter and Tompall Glaser that, for years, stood as the best-selling country album of all time. But the night he asked to be on my show, I flatly told Waylon Jennings that I didn't want to see anyone.

He drove into the night without a word right after I asked him to go away.

...14...

AT 5:15 A.M., ON ANY GIVEN WEEKDAY, NINE WEARY MU-
sicians saunter into WSMV-TV, the NBC affiliate in Nashville. They have sleep in their eyes and a drag to their step.
But they warm to the task of performing the opening theme
of the *Ralph Emery Show*. The title is unoriginal, the format
is unrehearsed, the attire is unglamorous, and the ratings
are unsurpassed.

Since the show's beginning in 1963, it has maintained the
largest lead-in audience for the NBC *Today Show* of any
local program in the United States. Arbitron surveys have
shown the program to garner as much as 68 percent of
Nashville's television viewing audience, leaving the other
32 percent to be split between the other two major network
affiliates, as well as the twenty-six cable channels.

I'm very proud of my local program.

International stars, such as Dolly Parton, Randy Travis,
the Judds, Roger Miller, Waylon Jennings, Willie Nelson,
and Loretta Lynn began their careers here. World-famous
celebrities walk in unannounced and involve themselves intensely in the local programming, even to the point of doing
commercials. They get so wrapped up in their impromptu
presentations, you would think they were the headliners on
Jerry Lewis's Labor Day Telethon.

MEMORIES

* * *

Bob Wills died in 1974, years after having been the most popular western swing bandleader in history. He and I were making small talk on the morning show, partially about automobiles. Since a Nash dealership sponsored the program, I asked Wills what he thought about the cars. I mentioned that I had heard he liked to drive a Nash. The man went into a ten-minute brag about the virtues of Nashes. American Motors would have had to spend a fortune to pay for the commercial endorsement it received for free that day.

The morning show is a venue where the early hour and the residues of the night before combine to loosen guests' tongues. They tell hilarious stories about each other.

The late Cowboy Copas told a yarn about Bob Wills's drinking bouts causing him to miss personal appearances. Wills's mammoth band, the Texas Playboys, would go on stage without him. He often slept off the booze in a car. Without Wills's appearing, the band would ask to be paid. Many promoters were angered.

"We sold tickets to see Bob Wills, and our customers didn't get to see him," they contended. "We're not going to pay the Bob Wills band 'cause Bob Wills didn't perform."

Growing weary of the hassle, one night a member of the entourage decided to put Wills on stage even though he was dead drunk. Wills was seated upright in a chair in view of the fans who kept clamoring for him to pick up his fiddle and play. Wills, the story goes, was too wasted to make a fist. Requests fell on his drunken ears.

Wills's signature gesture was his spoken "Ah-ha." He would yell the syllables in a falsetto, and made a fortune doing it.

Planted in the chair on stage during his intoxicated appearance, Wills began to tumble. A musician struggled to sit him back up, while continuing to play. Soon, Wills again melted into his seat, like a sack of potatoes. Someone in the crowd good-naturedly yelled "Ah-ha."

The band became disgusted, realizing they had fooled no

one and were not going to be paid. A player snatched Wills from his chair, and the troupe walked offstage, with Wills stumbling in tow.

As he passed a microphone, Wills's eyes focused briefly as he realized the band wouldn't be paid unless he performed.

"Ah-ha," he growled, into the mike. It didn't work. No one in the group got paid that night.

Nashville Now is seen in all fifty states, and throughout Canada, where the show's cable network, the Nashville Network, is the highest-rated of all American cable channels. The Nashville Network is seen inside 55.5 million North American households.

I have done many other network and syndicated radio and television shows but no program I've ever done has enjoyed the runaway ratings of the predawn, local *Ralph Emery Show* in Nashville.

I arise at 4:30 A.M. to do the local show not long after retiring at about 11:30 P.M., tired after the network show. I'm the morning show's executive producer as well, so it's my baby, Monday through Friday.

When I was on WSM, I simply went to the television station after doing the all-night broadcast. Some of the morning show guests come by after staying up to party all night.

I'm not always at my best during the morning show. RCA recording artist Lorrie Morgan, formerly a regular vocalist on the show, once introduced an up-tempo song she intended to sing.

"Good," I said, half-asleep, "I'm glad you're not going to do one of those draggy-ass ballads."

That might have been the only time in my career I used profanity on the air, but I didn't receive one letter of protest. A few people wrote that there was too much slow music on the program and wanted faster selections to wake them up.

In 1980, the Judds made their Nashville television debut

Ralph's high school graduation photo. "I was an unattractive young man, with crooked teeth, and what I would later call 'industrial-strength acne.'" *(Photo by the Cain-Sloan Company)*

Ralph, *right,* with then wife Skeeter Davis and Red Foley on the set of NBC's *Five-Star Jubilee,* 1961. "In retrospect, I am confident that Skeeter was in love with Ralph Emery the disc jockey, not the person."

Ralph and Tex Ritter on WSM's all-night show, March 14, 1967. *(Photo by Les Leverett)*

Loretta Lynn, Marty Robbins, and Bud Wendell exhibit plaques commemorating them as the most popular singers on Ralph Emery's all-night show on WSM, May 19, 1969. *(Photo by Les Leverett)*

Ralph Emery *(dancing, at left)* and Willie Nelson in a television studio in 1965; *below:* slightly older (and probably no wiser) on an all-night radio show in 1976.

The Everly Brothers (Phil, *left*, and Don) join Ralph in 1987 at *Nashville Now*. *(Photo by Jim Hagans; courtesy of The Nashville Network)*

Ralph and Reba McEntire at the "Music City News" awards show in 1988 in Nashville. *(Photo by Neil Pond)*

Ricky Van Shelton and Ralph backstage at the Grand Ole Opry House in 1990. *(Photo by Jim Hagans; courtesy of The Nashville Network)*

Then Vice-President George Bush and Ralph on the set of *Nashville Now. (Courtesy of The Nashville Network)*

From left: Johnny Cash, Ralph Emery, former President Jimmy Carter, and Mrs. Tom T. (Dixie) Hall in 1989 at the home of Tom T. Hall. *(Photo by Nate Crawford)*

Above: Ralph shares a laugh with Randy Travis on the set of *Nashville Now*. *(Photo by Jim Hagans; courtesy of The Nashville Network)*

Left: Singer Kathy Mattea thanks Ralph for his help toward securing her first gold album, 1990. *(Photo by Jim Hagans; courtesy of The Nashville Network)*

Below: Randy Travis, Minnie Pearl, and Ralph on *Nashville Now*. *(Courtesy of The Nashville Network)*

Ralph and Shotgun Red on *Nashville Now*, 1986. *(Photo by Jim Hagans; courtesy of The Nashville Network)*

K. T. Oslin and Ralph enjoy a playful moment on *Nashville Now*. *(Photo by Jim Hagans; courtesy of The Nashville Network)*

Ralph joins Clint Black on the set of *Nashville Now*. *(Photo by Jim Hagans; courtesy of The Nashville Network)*

Mrs. Maxine Everett (Ralph's mother), Mike Emery (middle son, holding the family cat) with girlfriend Marie DeNoto, Nathan Emery (Steve's middle child), Stacey Emery (Steve's youngest child), Steve Emery (oldest son), Shannon Emery (Steve's oldest child), Jerry Scott (Joy's stepfather), Jane Scott (Joy's mother), Kit Emery (Ralph's youngest son) with girlfriend Kristie Waltz, Ralph Emery, Joy Emery, Paul Everett (Ralph's stepfather).

Ralph Emery and Barbara Mandrell during the *All-Star Salute to Ralph Emery* in February 1990 at the Grand Ole Opry House in Nashville, Tennessee. *(Courtesy of The Nashville Network)*

on the show before going on to sell 6 million records in seven years and capture any number of Grammy and Country Music Association Awards. Naomi, the mother in the mother-daughter duo, talked about her rural rearing, and how she used to make lye soap at home.

Because my mind was foggy at 6:00 A.M., I sometimes could not remember the names Naomi and Wynonna. So I covered my embarrassment and called them the "Soap Sisters." I think they soon caught on to what I was doing, but they said nothing.

There is probably no country music performer who captured more headlines and major awards for about five years beginning in 1983 than Randy Travis. When he recently appeared on a tribute to me, he recalled the first question I ever publicly asked the then-nervous newcomer.

"Are you any good?" was my question. Videotape was projected, and sure enough, there I was, visibly sleepy, asking the Hank Williams of the 1980s if he had any talent.

There have been times when getting to that show was such a task, I barely arrived as the middle of the opening theme song was being played. There is nothing as suspenseful as seat-of-the-pants, live television.

Throughout this text, I will relate additional flashbacks from my local show, seen in a market of about one million viewers. Most of my national audience isn't aware that I have a Nashville show. In Nashville, more people see me on the local broadcast than on TNN.

The show began in June 1963, as a sixty-minute offering intended to lure viewers to stay tuned for the *Today Show* at 7:00 A.M. My show has since been expanded to ninety minutes. The initial show was the brainchild of Elmer Alley, then the program manager for Nashville's Channel 4. Elmer has been very good to me through the years, and has recommended me for several nationally syndicated shows, and even for my biggest break as host of *Nashville Now*.

The show's original title was *Opry Almanac*.

The television station made a deal with the local musicians' union to videotape about ten songs from about twenty Grand Ole Opry stars. I sat behind a table, situated in front of a mock sink. It was supposed to look as if I were in the kitchen, having coffee and chatting with viewers, who ostensibly were in their kitchens at home. I would talk for a while, then arbitrarily run one of the videotapes. I had to rerun them frequently, so regular viewers saw the same singers wearing the same clothes while singing the same songs.

We had been on the air for only a month when Channel 4 moved into its new and current studios on Nashville's Knob Road. My guest for the studio's opening was Loretta Lynn. Her life was the subject of an Academy Award–winning motion picture. She has been a Las Vegas headliner for years, and has performed for a number of United States presidents, but on that summer morning in 1963 she walked into my phony kitchen and sang for the early risers with no accompaniment other than her own guitar.

I wish I had a tape of that memorable day.

I did the morning show for three years, moved to afternoons for three more, left television in 1969, and returned in 1972. I haven't paused to this day.

The show never paid its performers very much. Most do it for local exposure, or as a favor to me. One time Irving Waugh, then the president of WSM-TV, suggested that I trim my already slender budget.

"Lad," he said (he always called me that), "be great, but don't spend any money."

Another time, Irving was complaining about the modest fee we paid some of the finest studio musicians in Nashville. He came by my table at a WSM Christmas party with the president of one of the leading advertising agencies in Nashville.

"Lad," he said to me, "I don't know what we're going to do about that band you have in the morning."

"I don't know what you're going to do without them," said the advertiser. "They're great!"

The band was finally accepted.

*   *   *

Today, the program retains its musical format and reports community activities. It's somewhat paradoxical, having national talent on a program that lists the school closings during inclement weather, or regularly gives notice of amateur art shows or charity dog washings. President George Bush sat with me on *Nashville Now,* and then eight and a half hours later I did the morning show with local used-car salesmen hawking their own vehicles. It's a dichotomy that never allows me to forget from where I spring. The broadcast still addresses the simple, grassroots themes on which it was founded. Of all that the program may or may not be, it's genuine.

Maude and Dorothy, the Paul sisters, are part of the show's authenticity. They have been in the studio audience since 1965. They have sung under the same lights that have illuminated the legends, rarely missing a morning. The band and I nicknamed their "act" the "Maudettes."

The ladies live in a senior citizens' home and have never been married. On the occasion of their twentieth anniversary on the program, we gave them a plaque, watches, and money. They always arrive earlier than the cast, and have coffee percolating for everyone else. They're afraid to drive on the interstate highways and come over city streets. I have no idea how early those women must depart in order to get to the show on time.

The Paul sisters are in their seventies. They have spent much of their lives acquiring opinions, and don't hold them back. A singer came on the show once with a bare midriff and the Pauls wouldn't speak to her, and shunned her efforts to be friendly.

They are the program's official greeters and are on a first-name basis with many of Tennessee's foremost politicians and entertainers. They are integral in keeping the show down to earth. I never wanted to be a part of a high-stress, pretentious program that aired when viewers were getting ready to gear up to go to work.

The Pauls are so genuine, a new viewer might think

they're caricatures, which was the case with a New York lawyer visiting my attorney, Tom Binkley.

"Those women are wonderful actresses," he said. "They really play those parts well."

I'll bet he thought they were both members of the Screen Actors Guild.

...15...

W**HEN** I **INTRODUCED** H**ANK** W**ILLIAMS**, J**R.**, **ON THE** Grand Ole Opry, it was one of the most historic moments of my career. It was 1962, the first year of three I served as an announcer on the Opry. I had visited the place many times before, and had even done a few guest appearances. But Opry and WSM officials, practically one and the same, waited until I had been on the *Opry Star Spotlight* for a half decade before they asked me to become one of three staff announcers on the longest-running live radio show on earth.

Hank Junior and I were in the same boat that night. The people in the audience had heard our voices, but not many had seen our faces. The difference was, of course, that I was not a victim of the famous-father syndrome. Hank Junior would eventually spend traumatic years trying to be his late father's son and his own man. He faced a public that selfishly demanded he sing like his father—then repeatedly let him know he couldn't.

Hank Junior, at age fourteen, premiered on the Grand Ole Opry stage and sang "Lovesick Blues," the song his daddy sang for his Opry premiere on June 11, 1949.

According to *The Country Music Story* by Burt Goldblatt and Robert Shelton, the senior Williams's debut as reported by Ed Linn in the January 1957 issue of *Saga* magazine, "stopped the show colder than it has ever been stopped, before or since, in its 31 years. After Hank had gone through six encores, Red Foley had to make a little speech to quiet the place down and get the show back on schedule."

In coming years, Hank Junior would have the same effect on a crowd reaching out to the son in hopes of somehow touching his dad. Hank Junior would record the soundtrack for "Your Cheatin' Heart," a movie about the life of his daddy, starring George Hamilton.

Opry performances are traditionally sold out months in advance. That day in 1962, many ticket seekers were still trying to get seats the day of the show to see the Williams legacy live.

"And now, ladies and gentlemen," I said, "here is the son of a legend. After all of these years, the memory of Hank Williams is reborn . . ."

That's about as far as I got.

Junior swaggered onstage, already over six feet tall. He kicked off with a signature yodel, and broke into song. I couldn't say its title for sure. I couldn't hear.

Watching the kid that night was viewing history repeating, and making, itself. The crowd kept him on stage the way they had his father thirteen years earlier. Someone had to walk out and practically physically remove the lad so that the show, thrown behind schedule, could go on.

The Grand Ole Opry is what country music fans have in common as much as country music itself. It is common ground between those in the business and those who patronize the business. It is the only thing in the entire country music industry about which every fan and employee has an opinion.

Some say the show is the Ringling Brothers, Barnum and Bailey Circus set to music. Others call it the South's answer to Broadway.

I think the show is a national treasure. I think the state of Tennessee should commission a sculptor to chisel the likenesses of Roy Acuff, Minnie Pearl, Hank Snow, and a few other Opry veterans into a cliff in the foothills of the Smoky Mountains. The busts should be country music's Mount Rushmore, situated along Interstate 40 East for motorists to behold who come to Music City, U.S.A.

The popularity of country music is fostered on WSM and nothing has been a greater conduit and boon for country music than the Grand Ole Opry.

Not every act can play the Opry and retain its composure. The show is informality bordering on pandemonium. There has never been a rehearsal in its sixty-six years, so the Opry is a beehive of activity in front of and behind its performers. When seats in the audience are filled, fans are seated on the stage. They talk and point and mill and flash plastic cameras in full view of the crowd out front, and only a few feet from the performer trying to concentrate on his act.

Fans visit with the stars, exchange telephone numbers, and present family photographs to one another while the show is underway. I've seen performers warm up with band members in the wings while another artist was singing on stage, the guy out front hearing the guy backstage, and both pressing on.

Sonny James was performing on the Hank Snow portion of the Opry. Sonny finished his song and received nice applause. Snow walked back to the microphone to solicit additional applause as Sonny left the stage. Sonny and three background singers ran to the spot where Hank was standing and nearly knocked him down. Hank staggered, Sonny continued singing, and neither missed a beat. Sonny had heard what he thought was enough applause for an encore—Hank wasn't so sure.

A famous story around the Opry concerned Hank's fiddle player, Chubbie Wise.

Chubbie was sawing on his instrument, and stood too close to Hank. Chubbie's bow accidentally dipped under Hank's wig and suddenly he was sawing away with Hank's hair flailing at the end of his bow. Hank retrieved his hairpiece, stepped out of the spotlight, placed it back on his head and reentered the beam to finish his song.

"Chubbie, you're fired," was all he said, off microphone.

I didn't see that incident. It's an inside story that has been told by so many Opry regulars, I have no doubt it's true.

In 1962, I was doing the Opry on weekends, the all-night show through the week, and local television on weekday mornings. I have been called a vocational man of steel. It has to do with my vivid memories of childhood poverty. I seize almost every opportunity to earn money.

When I first started in the Opry, I also did a weekend radio shift. The Opry ended at midnight, there was a live broadcast over WSM from the Ernest Tubb Record Shop, then I went to WSM's studios to play records from 1:00 A.M. until 4:00 A.M.

Ah, the stamina of youth.

It was anticlimactic returning to a nearly silent radio studio after standing in front of thousands of cheering fans. I used to walk out of the old Ryman Auditorium past convoys of idling buses waiting to take the country stars into the night and the matinees they were playing the next day. Their lives seemed very glamorous.

Eventually, I toured as an emcee with many of them and discovered the tedium behind the monotonous highway miles.

Life within the Opry itself was not the grandiose spectacle one might imagine from the other side of a radio receiver where the applause, music, and mayhem made it sound as if a genuine jubilee were underway every Saturday night in Nashville.

The Ryman Auditorium, from which the Opry moved in 1974 to its modern and more comfortable setting, was little more in the summertime than a microwave for the masses. The place wasn't air-conditioned because the antiquated roof could not support the heavy equipment needed to cool the massive room. I've been in the Ryman many times when it was 100 degrees outside, and perhaps 115 inside from stage lights and body heat. I'd be hard-pressed to estimate what the temperature was on stage, heated by footlights as well.

People have asked me if I could feel the legendary ghosts of the Opry whenever I stepped on the platform. It's hard to feel anything aesthetic when your shorts are saturated with sweat.

I remember once in the early 1960s, there was a film being made with Waylon Jennings inside the Ryman. It was so hot the cameras wouldn't function and had to be packed in dry ice between scenes.

For the performers, no alcohol, theoretically, was allowed on the premises. A stone's throw across the alley from the Ryman's stage door, however, sat Tootsie's Orchid Lounge, still a Nashville tourist attraction. Many times the Opry stage manager had to fetch an act from atop one of Tootsie's bar stools. His place and his drink were saved, since he would be consuming again at Tootsie's almost before the applause died down across the alley.

The Opry backstage was supposed to be "dry." The trip to Tootsie's was enacted by a discreet minority. The late Tootsie Bess, owner of the landmark watering hole, kept the Opry broadcast tuned in on the bar's radio. Performers in the bar listened for their "spot." They knew who sang before them, and when they heard the cue, they started toward the stage.

Tootsie's was initially called "Mom's" until Tootsie bought it in the early 1960s. Hank Cochran recorded a song about the place, and inexplicably referred to it as an "orchid lounge," and the handle stuck. Tootsie took no abuse from anyone, no matter how celebrated. When closing time came, she turned on the house lights. She had an enormous hatpin. If a partygoer was slow in leaving, she buried the business end of that pin in his flesh. It happened once to Charley Pride.

I did a live New Year's Eve show from Tootsie's on WSM. I got the idea for the program after hearing spot announcements all week for holiday broadcasts from the

Plaza Hotel in New York, the Palmer House in Chicago, and elsewhere.

Celebrities were to be interviewed over a microphone in Tootsie's. I didn't know who to expect. The Stoneman Family and the Wilburn Brothers showed up, among other stars.

We promoted the show for days. Fans drove from all over to hobnob with the singers New Year's Eve at Tootsie's. Visitors would even get the chance to extend their own holiday wishes over WSM. I started at 10:15 P.M., and the big gala was supposed to last all night.

I had to shut it down at 12:30 A.M.

The place was elbow-to-elbow. In all the madness, many of the drunken stars and fans forgot that their words were going out over fifty thousand watts.

I had feared as much, and thought I had taken precautions. I asked Tootsie to help me censor the party talk and she did, by evicting a customer whose language would have offended radio listeners.

Then Tootsie got caught up in the spirit of the evening herself.

The guy she threw out came staggering back into the bar, and was near my microphone when Tootsie grabbed him.

"What in the hell are you doing in here!" she shouted at him, her voice going over the air. "I threw your ass out a while ago."

That was it. Tootsie was my police force but now I needed someone to police the police. Fearing repercussions from the Federal Communications Commission, I shut down the broadcast almost immediately, a show I had been touting for weeks. I finished my New Year's Eve broadcast that year from inside the quiet WSM studios.

I probably would have terminated the show early anyhow. Maintaining momentum after midnight on New Year's Eve was next to impossible.

There is an incredible feeling of family among Opry entertainers.

In 1958, before I was even an official part of the Opry,

I went to see Don Gibson premiere "Old Lonesome Me," then the hottest record in country music.

I was the announcer for the Opry shortly after Patsy Cline, Hawkshaw Hawkins, Cowboy Copas, and Randy Hughes died in a fiery plane crash in 1963 en route home from a benefit performance. Hughes was Patsy's manager, and unknown to the crowd. The other three were big stars, especially Patsy Cline.

The Opry cast, and country music community overall, were badly shaken.

A thirty-minute segment of the show was devoted to the dead celebrities. The cast sang a medley of hits by the fallen stars, then assembled en masse for a Gospel selection. Emotions ran exceedingly high inside the old building.

Minnie Pearl, who celebrated her fiftieth year on the Opry in 1990, had to follow that emotion-filled segment of the show that sorrowful night in 1964. She went out and told her old jokes, and like the trouper she is, actually succeeded in shifting the crowd's mood from sadness to gaiety.

I stood in the wings as she came off and saw her forced smile and flowing tears. She had wept virtually throughout her comedy routine, and the audience never knew.

It used to be the dream of every serious country musician to play the world-famous Grand Ole Opry. One man had that in mind when he slipped past guards and into the wings while Roy Acuff was performing.

Acuff is known as the "King of Country Music," the father superior of the show, and vicariously he runs the whole shebang. No one, cast or crew, takes issue with him.

Acuff has a reputation as a man of charity to musicians down on their luck. Unemployed players often hung around the Opry and Acuff would let them play with him during his set. They'd sit in, and he'd see to it they were paid something.

That's probably why no one thought it strange the night the mysterious fiddle player appeared on stage with Acuff. No one knew him, not even Acuff. Opry security was loose back then. Almost anyone carrying a guitar or fiddle could walk in the back door.

The unknown player did some songs with Acuff, then abruptly left the arena. It wasn't known that nobody knew him until the girls who make the pay vouchers began to ask the other players his name. He was owed a check.

"I don't know who he was, I thought you knew," was the common response. Whoever he was, and wherever he is tonight, he can say truthfully that he played the Grand Ole Opry with Roy Acuff. It's too bad he left so rapidly. People said he played pretty well. Acuff might have hired him.

...16...

Tₑₓ Rᵢₜₜₑᵣ ᵥₐₛ ᵈₒzᵢₙg ᵢₙ ₕᵢₛ ₛₜᵤᵈᵢₒ ₒₕₐᵢᵣ ₐₙᵈ ₕᵢₛ soft snoring was gaining volume. I feared that it would leak into the microphone and go over the air. I had been doing the all-night show with the renowned cowboy as my cohost since I returned to WSM on January 1, 1966. I had intended to leave the station permanently but returned after fifteen months.

Tex was sixty-one when he and I joined forces. He maintained a busy personal appearance schedule, mostly from Thursdays through Sundays. By the time he returned to the overnight microphone on some Mondays, he was exhausted. The miles and matinees had taken their toll. He'd begin each Monday night shift in a talkative mood. Soon, however, he'd nod off. America didn't know that one-half of the Emery-Ritter duo was blissfully sleeping over fifty thousand watts. I'd cover for him by simply playing more music. We had the ratings, and Tex had his sleep.

The mood of the show the night in question was serene, as it often is in the wee hours. Fatigue and the lateness of the hour were probably apparent in my own voice. I loved to talk soothingly, as if the listeners and I were nocturnal, secret confidants. Suddenly, however, the spell was broken.

"A-w-w-w-o-o-o-l," screamed Tex, shattering the mood. I looked at him, now even larger than usual, rising up to his six-feet-plus height and heaving up and down.

He was beating his chest fiercely, and bellowing louder.

"A-w-w-w-o-o-o-l," he continued, totally unconcerned about the deafening noise going out over the broadcast waves. Then I saw the smoke and knew why. Tex Ritter was on fire.

He had done what he'd done so many times before—fallen asleep with his pipe in his mouth. As he gently exhaled into the stem, hot ashes were forced from the pipe bowl and fell onto his shirt. The garment was polyester or some equally flammable material.

There was no way I could ignore the mayhem so I told the listeners that one of America's national treasures was on fire in Nashville, Tennessee. Not long afterward, Tex's suite in the historic Andrew Jackson Hotel caught fire while he was there. I didn't have to wait for the fire marshal's inquiry to know why.

During his radio inflammation, he pounded his shirt until he smothered the sparks. The incident had been far more disruptive than serious. I teased the old gentleman over the air about nearly going up in flames. He said ours was truly a hot show. I chided him often and people loved the friendly fussing. The Tex and Emery coupling played for one and one-half years. It was the most enjoyable and fulfilling period of my career and I almost turned it down.

I was burned out in the wake of my divorce from Skeeter. I stopped staying up all night playing sad songs. But almost as soon as I left the program fans and friends began to ask if and when I would return.

I was trying to put the show that had been the cornerstone of my career out of my mind, but it was hard to forget something with so many reminders.

People are usually suspicious of show business retirements. They think that after a performer leaves a starring role, he is dissatisfied with the absence of accolades. A performer, on the contrary, might have an easier time laying down his role than the public does in allowing it.

MEMORIES

I was grateful for the heyday at WSM in the mid-1960s. But all good things come to an end, especially when they cease to be good. I had taken my broken heart from my last divorce and, with the exception of local television, I had gone into hiding inside myself.

Around Nashville, people might have seen Ralph Emery, but they weren't seeing me.

Opry Star Spotlight, of course, went on without me. The station hired a replacement from Chattanooga who didn't pan out. The guy really didn't have much of a chance, no matter how good he was. That show was associated with me, and the traditionally loyal country fans didn't want anyone else in front of my microphone.

Country people are resistant to change. Minnie Pearl, for example, is really Mrs. Sarah Cannon. She is a dignified woman and Nashville socialite yet fans don't want to see her without her inexpensive straw hat and the conspicuous price tag.

Porter Wagoner has worn ostentatious apparel covered with rhinestones for thirty years and his fans won't let him dress down. That same bondage to habit was extended to me and the all-night show. Fans seemed to want to keep me at that job. When I inherited the show in 1957, it didn't have a single sponsor. When I left for the final time in 1972, eighteen minutes of every hour had been bought by advertisers. Doing the show was no longer fun. The commercials broke up the time I used to have for sustained interviews.

In an attempt to revive the program's sagging ratings during my absence, WSM brought in Tex Ritter, a bona fide American legend. Tex worked two months with the legendary announcer Grant Turner, whose wife didn't want him staying up all night, so Grant also quit the show. In late 1965, Tex's deep and gravelly voice purred from AM radios coast-to-coast, and he was especially well received in Canada.

Tex had an interest in, and feel for, the country music he played. His cowboy image went hand in hand with the tastes of working people. They then composed the largest segment of country music fans.

In the fall of 1965, WSM management called and asked me to return to the all-night show. They even offered a salary increase. Financially tight as that place was, I knew the raise meant that they wanted me back badly.

In December, I said yes and almost instantly, the broadcast and published promotions began. The station got about the business of telling the public that I was returning. I was touched. My emotions were running high for the homecoming.

I was apprehensive, however, about working with a partner, even though the partner was the likeable Tex Ritter. I admired Tex the way I admire any American institution. When I was ten years old, I stood in line at a Nashville department store to get his autograph and carried it for years. But admiring him and wanting to work with him were two different things. As a longtime solo pilot, I feared it would be crowded in the cockpit working with someone else.

I couldn't have been more wrong.

He was a mammoth man in physique and character, a Gibraltar of a human whose heart was his largest asset. He had made sixty-five Hollywood movies and had sung the title song to the soundtrack of what many critics agree is the greatest western movie of all time, *High Noon*. He had made hit records, and would record more before his stint with me ended in 1967.

Some people in country music have inferiority complexes about their craft. They think they are second-class citizens compared to entertainers who have been in motion pictures, or appeared on Broadway or network television. They refer to entertainers who have done it all as "legitimate."

I never shared those ideas. If I had, I would have agreed that Tex Ritter was one of the most legitimate entertainers in our Nashville industry.

I felt humble sharing a microphone with him.

I worked the controls, and he sat across a table from me.

I tried to make the program follow the form of western movies. I would wear the figurative black hat, and Tex would wear the white one. I'd get on him about everything and anything, and he'd come back at me. He was very good at it.

I told him on the air that some of his western movies were ridiculous because he would shoot his gun forty-five times without reloading. He'd come up with an off-the-wall explanation, such as that his reloading skills were even faster than his draw, and he had popped bullets back into his gun without my even noticing.

Then he'd chuckle deeply, which made his pipe emit sparks. The man was jolly and warm, a cowboy version of an unseasonal Santa Claus.

And he had his defiant and mischievous sides.

Tex was a Republican well to the political right. He didn't like Muhammad Ali because Ali had resisted being drafted into the military, citing religious objections. Tex was always complaining about it, saying that the government ought to force Cassius Clay (Ali's former name) to serve.

I told Tex Ali didn't want to be called Cassius Clay, so Tex called him Cassius all the more vigorously.

Tex's passion for the things he liked was equally adamant. And he liked the state of Texas. The cowboy had griped about Ali for months, but was left speechless when Ali moved to Houston. Tex couldn't bring himself to bad-mouth a fellow Texan.

I've forgotten who Ali was fighting the night I walked into WSM and found Tex listening to the bout over a tiny radio next to his ear.

I "signed" our show on the air while Tex was standing across the studio listening to the final moments of the fight.

I think he wanted to cheer for Ali, but he would never have admitted it, just as he would never have used the champion's correct name.

Finally, Tex sauntered into our show, and went on the air.

"Who won the fight?" I asked.

There was a long silence and then he said, "Cassius won! . . . you just can't whip those Texans!" I never heard Tex Ritter say anything negative about Muhammad Ali again.

There was a campaign by members of the Country Music Association to admit fans to its membership. Many people in the country music industry, including Tex, resented the movement.

The idea was discussed during a CMA board meeting in Palm Springs, California.

Tex and Roy Acuff, among others, were on the board.

Acuff told the board, "I think this idea of admitting fans to our CMA is great. Why, on the plane trip out here, I met a stewardess who wanted to join. I'll bet I could have sold her a CMA membership, and she would have been a happy member of the CMA."

"R-o-y," came Tex's resonant drawl from the back of the room. "The CMA can do a lot of things for you, but it can't get you any poon-tang."

The meeting broke into uncontrollable laughter, and was adjourned.

Tex and I began to socialize off the air, and he became a friend and father figure to me. We often went to athletic events at Vanderbilt. His wife, Dorothy, was in California rearing their two boys. His son John eventually became a major television and motion picture star, and Dorothy was busy as early as 1965 sowing the seeds of his success.

Separation from his family made Tex as lonely as I was. Misery loves company, and perhaps that was one of the main staples of our friendship. He came to my house often and watched the first Superbowl there in 1967.

I used to enjoy being seen with him around town. His was an imposing stature. He looked like Hulk Hogan in a trench coat.

Tex and Dorothy were as much in love as newlyweds. She would fly from Los Angeles to see him once a month, taking the "red-eye" and arriving in Nashville about 3:00

A.M. He'd send someone to meet her plane and pace the floor nervously until she arrived at the studio.

He was excited to the point of nervousness. She'd bring us cookies, call him "Daddy," and the two of them would go off to his apartment. I always enjoyed seeing the look of adolescent love on a man who was nearly a senior citizen.

Dorothy Ritter has remained one of the most gracious people I've ever known. Joy and I have been to Europe with her, where she tirelessly took us on sight-seeing tours. She has done the same for us in Hollywood, and once insisted that we go see her son John. She wanted to drop by his house unannounced at 11:00 P.M. I pleaded with her not to do it, and we reached a compromise: We would not stop if John's house was dark. I prayed all the way to his address that his lights would be off, and they were.

In 1987, Dorothy had a stroke. Today, she resides in the Hollywood actors' home, unable to articulate. It breaks my heart, for she was one of the most delightful personalities I've ever known.

I'll always retain a library of Dorothy Ritter memories, such as the time she moved to a Nashville estate to be near Tex. I was at their house the Christmas after Tex died when Dorothy was sending her boys all over town to deliver presents. Dorothy didn't cook, and as John went out the door, she complained that she was hungry.

"As you make your deliveries and drop in on various parties, look to see if they have anything to eat," she said. "If there are sandwiches lying around, would you pick up a few for your mother?"

"What should I ask for?" retorted John, "a mother bag?"

Dorothy spent many hours calling Hollywood producers to nourish John's career, but I never knew how much Tex did to help his talented son, who was a star on *Three's Company*, one of the most successful situation comedies on television.

Tex never saw the show and was aware only of the beginning of the unfolding of John's career, when John played a preacher on *The Waltons* in the 1970s. At about that time the Grand Ole Opry comic, Stringbean, was walking from his car to his house on his farm late one Saturday night after an Opry performance. Assailants leaped from the darkness, stabbed and shot him to death, and took the hundreds of dollars that Stringbean always carried in the bib of his overalls. Everyone knew the money was there.

In November 1973, Tex, his eldest son, Tommy, and I went to Stringbean's funeral, along with virtually every entertainer in Nashville. Stringbean was a beloved and dignified man whose death pulled together again the family spirit among the country entertainers.

In January 1974, the guest on my nationally syndicated radio show was Tex Ritter. We talked about Stringbean and Tex's cowboy movies. As the show came to an end, I offhandedly muttered an impromptu closing cue.

"Tex," I said, "this is where you ride off into the sunset."

Tex gave his signature chuckle, and told the listeners that he would ride for about twenty-five yards, turn, and give a final wave from the saddle.

He didn't know how prophetic he was.

The last broadcast words he ever spoke were "Adios, amigo."

A week later, Tex was visiting a guitar player in his band who was in jail for overdue alimony. As Tex was about to enter the man's cell, he grabbed his chest, collapsed, and was dead before he hit the floor.

The last funeral I had attended had been with Tex Ritter. It had been two months before his own.

I flew with Tex's body to his funeral in Vidor, Texas. Funeral songs included Red Foley's "Peace in the Valley" and "Beyond the Sunset."

"Do you know what Tex would have said about that funeral?" Tom T. Hall asked me on the way to the graveyard. "He would have said, 'Well, the least they could have done was do one of my numbers.' "

I told Tex's widow about the closing moment on my syndicated show when Tex had unknowingly anticipated his death.

"I had no idea his good-bye to the fans would prove to be final," I said. "Dorothy, if you don't want me to, I won't release that show for broadcast."

She insisted that I play it.

I sent the program to the approximately two hundred stations that subscribed at the time. Only one declined to air it. Listeners, of course, knew by then that the cowboy waving his hat a final time was in his grave. Millions heard Tex say his last good-bye. There's no telling how many returned the farewell.

... 17 ...

ON EASTER SUNDAY, 1967, I SAT IN A RENTED CAR ON a parking lot in Tallahassee, Florida, with a woman who was bawling. I had flown there from Nashville and told her that I didn't want to marry her after telling her many times previously that I did. My plan had been to elope with Joy Kott. But I got scared.

Six hundred miles from home I developed two cold feet.

Because I had failed at three marriages to two women, I was sure that I couldn't get along with a female. I had a complex about it. I saw no reason to reenter marriage if the marriage was destined to fail. There was also the fact that I was heavily in debt, and I didn't think it was fair to offer financial stress to a young bride.

I probably would have adhered to my resistance, and flown back to Nashville, leaving Joy in Florida where she was a premedical student at Florida State University in Tallahassee. But Joy melted my armor with liquid tears. To this day, I weaken when she cries.

So inside the car, I acquiesced.

"Then let's get married right now," I said.

We went to the dormitory to pick up Joy's roommates. One woman served as her bridesmaid, the other as my "best man." That evening we were married in a church amid flowers left over from the Easter service earlier that day. By 10:00 P.M., the two-member wedding party was back in the dormitory, and Joy and I were inside the Tallahassee Howard Johnson's Motel.

We selected tiny Thomasville for the nuptial site because it was the first real town across the Georgia line. I didn't especially expect mass media coverage of my marriage, but as a safeguard I opted to marry out of town. There had been no press attention when Joy had taken the results of my blood test the previous Friday to the Georgia courthouse where she bought our wedding license.

I wanted to keep our marriage out of the headlines, which might read "Emery Takes Third Wife." I didn't want a story that pointed out the fourteen-year difference in our ages, which would have been frowned upon back then.

Mostly, I simply felt the marriage was nobody's business. I was trying to rebuild a life crumbled by booze, indebtedness, and indifference. I wanted the reconstruction to transpire privately.

With my having been back on the all-night show for two years, and the regional popularity of my Nashville television show, I was sure that my celebrity might be a magnet to uninvited guests. There was one person totally indifferent to my television show at the time of the wedding: Joy.

"I had never seen his television show," she said recently, when asked if she was initially drawn to Ralph Emery the person or Ralph Emery the celebrity. "I didn't know he was a celebrity when I met him," she said.

Tom Carter, who helped me write this book, teased that I must have found Joy's unawareness of my show business career very reassuring regarding my popularity.

"I've never cared about Ralph Emery the entertainer," Joy said. "I'd love him no matter what he did."

She would and she has.

It's expected that I brag about my wife. But I brag about her with no regard to expectations. I have met the world's leading celebrities and responded to White House invitations during two presidential administrations. I could go on almost indefinitely about the important and influential people I've known, some of them intimately.

But no single person and no single force has been a positive and supportive influence like Joy. To paraphrase a song, I'd rather die young than grow old without her.

Joy's mind is as expansive as her heart. Her brightness is commensurate with both. Her intelligence quotient has tested at 145. She was enjoying an academic scholarship to Nashville's Peabody College when I met her.

She was employed part-time at Nashville's Channel 4 where, among other things, I supplemented my income by being a freelance booth announcer. Joy would come in evenings when I was doing my spots. She had never seen my morning show on the same television station, saying years later that she didn't get up in time.

Our meeting came during my fifteen-month absence from all-night radio.

On Saturdays, she would get off at 11:30 P.M. She would come to my announcer's booth and sit with me until 12:30 A.M. when we would go for pizza. That routine began as early as our second date.

I fell in love fast.

Joy later would say that she met me after having had a vision. It seems she had had a premonition about meeting a man whom she would see for the first time in three-quarter profile. That's how I was standing the first time she laid eyes on me. Who knows, if I had been looking at her straight on, the marriage might never have happened.

Not only had she not seen any of my shows, but, I later learned, she had never heard of me the first time she saw me. Furthermore, she didn't like country music. My broadcasting and country music are the Alpha and Omega of my life.

"Why then," I eventually asked her, "were you attracted to me?"

"Well," she said, "there was that three-quarter profile that I had envisioned as the way I would meet my husband, and I liked your fingernails. They were clean and pristine."

"You developed a romantic interest in me because I had clean fingernails?" I asked.

"Not entirely," she said, "your pressed shirts had something to do with it too."

The whole thing might not have happened if I hadn't owned an iron and manicure set.

I called Joy two days after having met her. I have spoken to her almost every day of my life since. We'll celebrate our twenty-fifth wedding anniversary in 1992—a quarter century and two sons later.

Her parents didn't like me because I had been married previously and because there is fourteen years' difference in our ages. They were against the wedding. They sent Joy to Florida State University to get her away from me. Her father predicted our courtship would last less than two years. He made no prediction about a marriage he didn't expect.

During our courtship, Joy gave me a beagle which, for no reason, I named Margaret. Her mother had a fit whenever Joy came to my house on Saturdays and cleaned the garage where the dog stayed all week. Joy has been forever attentive to me, while retaining her own identity. Joy is a master at giving and taking mental space.

There is only one significant negative thought I have about our marriage. It has nothing to do with Joy, and everything to do with the way some people treat her.

It's difficult for her to be a celebrity's wife because people tend to ignore her when she's with me. It's rude.

I've seen the same thing happen in many of my friends' marriages.

"Sometimes, I feel as though I would have to rob a bank to be noticed," Joy said, regarding her treatment from others. Unfortunately, treatment from the press toward a celebrity or his spouse isn't always as inattentive.

In December 1990, our youngest son, Kit, was sworn into the United States Air Force. The ceremony transpired live on *Nashville Now*. He left the next day amid news that the United States was moving closer to war against Iraq in the Persian Gulf.

My son Mike is now a junior at Middle Tennessee State and lives in Murfreesboro. Steve is grown and has been gone for years.

Joy and I are adjusting to the "empty nest syndrome." There were times when all three of my sons joined Joy and me in a house that rang with laughter and love.

My wife and I will try to make up for the departures of our sons by loving each other even more. It will be a challenging task that will fulfill each of us. We love to work on our love.

When I come off the air at 9:30 P.M. Nashville time, I go home to a dinner that Joy always has waiting. She foregoes her own dinner at a conventional hour to dine with me at 10:15 P.M. We line out the next day's activities, then retire until my alarm rings at 4:30 A.M.

That was our routine when Joy and I returned home after Kit had been inducted into the military. He went out with his friends and we put him on an airplane the next day for San Antonio.

The next night, I was entering the house as the telephone rang about 10:00 P.M. Kit was calling to say that he had made it to his first military destination.

Suddenly, I realized vividly what had failed to seep in all along—that my youngest son was gone from home.

Joy and I each talked to him, hung up the telephone, and didn't say a word to each other for what seemed like the longest time.

...18...

IF THE TELEVISION INDUSTRY, ALWAYS IN LOVE WITH RE-producing itself, ever does a remake of the popular 1960s series *My Three Sons,* I could play Fred MacMurray's lead role. As for *my* three sons, there is almost twenty years' difference in the ages of my eldest and youngest. There is a century's worth of memories. The recollections began to come on relentlessly in the wake of Kit's departure for the United States Air Force in December 1990. He is the youngest, and the last child to leave home. The predominant symptom of the empty nest syndrome is the uncanny ability of those left behind to fall into spontaneous laughter, given the slightest hint of a memory, and to continue laughing amid a shrinking smile and ever-moistening eyes.

I do miss my sons.

I have essentially reared two families in two decades, with the second containing twice as many children as the first. Steve, my son with Betty, was old enough to drive when Kit was born. We were five people who made uncountable memories. Ours was happiness by the numbers, although Joy spent much of her married life trying to suppress the daytime noise of the all-boy boys so that her night-working husband could sleep.

Writing about my sons is difficult. It's easy to fall into a sentimental trap and write things that would only be of interest to members of my immediate family. I don't want these pages to be verbal portraits that are the equivalent of family photographs.

But indulge me as I talk about my boys. Until my last son left home, weekends were almost always reserved for the parade of torn denims, dirty faces, dental braces, and the unwilling enrollees in apprentice masculinity. I watched my sons evolve from crying over frogs that escaped their pockets, to tears over girls who broke their hearts. As for Kit, there were so many girls, I can't remember all their names. But I can the frog's.

Freda the Frog was an amphibious ambassador of companionship and entertainment. She had an extraordinary ability to snatch fireflies from the air with no more than the lightning flick of an elongated tongue. Her oral dexterity prompted cheers from Mike and Kit, whose ravings grew even louder after Freda swallowed her prey.

"Look, you can see a light in her belly," Kit screamed.

Sure enough, the frog's torso was illuminated when the insect flashed inside her tummy, visible through her thin and shining skin. Her body was an amber glow with legs, and this family, who sometimes watched on all fours, rose to our knees to laugh and applaud that gluttonous frog. She then emitted a guttural sound that was either her natural croak—or an insect burp.

Steve Emery is one of the hardest-working and most disciplined people I've ever known. He majored in premedicine in undergraduate school. When he finished and felt his grades weren't all they could be, he reenrolled and took many of his courses again, scoring a grade point average that was a ticket to admittance to dental school. He practiced general dentistry for eleven years and decided to become an endodontist, a root canal specialist. He underwent a divorce during that period but nonetheless finished number one in his class at Boston University. Today, at thirty-eight, he is one of Nashville's leading endodontists. He married his high school sweetheart and they have given Joy and me three grandchildren, the eldest of whom is only two years younger than Kit.

While still in school in Boston, he surprised me by flying to Nashville in February 1990 to observe the *All-Star Salute to Ralph Emery*. In his seat in the front row, and from mine at center stage, I could see the glint in his eyes as millions watched the televised tribute and my proudest hour.

I should have known Steve would become a dentist because of his compulsion to be meticulous. When he was a teenager, I hired him to paint our living room ceiling and, stupidly, offered to pay him by the hour. The task took almost an entire summer. He worked at a snail's pace because he was obsessed with detail, moving his brush in short strokes as if he were painting a portrait, not an enclosure.

My all-night radio show commenced at 10:15 P.M., and during its theme song on November 27, 1967, the studio telephone rang. It was me calling whoever was taking my place to tell him to tell the listeners that Joy had given birth to Michael Emery. The same thing happened at the same hour twenty-three months later regarding the birth of Kit.

Twenty-three years ago, I was driving down Nashville's Franklin Road with Joy as we talked about our financial stress.

"And there is going to be another expense," she said. "I'm going to have a baby."

"Oh, no!" I said.

I didn't recall that enthusiastically negative response until Joy helped me with the recollection recently. In retrospect, it's understandable how a provider strapped for funds would fear the arrival of a baby. The remark is regrettable. I thank God for the prosperity that I've found, but if I were still poor, I could not put a price tag on the pleasure afforded me by my boys.

I was so excited the day after Mike was born that I couldn't contain myself.

"Have a baby," I told my television audience, "my wife just had a cigar!"

Joy and I named our firstborn Michael, after a song popular then, "Michael Row the Boat Ashore."

A month before Mike was born, Joy and I went to Sears and charged a baby bed. We were positive that Mike was going to be a girl because that's what we wanted. So his bed was French Provincial with flowers, lace, and eyelet. He looked out of place among the feminine frills, he in his tiny canvas gym shoes.

Mike was an extremely boisterous child. He is the only baby I have ever known of who wore out one baby bed and almost went through a second. He used his sneakers to kick the sides off the contraptions.

Mike was also inventive. He hadn't been walking long when he learned how to remove the vertical bars from his baby bed. He twisted and turned them until eight were missing.

He always had a compulsion to disassemble things, such as dresser drawers and their contents when he was little, and car engines when he was a teenager. He always reassembled the engines, and is currently enrolled at Middle Tennessee University, studying environmental science and technology.

Joy has been an excellent mother who read all the books on parenting but abandoned the task in the wake of conflicting texts. She never left Mike alone when he was a baby—except once.

Mike was five months old. I was asleep, and rather than wake me, Joy darted out of the room for a second to get something for him. Mike chose that instant to turn over for the first time in his life. He rolled off the dressing table and onto the floor perhaps five feet below. He was uninjured, but terrified. He screamed for eighteen hours, during which time Joy rocked him to restore his better temperament.

Michael was responsible for Joy and me making a big adjustment in our schedules. I worked all night and we slept all day. Her mother would often call at 2:30 P.M. and we would still be in bed. She thought that was terrible. We finally bought one of the first telephone answering machines ever made so we wouldn't be disturbed. The early models were expensive, and we paid $21.67 a month for four years.

So with Michael's birth Joy was up during the days and we didn't see as much of each other.

I was announcing the *U.S. Navy Recruiting Show* for extra money when Mike was born. At the time, I was only earning enough to stay alive, and the hospital wanted six hundred dollars for the delivery and subsequent stay. A government check for the show came just in time to enable me to pay for Joy's and Michael's discharge.

Michael showed me the human frailty that characterizes childhood. Joy and I took him to a basketball game in Memphis where Steve's high school, Stratford, was playing in the tournament. Michael was still a babe in arms. When the home team came onto the court, the crowd cheered madly, and the noise terrified Michael. Joy had to take him to the car where she held him throughout the game she never saw.

He cried that same hysterical way during the entire return flight from New York, where I had taken him with Joy for a syndication taping. His tears and wallowing left my tie so irreparably wrinkled that I threw it away.

But, despite the chaos, almost whenever I went anywhere, my family went along. To this day, I still don't like to take vacations without the children.

I remember a time Joy and I went without the boys. Our babysitter could not deal with their high energy, and she quit. Joy's mother called to say the boys had been unexpectedly placed with her. We were skiing in Colorado and had to cut short the holiday. But that wasn't the extent of the hassle.

The motel where we spent our nights had extremely thin walls. Joy and I set our alarm for a predawn awakening, and I was afraid the ringing clock would disturb other guests, many of whom were our friends. The instant the clock began to sound, I leaped from the bed to silence it. Groping and staggering in the dark, I bolted into a wall. The impact sliced my forehead from above the corner of one eye to above the corner of the other. I had to be taken to Aspen Valley Hospital to stop the bleeding.

The next day, my face turned black and blue but I decided to appear on my morning television show with no explanation to viewers about my facial discoloration. They probably imagined that Joy and I had been in a fight. I didn't wear makeup during my recovery, and I never did make a public explanation. The stitches and bruises would never have happened, however, had it not been for my errant boys and their indirect summons to come home.

All these boys, especially Michael, had many physical accidents. Mike fell down the stairs once and was pushed out of a treehouse by a little girl. His teeth went through his lower lip, and his tongue protruded through the hole when Joy took him into the doctor's office. He had to be restrained in a straitjacket as the doctor sewed stitches, and Joy passed out.

The power of a child's love came home to me when Michael was twelve. He attended a public school with children of lesser economic means. They resented Michael's nice clothes, and a gold coin and chain I had given him. Three boys attacked him one day after school, tore his designer shirt off, and threw away the chain. When Joy arrived to pick him up, she found him scratched and battered in the grass. He was parting the blades looking tirelessly for the jewelry I had given him. It was more important to him than his wounds, including the invisible ones on his broken heart.

Kit was born only eight months after he was conceived. He was delivered with immature lungs and the doctor told us that he had a fifty-fifty chance to live. Despite the rigors of childbirth, Joy could not sleep the first night of Kit's life because she feared that her newborn might not live. For days after Kit's birth, she feared that anyone entering her hospital room, even the orderlies, was coming to say that her baby had died.

He spent the first seven days of his life inside an incubator. With each breath, his chest would rise and fall as he struggled to get oxygen into his system. His strong will to live was overpowering. Joy stood at a hospital window watching her week-old son whom she had not been allowed to touch. As his chest heaved, she prayed and bargained with God, saying that she would do anything He wanted as a mother if only He would let her baby survive.

Joy was released from the hospital but our baby had to stay. Sleep was fitful for us, and each time the telephone rang, we feared it was the hospital calling to report his death.

When Kit was finally released, two-year-old Michael went with Joy to take home the baby, who had been named Walter Ralph Emery, Jr.

"Oh, what a cute little kiddy," Michael said of his brother. The name stuck, and the boy was called "Kiddy" until he was ten, when he decided it did not sound masculine. He wanted to change his name and we told him he could select a new one. He chose the name Kit. Joy told everyone in the family to call him Kit.

Kit is one of the biggest extroverts I've ever seen. When he was small, he would walk down the street and speak to everyone, and couldn't understand why they wouldn't return the greeting.

Within two months after his induction into the Air Force, Kit was a dormitory leader. His ambition is to become an honor graduate at the Combat Arms Technical School. They have an inspection scheduled at 6:00 A.M. one day a week, but Kit is not told which day, so he rises at 4:30 A.M. daily to be prepared. I'm enthralled at the way he has adjusted to military life and accepted responsibility.

I've heard people say that happiness begins when the kids leave home and the dog dies. Our dog, "Sugar," a family member for thirteen years, died in 1990. So having undergone that prescription for happiness, let me tell you it's a lie. Having children is a tremendous stress on a male-female relationship. But the rewards exceed the sacrifices. Children have no idea how much they are loved. Parents suffer with them more than they ever know. If you've never been a parent let me say simply that when your children are hurting, so are you. You find yourself trying to live their lives vicariously while struggling to maintain your own.

The strain is nerve-wracking and heartbreaking. You give them all the wisdom and love you have, and hope that God and luck intercede to do the rest.

While Kit was in basic training, there were a few hours on Christmas Day when he was allowed to visit with us. Knowing he would have the time we flew to Lackland Air Force Base and visited with Kit for seven hours.

"You know," Joy said, on the way home, "I think he was actually glad to see us. For the first time in his life, I thought he was actually glad to see us."

I don't think it was the first time he was glad. I think it was the first time he realized he was glad. That was an unspoken but glorious realization to us all.

...19...

My RADIO SHOW IS CURRENTLY AIRED ON 440 STATIONS in 225 markets for the largest distribution I've had in twenty-three years of intermittent syndication.

It all started with a dream, and it wasn't mine.

I was doing a Nashville television show on WSM-TV and so was singer Bobby Lord. When station officials decided to syndicate his program, I was disappointed that they hadn't done the same for me.

I was bemoaning the situation to Merle Kilgore, who wrote "Ring of Fire" for Johnny Cash, and who is currently executive manager for Hank Williams, Jr.

"Ralph," he said, "you know I have extrasensory perception and people say I'm crazy. But I'm going to tell you three things that are going to happen to you. First, the bushes around your house are all going to die. Second, your wife is planning a most unusual bookcase and she's going to build it. Third, you are going to get a syndicated show."

I assumed he meant television.

I never mentioned the prediction to anyone until I noticed the dead bushes around my house.

"Joy," I said, "are you thinking about a new bookcase for our house?"

"Why yes," she replied. "I haven't said anything before but you know we have that big picture window in the living room and I thought about a bookcase beneath the window with a seat on top."

My astonishment was surpassed a few days later when I was called by a representative of Cinevox Corporation in New York asking me to discuss becoming a host on a syndicated radio show. I had never heard of the man or his company.

He had gotten my name from the late Jack Stapp, founder of Tree International, the world's largest country music publishing company.

In October 1968, I flew with trepidation to New York City for a meeting in the Pan Am Building with my potential syndicators. I left with a deal for four hundred dollars a week for broadcast in forty markets. It was considerably more than I was making at WSM. And it was syndication.

The terms of my contract called for me to record in New York beginning at about 11:00 A.M. every Monday, depending on the plane's punctuality. On those days, I recorded one week's worth of two-hour shows. (The majority of the time was filled with recorded music. I only recorded my talk in New York.) I began the recording weeks by leaving Nashville before daylight. I recorded until 5:00 P.M., flew back to Nashville, and signed on the all-night show at 10:00 P.M. I played records until 5:00 A.M. Those Mondays were twenty-four hours and three thousand miles long.

The New York shows were produced by Maury Benkoil, a Turkish Jew and former program director of WCBS in New York. He was wonderfully upbeat and I liked him a lot. The only thing he knew about country music was that he knew nothing about it. He let me call the shots.

Within eighteen months after I adopted the hectic schedule, Cinevox closed its New York operation and sent me on alternative weeks to Chicago. There, I recorded my show with the great Dick Orkin, who does the *Time* magazine commercials today. I worked Chicago for six weeks, during which Cinevox was consistently behind with my pay. I was buying airplane tickets with my American Express card and the bill exceeded $2,000.

I wanted continued syndication, but I didn't want to work for free. So I personally contacted each of the stations that had been subscribing through Cinevox, and asked if they would buy directly from me.

I was suddenly the star, and distributor, of the *Ralph Emery Show*.

Joy and I took reel-to-reel tapes, packed them in boxes, and sent them out. She kept records indicating which stations were paying, and our living room looked like a minefield of recording tape and pasteboard box. She never complained once.

To this day, Cinevox Corporation is listed on the unfair list at AFTRA (American Federation of Television and Radio Artists) for not paying my and other salaries. They owed me about three thousand dollars, which I've never collected.

My collection woes continued with the stations to which I was selling. Many paid late or not at all. The stress of performing on two shows, while producing and distributing one, became too much. I was called by Jane Dowden at Showbiz, then the hottest syndicated country music television company in the business. She wanted to take over distribution of my radio show. I wanted to let her.

My memories of celebrity interviews are as voluminous from radio syndication as they are from the all-night show.

Jim Ameche, brother of actor Don Ameche, played "Superman" on a 1933 radio series sponsored by Wheaties. He told a story that epitomized the godlike stature of Babe Ruth during his prime.

Ruth was hired to do a live commercial and rehearsed all day. He nonetheless always failed on one line. Despite continued practice, the line continued to come out wrong.

Eventually, it was showtime. Ameche recited the following scenario.

"Now," said the announcer, "here is Babe Ruth for the breakfast of champions."

Ruth stumbled on the same line and said, "Son-of-a-bitch, I did it again." His words went over the air.

That was during a time when the words "hell" or "damn" would have prompted public outrage. But there was not one telephone call or letter of dissent regarding the Babe's slip. I thought the story was a telling essay about a more innocent America's tolerance for its heroes.

In 1980, I was visited on my syndicated program by Kris Kristofferson, a first-class songwriter who was fast becoming a fixture of the motion picture industry.

He's the only person I've ever met who has trouble pronouncing his own name.

Each guest was asked to make a promotional announcement for his upcoming show with me. We tried numerous times to record Kristofferson's announcement because he kept stumbling over his surname.

Kristofferson's career is perhaps the most enigmatic in Nashville. He was a Rhodes Scholar at England's prestigious Oxford University and his father was a United States Air Force major general. Kris became an Army captain.

He could have had a distinguished military career and was supposed to teach at West Point. He could have had a solid civilian career teaching English literature or composition at the university level.

He opted to become a country music songwriter and, while awaiting his break, worked as a janitor at Columbia Records.

He told me that his father was, to put it mildly, disappointed. There was an estrangement whose end was signified by a letter of apology from his father shortly before his death.

Kristofferson said that his willingness to accept a pedestrian job to gain a music business foothold was at times a liability.

"I met a lot of stars who were recording at Columbia, but many of them didn't want to take songs from a janitor," he said. "They thought if I had any talent as a songwriter, I wouldn't be working as a janitor."

He had done his initial film, entitled *Cisco Pike,* years

earlier with Gene Hackman. When Kristofferson did my radio program, he was touting *A Star Is Born*, a blockbuster movie he had done with Barbra Streisand.

Kristofferson played an established rock star, and Ms. Streisand played an up-and-coming singer. Their characters fell in love, and Kristofferson relayed a behind-the-scenes story about the pair's first screen encounter.

"Remember the scene where we are at the piano?" he asked. "It's the first time we got together and I'm trying to put the make on her."

The scene called for Kristofferson to sit next to Streisand on a piano stool where she had been struggling to match lyrics with a new melody. He suggested some words, she was touched, and became putty in his arms. At that point, he was supposed to pick her up and carry her off to bed.

In a shot the public never saw, Kristofferson said he struggled to hoist Streisand while he was sitting down. He wasn't strong enough to lift her high enough. As he turned her horizontal torso, he accidentally raked her feet across the top of the piano, ridding the instrument of ash trays, glasses, and other objects. He nearly dropped Ms. Streisand, but not before he got his feet tangled in production cables and began to stumble. The first rule of film production is to continue a scene, no matter how disastrous, until the director yells "cut." The director couldn't yell, Kristofferson said, because he was mute with laughter.

That movie contained a delicately erotic scene where Kristofferson and Ms. Streisand sat nude in a bathtub surrounded by scores of flickering candles. Their caressing bodies were shadows in the faint glow. The spell was broken for me when I recalled Kristofferson's clumsy and unintentional dance with one of the world's biggest stars clutching to avoid falling from his flailing arms.

There was additional comic relief during filming, Kristofferson remembered, when a makeup man smeared Streisand's white dress with fake dirt. A substance in the makeup had spoiled and smelled like excrement.

Kristofferson said that he told the director that the star of his film literally smelled like shit.

"I don't want to hear it," was all the director would say, Kristofferson said.

Kristofferson and Streisand began shooting another passionate love scene and the odor rose into his nostrils. Streisand claimed she could see the pupils in his eyes dilate because of the stench, and she fell out laughing. The scene was done again.

Kristofferson said the public never knew that the pair portrayed romance to an aroma resembling a barnyard's.

He spoke later on my show about how he happened to write one of his biggest hits, "Bobbi McGee." The song was probably Janis Joplin's biggest record, and was perhaps the most successful "story" song of the 1970s. There were all kinds of romantic rumors about the song, rhapsodical stories about Bobbi McGee being a former Kristofferson lover, and the like.

Kristofferson said he named the character because he was drunk and misunderstood Fred Foster, then owner of Monument Records, who assigned him to write about a fictional Bobbi McKey. The latter name doesn't invoke as much imagination as the first. Who knows what would have been the fate of that tune had Kristofferson been sober when it was suggested?

Kristofferson talked about having read an article about Frank Sinatra in a national magazine. He remembers it as being *Time,* although I think it was *Esquire.* Sinatra said he believed in broads, a bottle, a Bible, or anything that would help him make it through the night. Kristofferson penned "Help Me Make It Through the Night."

Hearing him spin the stories behind the songs was magnetic to listeners and to me.

In 1976, the hottest act in country music was Willie Nelson, an old friend who did my syndicated show when his biggest hit ever, "Blue Eyes Cryin' in the Rain," was coming off a spectacular popularity run.

We reminisced about the first time he came to the all-night show in the early 1960s. He was plugging a record under his actual first and last name, Hugh Nelson.

He told me he had sat up with me all night. When I

asked if I had been nice to him during his premiere, he said that I was.

"But you never did play my record," he added.

I couldn't believe that, and am happy he nonetheless chose to see me again throughout the years.

During one syndicated show, Willie spun the story behind one of his stellar compositions, "What Can You Do to Me Now?" The song is about a man who is overly abused by a woman, of whom he asks, "What can you do to me now?"

"How did you come up with that title?" I asked Willie.

"I wrote that the year I had gotten a divorce and wrecked four cars and a pickup," he said. "I wrote the tune, and the next day my house burned down. It's true. The record came out, it was sent to my manager in New York, and inside the jacket someone had mistakenly placed a Waylon Jennings record instead of mine."

Ronnie Milsap was the hottest new act on RCA Records the first time he did my syndicated program. The blind singer-pianist brought along an apparatus that enables him to write and read braille called a "pecker." He made braille notes during our conversation, felt them, and read aloud. He was fascinating.

Ronnie had put away the device when I unexpectedly asked him another question.

"Just a minute, Ralph," he said. "I'll tell you but first I've got to pull out my pecker."

He instantly realized his mistake and was deeply embarrassed.

Mack Wiseman, my other studio guest, and I howled with laughter. I edited the remark out of the tape and it was never broadcast.

My syndicated show ran for twelve years through Showbiz. It was sponsored by General Mills, Ford Trucks, Bayer Aspirin, and others.

During the span, Jane got the idea for *Pop Goes the Country,* the syndicated television show I did for several years in more than two hundred markets. In most places, it aired on Saturday afternoons opposite college sports. It was always strong in the ratings. People were astounded when I quit the program.

I'm especially proud of my days with *Pop*. I booked the talent on the show, and think I put together some tremendous packages. I did a show opened by Barbara Mandrell and Anne Murray, marking the only time they ever sang together. I assembled another package with Mickey Gilley and his cousin, rock 'n' roll legend Jerry Lee Lewis.

Booking the talent from the roster of inaccessible country stars was no small feat. Once I chased Charley Pride via telephone all over Texas. I finally caught him in his Dallas barber's chair.

"Why are you calling me here?" he wanted to know.

"I want you to do my show," I shouted into the receiver, and he did.

Mickey Gilley wanted to be on the show and asked if he could bring a would-be star named Johnny Lee, then the rhythm guitarist in Gilley's band. I frequently had to book a lesser act to get a greater one. I put Johnny Lee on as a favor to Mickey. I wasn't particularly impressed with Johnny Lee at the time. Little did I know that the following year his "Looking for Love" from the motion picture *Urban Cowboy* would be the biggest country song of the year.

Kenny Rogers had a new record called "Lucille," the song credited with giving him a second career, after his celebrated years with the band First Edition had petered out. I returned his call on the set of the *Dick Clark Show* in Philadelphia. He had made a small fortune with First Edition but was broke.

"Could you bring my money [performance fee] to the show?" he asked.

"Lucille" became the biggest country song of the year, crossed over onto popular music surveys, and Kenny followed it shortly afterward with "The Gambler." By the end of 1978, he was touring with Dottie West and the Oak Ridge Boys. The package was the highest grossing in all of country music that year. That was just one of hundreds of rags to riches stories I've seen firsthand.

Pop Goes the Country continued to garner more markets and increased viewership, becoming the most popular syndicated television show in country music, except for *Hee Haw*. My life was stretched to the limit once again, with my morning television show, a morning radio show, and my syndicated radio show. The most taxing part of my schedule was booking the talent for *Pop*, a task I hadn't wanted in the first place.

Sometimes, entertainers who had been longtime friends would ask me to be on that show. I'd suggest it to the producers, and they would tell me to tell the artist no. That put me in a difficult spot.

That was the case with Hank Williams, Jr., who in 1979 was a big act with a lot of hit records under his belt. He wasn't the megastar he would become, but he was popular among country fans. I had known Hank since he was fourteen, and I grew tired of making excuses to him and his manager, the late Shorty Lavendar, about why Hank couldn't do the show. Lavendar was also railing for me to use Tammy Wynette, one of the greatest female song stylists of all time, and another personal friend. Again, I had to make embarrassing excuses because the producers didn't want her.

They thought her best days were behind her, and that she was too old. Today, I find the attitudes particularly amusing, since Hank is about the biggest box office draw in the business, and Tammy's career is still going strong on radio and television.

The only talent the narrow-minded producers could think of was Waylon Jennings and Willie Nelson. They were the hottest country acts of the day, in the wake of the "Outlaw" album with Jessi Colter and Tompall Glaser. I actually put together one show, with all four names, and the producers were relentless in hounding me to get them back.

I was paid five hundred dollars for each show, although I figure I had put ten hours into each half-hour production.

After doing the show for six years, I reached the point where I was tired of wrestling with the problem of booking the talent. I decided to ask that I be relieved of my responsibilities as host and talent coordinator. The Hank Williams, Jr./Tammy Wynette ordeal was the reason.

I went to lunch with the owner and the chief executive officer of Showbiz. We dined at Nashville's exclusive Belle Meade Country Club. I used the opulent setting to resign.

They asked me to suggest a successor, and I selected Tom T. Hall. They asked if he would do it and I said I'd have to ask him. He said he was happy to do it, but that he wouldn't book the acts. He didn't want to duplicate my despondency.

When I left the program, the producers didn't immediately have an easy time getting talent. I think the producers saw how many of the acts had done the show simply because they had a personal relationship with me.

The producers therefore tried to recruit talent through doors that had already been opened by me. One of the first casts they assembled for the new season after my departure starred Hank Williams, Jr., and Tammy Wynette.

That really made me angry.

Showbiz later sold to Multi-Media. Multi-Media officials announced that they didn't want to be in radio syndication. I once again took over the distribution of my radio show, and do it to this day.

Goody's Headache Powder sponsors the program, and also retains me as a company spokesman.

By 1979, when *Pop Goes the Country* was a continuing hit without me, I was fed up with syndicated television. I'm basically a sensitive person, and I had been made to feel like a second-class citizen through the irony of being wanted by producers to recruit talent, then not being allowed to recruit the talent I wanted.

In retrospect, I feel the only reason I was host of that show was my contacts in the world of country music.

In 1981, Elmer Alley, a producer with whom I had worked since my first live local television show, told me that WTBS, Ted Turner's station in Atlanta, was going to air a weekly, hour-long live show.

"Live television is your specialty," he said. "I'm going to produce the show, and I want you to host it," he said.

We did the program for two years from the Stage Door Lounge at Opryland Hotel. My only role was to act as host to the program, whose format consisted mostly of celebrity interviews. I was paid $2,200 per show.

I did twenty-six first runs, and there were twenty-six reruns per season. The last show in the season was produced exactly one month before the Nashville Network hit the air. I assumed the TNN birth caused the termination of the Turner Broadcasting–Opryland association. I accepted the job as host on the first night the network went on the air.

On March 7, 1983, *Nashville Now* premiered with me in the commander's chair on the Nashville Network. We started with 6.5 million subscribers and have about 55 million today. I was fifty years old and had a distinguished career behind me. It was nothing compared to the exposure and success I've derived through the most powerful venue ever to program country music—TNN.

...20...

FIVE YEARS AFTER MY MARRIAGE TO JOY SHE PROVED TO me how little I knew about her. I don't think about George Bush's wife, but if I did, I would think that she approves of her husband being president. I don't think about Larry Bird's companion, but assume she wants him to play basketball.

I had never thought that my wife might not want me to be an all-night disc jockey. She said something one day that started me to thinking a great deal.

"I've never been completely easy with you gone at night," she said.

"Really," I responded, "you've never mentioned that before."

"I realize that's how you make your living," she said, "and I couldn't interfere."

"But if you have been scared at home, you should have mentioned it. Life is too short. I don't want you home and alone and scared every night."

"I know," she replied, "but that's how I feel. I wish you were here at night."

I had been inattentive, and hadn't known that the dearest person in my world was unselfishly suffering because of what I did. Joy had been considerate toward me, and had been victimized because of it. She had been living uneasily for months.

That realization was all it took. The conversation of a moment was about to eradicate a radio career of fourteen years. (Remember, I had taken off fifteen months from the all-night show during a recess that ended on January 1, 1966.)

Joy and I, of course, had more conversations about my walking away a second time from country music broadcasting's dean's chair. We hashed out my alternatives, weighed the value of my other incomes, and more. Joy never directly asked me to quit that job. And although I was terribly burned out, I might have remained behind that microphone indefinitely. I don't always make changes easily.

Yet Joy's intimation about what would make her happy was all that I needed to make a life-changing decision. Sometimes, with Joy and me, a mere mention will prompt more change than begging will from someone else.

The instant Joy indicated that she wanted me at home at night, I knew where I'd be at sundown.

I'd like to tell you that mine was a weepy and sentimental departure that marked the closing of a page in my personal history. Actually, it closed the entire book on overnight radio and it's never reopened. If I had wept, it would have been tears of joy. There is a time for everything, and for me, it was past time to go. Man, I was weary of that shift.

Leaving was like getting a ball and chain off my neck. After about one-and-one-half decades of seeing the world through ebony, I can tell you what I told the *Tennessean* newspaper at the time.

"Man was not meant to sit up all night."

On July 28, 1972, I sat up for the last time.

I stayed at WSM and did various daytime shows. None of them attracted a fraction of the attention of the all-night show. During daylight, the WSM signal was significantly decreased. Besides, my forte had been intimacy. I had been the night person's confidant. Daytime radio won't allow a disc jockey to be as personal with his listeners. The element of intimacy is absent.

I remember when Walter Cronkite left the *CBS Evening News*. There were weeks' worth of press preceding his departure. Every time mere insiders simply surmised that Johnny Carson might be leaving the *Tonight Show*, there were mountains of publicity. My role as a broadcaster was far less significant. Yet I had a following as loyal as that of anybody who ever graced a microphone, and in parts of the country, it was just as expansive. By the time I rose from the all-night chair the final time, I had been "disc jockey of the year" six times.

My final night and the days preceding it, however, were relatively unceremonious in the eyes of WSM managers.

The people in front offices never truly know what's happening on the front lines. I was being paid by persons who were asleep when I signed on the air. If they had thought, they of course would have realized I was on all night. But they never thought.

There was no pomp and circumstance from the bigwigs.

The nation's little people, who had made me, were true to form and reached out through the telephone and mail as they had since my first night.

The world is filled with lonely people to whom my voice in the dark had been comfort to the soul. Thousands had told me about lying in darkened rooms where I was the only sound. They had talked of a kinship with others who they knew were doing the same.

"It's not as hard being alone when you know there are others alone too," I had heard time and time again.

One guy called to tell me he was leaving town after having been a regular listener for years. I wished him the best, and mentioned his departure over the air. Then the next night, he called with the same story.

"I thought you were going to leave today," I said.

"Oh, no," he said, "it's tomorrow." I publicly wished him farewell a second time.

He called with the same story for several nights in a row before I realized he wasn't moving anywhere. He was just lonely, and wanted to hear someone say that they would miss him when he was gone.

I used to be called regularly by the prostitutes at a whorehouse on Woodland Street until the police busted the place and shut it down. The girls told me their names, and would take turns chatting with me. They were among the callers I didn't put on the radio.

Sometimes, I'd ask one girl about another. If she was with a customer at the time, the first girl would always say, "She's busy now."

One night I played the Woody Herman theme, "Wood Choppers' Ball," by Pee-Wee King's western swing band.

"I really liked that version of the song," said a long-distance caller. "I'm in a hotel and was scanning the radio dial."

He mentioned that he and Pee-Wee were from the same hometown. "Who are you, please?" I asked.

"This is Woody Herman," he said nonchalantly, "calling from Indianapolis." Something about the way he talked convinced me he was.

People called regularly to talk about marital woes, teenage pregnancies, drinking problems, job promotions, the foal of a mare, and more, including family deaths, all the things that you tell a friend—even if you've never met him.

There was an outpouring from those folks. I'll never miss that shift. I'll forever miss its followers.

I gave personal remedies for toothaches, looked up ZIP codes, and directed travelers to Nashville when they were lost along interstate highways.

One woman from Atlanta called in total distress.

"Your signal is fuzzy tonight," she said. "I can't hear you clearly."

I could tell she was genuinely upset, and among those listeners who set their watch by that show. I didn't know how to help her, since she was pointing out a technical problem over which I had no control.

Then I realized she didn't know that. I gave her a mental placebo.

"You can't hear, huh?" I said. "Well hold on just a minute and let me try to fix it. I just need to turn one dial. . . . There, is that better?"

"Much better," she gleamed, not knowing that I hadn't done a thing.

The fans especially expressed their unhappiness about my going after the Associated Press circulated a story nationally with a headline that read, "Ralph Emery Gives Up the Most Desired Job in Radio."

On my last Friday night, I moved the show from the WSM studios to the stage of the Grand Ole Opry. The Opry was signed off at midnight and most of the crowd adjourned. I sat center stage behind a portable table and played records on two turntables. In physical proportion, I must have looked like a gnat in the living room of God. The awesomeness of the old Grand Ole Opry House swallowed me. Feeling that tiny was incompatible with the mood I wanted for the final night. I had been touting the final show during the all-night stint for about two weeks.

I began to ask the radio audience to come by if they thought they could be in Nashville by 4:00 A.M., my sign-off time. I was asking America to drop by. And part of it did.

I had hired a band, and celebrities from around town popped in to sing. I put them on the radio. The Ryman Auditorium's front doors were propped open, and fans and well-wishers strolled in and out until my final farewell.

One of the most popular country entertainers of the day was Tom T. Hall, who had a monster hit record entitled "Clayton Delaney." He had promised he would visit me on the last night.

He was coming back from a show in Georgia where his flight was delayed. Under an agreement with the musician's union, live music had to be stopped at 2:30 A.M. By the time Hall arrived, the band had gone. So he joined me at the footlights with only his guitar for musical accompaniment and sang for guests and me. He soon was joined by Connie Smith, Jackie Ward, Jeannie Pruett, and others.

They did "I Saw the Light" and other Gospel songs. Hall had recorded a hit entitled "Me and Jesus," but the tune wasn't performed because Connie Smith, who is very religious, doesn't like the song.

That's a condensation of my last night on WSM. My greatest regret about that show is that it didn't include Marty Robbins, who was just years away from suffering a fatal heart attack. Marty had visited me more than any other entertainer on the all-night show. He had sung more "live" songs, answered more telephone calls, and responded to more requests. He was absent in body, but present in my mind, during my overnight swan song.

For fourteen years, I used to go to the water faucet during news breaks and douse my face to stay awake. I drank an ocean of coffee. I developed my skills as an interviewer and formed stronger bondings with entertainers than any other nonmusical personality in country music.

I was there when Fidel Castro's regime began to intensify in Cuba and yielded my microphone to the United States Information Agency, which sent a Spanish-speaking propagandist to WSM. Our signal went as far south as Cuba, and my show was used as an anticommunist vehicle aimed at Cubans inclined toward democracy.

People have asked what I played for my final recorded song. I've truthfully said I don't remember. The idea of my doing the all-night show once annually as a WSM promotional has been broached. I've adamantly refused.

Tom Carter suggested it as a promotional gesture for my book.

"Forget it," I snapped. "I've seen that movie, and have no interest in the rerun."

At 10:15 P.M. the following Monday, Hairl Hensley took over *Opry Star Spotlight* and I was asked to introduce him to listeners. Hensley is a WSM human institution to this day, and had a daytime following back then. He only lasted a few months on the all-night show. I signed on the first Hensley show on July 31, 1972, thanked the fans for their kind expressions to me, and turned over the microphone to Hairl. I don't recall how long Hairl played records all night, but he finally succumbed to his wife's wishes to have him at home at night, and he too left the shift. To this day he remains an important fixture on WSM and the Grand Ole Opry.

On his all-night premiere, he wished me the best, we exchanged other pleasantries, and then he put on a record. I was out the door and in my car before the song quit playing.

...21...

AT 5:00 P.M. MONDAY THROUGH FRIDAY, NINE MUSI-
cians, four background singers, a production crew, two
guest bands, and three or four guest celebrities assemble
behind the curtain of a thousand-seat theater adjacent to
the Grand Ole Opry House in Nashville. For two hours,
Jerry Whitehurst and the *Nashville Now* band, the most
award-winning band in the history of televised country
music, rehearses what will be broadcast live in three hours.
(The program is videotaped and rerun from 11:00 P.M. until
12:30 A.M., Nashville time.)

Nashville Now is the most successful program on the
most successful television network programming country
music. Much of the credit goes to producer Bill Turner.
The show is the only live, prime-time talk/variety show on
television. The show is owned by Opryland Productions, a
division of Gaylord Broadcasting. Paul Corbin, TNN program manager, has told me about plans to permanently
move the show into the Roy Acuff Theater, a sixteen-hun-
dred-seat arena, in 1992. Admission to the show is five
dollars. Throughout the year, people travel thousands of
miles to sit for ninety minutes within a few yards of their
favorite country stars.

The colossal network was just a rumor when I first heard

of it in the halls of WSM-TV. No one had any idea that the Nashville music scene would ultimately be televised on such a grandiose scale. I thought it would just be a glorified version of my local show. I even talked about putting Maude and Dorothy on as regulars and wondered how they would go over in the rest of the nation.

I went to New York City a couple of times before the network's launch night. I was expecting to do interviews with entertainment writers from *The New York Times* about TNN. Mass media from around the nation ate at the Lone Star Café and Tavern on the Green as guests of the Nashville Network. The writers ate free food and guzzled free whiskey.

Country music was going onto its own television network, but it wasn't going onto the hallowed entertainment pages of *The New York Times,* whose entertainment reporters were uninterested.

The TNN marketing people, Group W Satellite Communications, are very smart. They went back to *The New York Times* and asked to speak to a business writer.

"You don't understand country music, but you do understand dollars, don't you?," I'm told they said.

The Nashville Network was first reported on the financial, not the entertainment, pages of the world's largest daily newspaper.

The TNN ownership was brilliant in its financial prognostications. It said the network would lose money for four years before entering into substantial profits. That's exactly what happened. I'm thankful to the men who had the vision, and the courage to stick to it, during those lean years.

The Nashville Network was to have premiered in October 1982, but due to technical problems, did not go on the air until March 7, 1983. History will record that date as a country music milestone comparable to the initial airing of the Grand Ole Opry on December 26, 1925.

Two words explain why I was asked to be the host of *Nashville Now:* Elmer Alley. He is the producer who has drafted me to just about every live television show I've ever done. I'll be forever grateful.

He took me to meet David Hall, TNN general manager, to discuss my becoming host. I've been asked if I was represented by an agent, and if bargaining sessions were lengthy. The answer to both questions is no. Hall and I discussed my potential duties and prospective salary for thirty minutes. It took me two seconds to decline the offer.

I thought the offer was embarrassingly low.

We eventually resumed negotiations, settled on a salary, and you know the rest. The network has been very generous with me, and my salary has increased in the wake of TNN's burgeoning popularity.

WSM and the all-night show were the launch pad for everything significant I subsequently did. *Nashville Now* has been my orbit.

In January 1983 I met with Alley and coproducer Joe Hostettler many times in Michael's Restaurant on Nashville's Murfreesboro Road for preproduction meetings. We had seven and a half hours of live programming to fill each week during our format. The show was rerun three times every twenty-four hours during the early days of TNN. In planning the program, we wanted to be different, but not threatening. Country music fans aren't famous for tolerating controversy.

We decided we would let fans call in to ask questions of the celebrities. The idea had done well for me on live radio, so why not on live television? It was a novel idea in 1983 that has since become hackneyed. The practice was comparatively short-lived because many fans would call merely to chat with entertainers and tell them how much they admired them.

"I just think you're wonderful," the caller might say.

"Thank you very much," the bored and embarrassed celebrity would reply.

"I have all of your records," the fan might continue.

"Thanks again," the star would reply.

Then there might be a few seconds of dead time, and finally I would pipe up to Joe Fan from Des Moines.

"Joe, this is Ralph Emery, do you have a question for so-and-so?"

"Oh yeah," he'd say, "when are you coming to Des Moines?"

What we had planned as the unique characteristic of our program often became thoughtless and interchangeable banter. Many fans were racing to dial their telephones when the lines were open, and not thinking about what they would say when connected. Many were innocent victims of old-fashioned stage fright.

We also had trouble with songwriters who would call an entertainer to ask how to get a song to him. That would be embarrassing to the entertainers, many of whom don't accept unsolicited material.

Occasionally, a heavily breathing woman would call and purr romantic insinuations over live television. That became discomforting when she referred to behavior she had performed with the male celebrity she was calling. If a woman started talking, for example, about the good time she had the other night in San Antonio with so-and-so, it created problems for him with his wife.

Yet the telephone call-ins were an extremely popular part of the program.

The long-distance calls don't ring, but are signaled by flashing red lights inside the control room. When the show isn't on the air, the phones aren't answered, although they ring almost incessantly.

A new engineer one day picked up one of the flashing telephones.

"Hello," said the caller, "this is so-and-so calling from West Virginia. May I speak to Ralph Emery?"

"I'm sorry," he replied, "but the show won't be on for three and a half more hours."

"Okay," she said, "may I hold?"

The telephone part of the program, for the above reasons and others, was discontinued on a regular basis a few years ago. It was revived in January 1991, after being purchased as a feature attraction by American Telephone and Telegraph Company.

Then there are the blue cards. Audience members write questions on the cards and turn them over to me through a courier, and I select the most interesting. I then approach the studio authors, ask them to stand and discuss the cards on the air. One of the regular requests we make of persons who fill out the blue cards is to tell us something interesting about the person who accompanied them to the show.

Sometimes, fans will write total falsehoods on their cards just to be selected for chat on the air. They admit to it on television.

"I just made it up so you'd call on me," they'll say.

I avoid audience members who have been drinking and sometimes seek out overly aggressive and overweight women who want to bear hug a celebrity. That's very risky on live television.

People have hissed, poked, and done any number of things so that they would be chosen to stand and be queried about their blue cards.

Nashville Now is one of the few charter programs on TNN. On launch night, we did five hours' worth of live television. That's longer than some telethons.

We started at 8:00 P.M. and did five remote broadcasts as well as the studio portion from two Nashville locations— the Grand Ole Opry House and the Stage Door Lounge of the Opryland Hotel.

We broadcast from New York, Los Angeles, Austin, Denver, and Chicago.

Con Hunley, Don Williams, Emmylou Harris, T. G. Sheppard, Hoyt Axton, Roy Acuff, Patti Page, the Nashville Symphony, and others were hosts at the remote locations. They interviewed other artists and fans. Fans have always had a big role in TNN.

The list of *Nashville Now* guests reads like a "Who's Who of Show Business." I don't book the talent on the show, so I can't be accused of bragging when I say there has never been a country music show, in radio or television or otherwise staged, that can boast of having had such luminaries.

George Bush appeared on the program when he was vice president. Bush is a friend of sausage magnate Jimmy Dean. Dean asked me if he could bring Bush on the program during his presidential campaign, although Bush had not officially announced his candidacy.

"I want him to be on the program because I think people think he's stuffy and I want to show that he isn't," Dean told me.

Bush's portion of the show was videotaped, the only segment in the history of *Nashville Now* that ever was. The studio was crawling with Secret Servicemen who would allow no one on the premises except a skeleton production crew.

Bush seemed to enjoy his appearance and asked for a copy of the videotape.

"That's the way I want to look on television. Make me look like that," he told an aide.

Following his appearance Bush was photographed with David Hall, vice president and general manager of TNN and Opryland U.S.A., and Tom Griscom, senior vice president, broadcasting, Opryland U.S.A.

"I want to have my photograph made with them," Bush said, pointing to the production crew, dressed in their working clothes. The photograph still hangs backstage at *Nashville Now*.

Former presidential candidate Gary Hart appeared on *Nashville Now* and he didn't go over very well. His delivery was stilted, and he came off as an elitist who lacked the common touch to communicate with people. He was devoid of the back-slapping, glad-handing skills that usually work for a politician addressing a largely southern crowd.

I gave him a gift, a pair of Tenny Lamas, made by the Tony Lama boot company. They are cowboy boots whose soles are designed like athletic shoes. Politicians spend so much time on their feet, I thought the unique footwear would prove useful.

He didn't respond to the gift, and when he left the building, he didn't take the gift with him.

Other celebrities who have graced the *Nashville Now* roster include Dr. Joyce Brothers, Mickey Rooney, Lily Tomlin, Kenny Rogers, Dolly Parton, Ronnie Milsap, the Pointer Sisters, Merle Haggard, Clint Black, Barbara Mandrell, Reba McEntire, Wayne Newton, Della Reese, Carol Lawrence, Shirley Jones, Jay Leno, Patricia Neal, Anson Williams, Jimmy Stewart, Dennis Weaver, Tommy Lasorda, Orel Hershiser, Vin Scully, Vic Damone, James Garner, Steve Allen, Jayne Meadows, Tiffany, Robert Duvall, Barbara Eden, George Strait, Willie Nelson, Robert Goulet, Loretta Lynn, George Jones, Randy Travis, Cybill Shepherd, Tommy Lee Jones, Wilford Brimley, and Jamie Farr from *M*A*S*H*.

Any country artist who has ever achieved a modicum of success has appeared on the program. There has never been a country show to attract so many stars from other art forms. Country stars, however, are still the backbone of the show. They are much preferred by both live and television audiences.

The show has always devoted generous time to up-and-coming entertainers, as well as to those whose celebrated years are past.

In April 1987 we took the show to Las Vegas for a five-day run. Many Vegas acts wanted to be on, and the show became overbooked, so we had difficulty getting everyone on.

Norm Crosby, who I mistakenly thought was playing Vegas, had in fact flown out from New York just to do the show. He was the last act on the last night of the run, and there was room for him to do only three minutes.

During the commercial break, he expressed his frustration.

"Three minutes?" he said. "I flew all the way out here for three minutes?"

"Norm," I said, "look at it this way. The other night we had a singing pig on, which we brought all the way from Missouri by truck, and he only got four minutes."

On our second night of broadcasting (in 1983), we cut the program to ninety minutes, its current length, and shed our black ties and tuxedos.

I was incompatible with the early production crew whose members worked strictly by the book. I was much less formal in my approach, accustomed to the relaxed techniques of my morning crew. I was used to "feeling" my way through a show and had little concern for the clock. Experience had given me a sixth sense that told me when it was time to go to a commercial break, or when to end the show.

That first crew and I had some difficulty understanding each other. Tennessee Ernie Ford, a guest on the show's second broadcast, also had difficulty.

Ford had no sooner sat down on the interviewees' couch when the floor director held up a time card. It said "Three Minutes!" in big letters, underlined.

Ford looked at me and looked at the card and felt confused. If we had been videotaping, he might have asked that the tape be stopped while he sought direction.

Instead, he thought out loud.

"Three minutes?" he said. "I can't even say 'hello' in three minutes." I'm sure the television audience wondered why he brought it up.

My personal preparation for *Nashville Now* began a month before the premiere. I had a radical facelift. In 1957, because heredity had graced me with an overly large lower jaw, I had undergone bone surgery to correct this condition. My mouth was wired shut for six weeks and I lost thirty pounds. It was an unpleasant recovery.

During that time, my jaw muscles became soft. I feared they had stopped working altogether when I had the wires that had held my mouth shut removed.

The surgeon was a practical joker. He cut each of the binding wires, then intentionally left one intact.

"Open your mouth," he commanded.

"I c-a-n-n-n-t," I said, through clenched jaws. I briefly feared I was paralyzed before he snipped the final wire, and I was able to speak properly.

In February 1983 I had my eyelids lifted and excess skin on my cheeks and jowls pulled tightly behind my ears. Incisions were made behind the cartilage and the skin was stretched to eliminate wrinkles. (I have also undergone a hair transplant. All of this had to do with my complex about my appearance that began when I was a teenager.)

After the 1983 surgical go-round, my face swelled significantly. I felt like a basketball with eyes. I had intended to take several days off before being seen publicly. My plans were interrupted by a TNN official, who said he wanted me to go on the *CBS Morning News* to promote the TNN premiere.

I wore what must have been a pound of makeup when I did that program. If I had smiled, I would have cracked.

The test of my interviewing skills on *Nashville Now* is unprecedented. Doing ninety minutes a day, after doing ninety minutes of live local, is tough. I only have three writers for *Nashville Now*. Other talk shows have as many as fifteen.

There is nothing more difficult than having a guest on a talk show who is reluctant to talk, as is often the case with Vern Gosdin and Charlie Rich. Some personalities are quiet. I wonder sometimes why they agree to appear on the program. I try not to phrase questions in such a way as to allow a yes or no answer. With some guests, the task is futile.

The entire thrust of my interviewing approach has been to try to impart dignity to country music talk. There have been thousands of times when I've wondered if some listeners or viewers understood what I was trying to do. I fear that some will think I'm boring.

Two of my idols were Dave Garroway and Arthur Godfrey, neither of whom had dynamic personalities. They were not high-energy men. But they were effective communicators. That's what I strive to be.

I think there is an additional obstacle to the interviewing process in that my guests and I often have different ideas about why they're on the program. I think they're there to entertain. They often think they're there to promote. Many only appear when they have something new to sell, such as an album or upcoming concert tour.

I'm always glad to help anyone's career. But ultimately, I have to think of the fan. He won't tune in night after night to hear each of my guests tell me about their forthcoming new record. That's repetitive and boring.

Some entertainers have become annoyed with me because they come onto the program with a list of suggested questions prepared by their publicist. The questions aren't really questions at all. They're more like verbal springboards intended to allow the guest an opportunity for sales pitches. If some of the guests had their way, none of the viewers would ever know anything about them other than the fact that they had recorded a new album that would be out soon.

Broadcasting is the only form of live entertainment that is not geared primarily toward the live audience. You depend on ratings, not applause, to tell you how you're doing.

I therefore seek any and all input I can about what the fans do and don't like about *Nashville Now*.

Much of the information comes from the audience members themselves. Next to directness, the greatest characteristic of the *Nashville Now* audience just might be patriotism. They are grassroots America and Richard Nixon's "Silent Majority."

The most spontaneous and explosive standing ovation I've ever seen came for a group of elderly gentlemen who were on the Bataan Death March in the Philippines during World War II. I had a chance to talk to a few of them on the air. The crowd leaped to its feet and had to be quieted so we could proceed with the show.

In January 1991 a member of the studio audience wore his World War II Army uniform for the first time in fifty years. He said he merely wanted to be seen on television showing support for soldiers engaged on behalf of the United States in the Persian Gulf.

The most encouraging input I've ever received in my entire career came in 1986. *Cable Guide* magazine is the Bible of the cable television industry. It is to cable what *TV Guide* is to major network television.

It ran a popularity survey of its subscribers. More than sixty thousand viewers took the time, and spent twenty-five cents, to select Steven Spielberg as their favorite film director, Jack Nicholson as their favorite actor, Sally Field as their favorite actress, and me as their favorite cable personality. I was in very distinguished company and garnered my award ahead of Max Headroom, the Bart Simpson of the day.

In that same poll, I was voted Best Host of a Talk/Entertainment or Information Series. Readers named me number one ahead of Dick Cavett and Larry King.

I have the utmost admiration for both men. I was elated and humbled at my winning, especially since the voting was done by the fans themselves.

Soon afterward, the Nashville press screamed with the story, and it was carried via the newswire services all over the nation.

I felt more secure in my inclinations as a broadcaster than I ever had. I had experienced the empathic response for which I had yearned for years. The greatest thrill I ever received from an award was my first winning of disc jockey of the year, and the second-greatest was the pronouncement by *Cable Guide*.

... 22 ...

THE STATUS OF *NASHVILLE NOW* WAS APPARENT SOON after its debut. By 1990, when TNN went onto the Manhattan Cable System, the network had become a part of every regional cable system in the United States.

If, in 1983, we had had a crystal ball, my level of stress concerning our multi-million-dollar experiment would have been considerably lower.

I racked my brain about ways to increase the viewership. I didn't dwell on promotions, contests, or other conventional means to the ratings end. I relinquished that to the promotions department. I was more concerned with my show specifically. I thought that since the network had entrusted its prime time to me, I had to come up with someone or something that was unlike anything else on TNN.

I've heard a lot of entertainers who have played a lot of nightclubs say, "If you want to get the male customers, attract the women."

I hit on a similar rule regarding variety television.

"If I want to get the adult viewers," I surmised, "I must get the children."

I recalled how my own boys would fuss when they were small if I endeavored to change the television channel from a program they liked. They made such a stink that I gave in to their viewing preferences for *Mister Rogers, Sesame Street,* and similar shows.

I believe that history repeats itself. I thought of historic, televised adult fare that captured the fondness of youngsters. Ed Sullivan always had clowns or ventriloquists. Jimmy Dean, decades before he manufactured sausage, had a puppet named Rowlf, which he mispronounced as Ralph. That doll was a creation of the late Jim Henson. My mind raced to the 1950s package shows on which Edgar Bergen and Charlie McCarthy and Shari Lewis and "Lamb Chop" were regular guests.

There hadn't been an established personality puppet on the scene in years and the idea seemed highly experimental. But *Nashville Now* itself was experimental. Why not keep with the trend, I thought. I began to think puppet.

My mind raced to one of my local shows about 1982 and a puppeteer named Steve Hall, who was also a singer. Hall was in town to compete in a talent contest and came by unannounced. He sat in the audience during the program and held a cowboy doll, which he waved conspicuously. After the program, he introduced me to "Shotgun Red."

I thought then that Red would be a charming addition to somebody's show, but never considered him for mine. Hall, who lived in Brainerd, Minnesota, returned at the end of the talent contest. I never expected to see him again, and never thought about him until I decided we needed a puppet on *Nashville Now.*

I told Elmer Alley that I knew a cowboy puppet up north who would be perfect for our show. The doll wore a hat and western clothes and looked nothing like a stereotypical puppet.

As I relayed my convictions about the wealth in children's viewership, Elmer listened intently.

"All right," he said, "if you feel that strongly about it, get the guy down here. We'll let him do an audition tape."

The network staff began to search for Steve Hall, who was found living in a trailer and earning very little money with his band, "The South Bound Seventy Sixers," working in Minnesota nightclubs. That would be changed in a matter of days. A puppet was discovered and a star was born. Today, Hall earns much of his living doing personal appearances because of the celebrity he gained on *Nashville Now*.

Shotgun Red is as much a part of *Nashville Now* as three-chord music. He gets more fan mail than any guest we've ever had, and was host to his own video music program on the network. He has done personal appearances. There was a forty-foot-tall likeness of Shotgun Red, inflated with helium and held by straps, that was erected by Johnny Hobbs, a restaurateur, near the entrance to Opryland U.S.A. In June 1990, during "Fan Fair," an annual mixer of fans and celebrities in Nashville, someone stole the mammoth doll. A five-thousand-dollar reward was offered, to no avail, for his return.

Hall was blown away when he came to *Nashville Now*. He'd never met any stars and never expected to. He'd only sung other people's songs. Suddenly, he was thrust into the middle of Nashville show business.

I remember Hall looked at the musicians in the *Nashville Now* band and said, "God, these guys are lucky, to get to play around these stars every night."

I assured him that celebrities were a way of life, and that each edition of *Nashville Now* was just another show to those of us who appeared regularly.

Shotgun Red stands tall in the entertainment world, but was found inside a Minnesota pawnshop. Hall saw him in the display window and bought him for forty dollars. To this day, no one knows who created him.

Hall and I have often talked about how prosperous the inventor would be if he had copyrighted the puppet. We've wondered if he is alive and if he has seen the show to witness how far his creation has gone.

Hall lies at my feet on a wooden wedge, covered by foam rubber, that is slanted at about thirty degrees. Concealed by my desk, he has a television monitor on which he watches the show, and a microphone into which he speaks Red's growled intonations. I have immense respect for the talent of a puppeteer who can recline, extend his forearm, watch a television screen, and be witty simultaneously. Hall is a mischievous sort who enjoys pulling the hair on my legs. Hall is also ticklish. I keep a drumstick on my desk and poke him with it in self-defense. Sometimes, the studio audience catches on to our antics.

Hall and Shotgun Red have never been visible on the screen together. Zealous fans have tried, at the end of programs, to walk behind my desk and photograph the person with the extended arm that is the backbone of Shotgun Red.

Neither Hall nor I will allow it.

A lady caller with a question for the stars once asked during our live broadcast for the name of the person who is the voice of Shotgun Red.

"Honey, let me tell you," I said. "Shotgun Red is as real to me as any of these guests sitting on this couch. As far as I'm concerned, Shotgun Red speaks for Shotgun Red."

The studio audience broke into tumultuous applause.

Porter Wagoner was a guest that night. During a commercial break, I asked him if he would like to sing a song with Shotgun Red. When the program resumed, Wagoner moved into my chair where he and Shotgun Red did "Y'all Come."

The tune prompted a barrage of clapping and warm smiles.

On the next break, Wagoner whispered to me.

"Boy," he said, "you sit right next to him, and work with him, and he becomes real."

Barbara Mandrell brought her four-year-old son, Nathan, on *Nashville Now*. The lad began to talk to Shotgun Red, totally ignoring his mother and me. He later gave me a nickel to give to Red so that Red could buy a pair of skis, and asked me to ask him to come to his house to go swimming.

Children believe in Shotgun Red.

Shotgun Red has been the closest thing to a cohost I've ever had in my entire television career. Many nights, I allow him to introduce and interview guests. I have enjoyed many three-way conversations with Shotgun Red and a celebrity.

Then there were the record albums. Shotgun Red and I have recorded two of them for RCA Records. One was a Christmas album, the other a children's record. The discs were sold at record counters throughout the English-speaking world, as well as through an "800" number on the Nashville Network. The records outsold many that have been recorded by big stars, although neither Red nor I fancy ourselves as singers.

A few years ago, Steve Hall was married and Johnny Hobbs chartered an airplane for a group of us to fly to his wedding in Minnesota. I took Shotgun Red to the ceremony.

I sat near the front of the church sanctuary with Red on my arm. Red wore a tuxedo. When the minister prayed, I saw to it that Red bowed his head. When the bride entered and the congregation stood, Red stood with me, again on the end of my arm.

Red's presence was almost disruptive. Guests kept coming to the front of the church to photograph him. Much of the film intended to photograph the bride and groom was spent on Red and me.

As the bride, Miss Daisy, walked down the aisle, I turned Red's body in relation to her presence. He moved at exactly the same angles as the human guests. The bride noticed Red in the audience, stepped over to his pew, and kissed him. The entire gathering began to giggle and coo.

Country music has long been known for its realistic portrayal of life. Shotgun Red is the unrealistic and comic relief from that. Of all the luminaries about whom I've been questioned, none has drawn more queries than Red. It would suit me if he remained my sidekick for the rest of my career.

There are four people who were a part of my life before I'd ever heard Red's name. They've become his friends too. I want to tell you about them at length.

...23...

A COUNTRY MUSIC INTERVIEWER GETTING AN EXCLUSIVE
with Johnny Cash is the equivalent of a boxing writer getting a one-on-one with Mike Tyson. I had my last exclusive
with Cash in 1989.

I asked him when and where, underwent two of his post-
ponements, and still arrived before he did. Much of our
interview was broadcast; much was not, due to time limita-
tions. A barrage of mail was prompted by Cash's candidness about religion, the Reverend Billy Graham, prisons,
poverty, his infamous drug addiction, and more. I was not
intimidated by our session, as I had been the first time I
interviewed Cash on the radio, the night he threw his boot
at me in the WSM studios, and any other time our conversation has been public.

I could have interviewed the late Elvis Presley, or members of the Beatles, and not been as uneasy. My discomfort
has to do with Cash's larger-than-life presence—physically
and artistically. He is the most influential living singer in
the history of country music. Merle Haggard is a keeper of
the flame. Cash built the fire.

In 1969, Cash reportedly sold more songs for Columbia
Records than any other artist in the label's history. Some
of his compositions, such as "Folsom Prison Blues" and

"I Walk the Line," rank with "Tennessee Waltz" or "Gentle on My Mind" as the most recognizable country melodies of all time.

He receives Bob Dylan, Kris Kristofferson, Robert Duvall, the Reverend Graham, and equally distinguished guests at his sprawling estate on Old Hickory Lake near Nashville.

He hasn't had a hit record in years but is still a bigger concert draw than many young singers whose recording careers are hot.

He is pursued by music lovers and curiosity seekers. He is Americana on two legs. Like Babe Ruth's bat or Bob Hope's jokes, Cash's songs belong in the people's archives.

Fans, however, don't always think immediately of music when they think of Cash. They instead sometimes think about the most violent, publicized drug habit ever to hold a guitar. Cash never went to his closet. He talked freely about his problem while tirelessly trying to overcome it. He went for years without amphetamines after claiming to have ingested fifty, and fifty barbiturates, daily. He was hospitalized for an unrelated affliction in 1983, was administered morphine, and fell back into addiction.

Cash, in 1983, checked himself into the Betty Ford Center, an addiction recovery facility in Palm Springs, California. He stayed for forty-three days.

"Those were six of the greatest weeks of my life," Cash told me. "It was like inner therapy, self-unfoldment."

He said he grew to like himself through weekly assignments. He remembered walking to the front desk where he was queried about that day's assignment.

"The girl said to me, 'What's your assignment?' " Cash recalled.

"Trying to diminish my inflated ego," he dutifully answered.

"What can I do for you?" the girl asked.

"Nothing," Cash said, "I just came by to brighten your day."

Cash was discharged from Betty Ford while sober, nonusing and unrecovered.

"I didn't ever kick the drug habit and I don't think I ever will," he said. "There will always be that gnawing."

Seconds earlier, Cash had indicated that he did not want to talk about his chemical problem, and then he proceeded to do so anyhow. He had digested that in his book, *Man in Black*, published in 1975. The drug discussion was painful for him then but was undertaken in part, he wrote, because "if only one person can be saved from the death of drugs; if only one person turns to God through the story which I tell . . ."

Perhaps it was similar thinking that motivated his discussion of the tired subject with me again. It's my job to know what the fans want to know about. So I pressed him.

"There is a gnawing, a craving that comes by every day and then passes, thank God," Cash replied. "Sometimes it lasts a few seconds, sometimes an hour. I make a daily commitment to God and ask Him to take away the problem. I never did acid or cocaine. I did amphetamines, mixing them with beer and brandy."

I realized why Cash's career had remained on top. Even when discussing something he didn't want to, he discussed it openly. His spoken words were as honest as his sung.

Listeners believe him because his frankness forces trust. If Abraham Lincoln were reincarnated as a country singer, he would be called Johnny Cash.

"I don't like drugs," he continued. "I hate them, I despise them, I hate everything they've ever done to me, yet I crave them. I don't know the answer except to make a daily commitment to God."

Cash is a deeply, fundamentally religious man who, I thought, must be tormented by guilt whenever he has a chemical accident. I thought about the ruthless unfairness of a giant of a man never totally escaping the control of a pill weighing a fraction of an ounce.

People who contend that drug addiction is a sickness and not a moral failure have a case in Cash. You can't listen to him and suspect that his infrequent drug use is recreational. There is no amusement for him in the torture he obviously feels.

"How do you work your way through that time each day when you want the drugs?" I asked.

"I pray, or call Waylon [Jennings], or somebody who is recovering too," he said. "I might not even talk about it. I might just talk about anything positive to get my mind off of it."

I recalled to myself the losing fight staged by George Jones for years against alcohol. My anger was tapped whenever I was backstage and saw so-called friends, who knew Jones was fighting alcoholism, offer him a drink. I mentioned the incidents to Cash, and asked if he had undergone similar ordeals.

"I used to have [to]," he said, before he made his recovery struggle public. "People used to come by and say, 'Hey, try this one.' But nobody has told me that in six years. I have cleaned up my playmates and playgrounds. I don't go to nightclubs 'cause I know there are things I'd be around that I don't want to do."

My questions had ceased, yet Cash's answers continued. He was on a roll of self-exposition. He was using my program as a personal podium to testify against consumption. Cash is not the first country star to go to the Betty Ford Center. He is among the few who stayed. Some left when they were asked to do their laundry and clean their room. I thought about Johnny Cash pushing a dust mop, and likened it to an elephant knitting a doily. My heart went out to someone who, after almost sixty years, still fights his demons daily.

Cash talked about the role model he had as a lad in his brother, Jack Cash, who was two years older. When Jack was fourteen, he died seven days after being sliced in a violent table-saw accident at school.

"When I dream about Jack today, I do so with him still two years older," Cash said. "He saw Heaven when he was dying and he asked my mother, 'Can you hear the angels?' Those were his last words."

I asked him if he thought he might have forgone some of

his mistakes had his brother's positive influence remained alive.

"I can't blame anybody for the trouble I got into," Cash said. "It all boils down to the fact that we have free wills."

I wondered how he could associate a "free will" with the sickness of addiction, but didn't ask.

I had just begun doing the all-night show when Nashville vibrated with rumors about Cash's outrageous behavior during performance tours.

He told me he was under the influence of pills and boredom when he bought five hundred baby chickens and turned them loose inside a hotel. Another time, he said, someone in his entourage painted a hotel room, including its furniture and appliances, totally black.

"The two hours you're on stage is what you live for when you're on the road," he said, "but the other twenty-two are boring."

Cash is country music's greatest diplomat. He can mix with blue-collar fans, then answer an unexpected call from the Reverend Graham, who Cash said wrote his last three books at Cash's Jamaican estate.

"Billy Graham never preaches to me," Cash told me. "He lives it [Christianity], and he gives me spiritual advice when I ask for it. He's never 'preachy' toward anybody."

Johnny Cash is the one entertainer in country music who has a considered opinion about almost everything. He's among the few whose opinions are sought after by fans as much as his music. People want to know how this country-folk music patriarch feels about topical subjects. Perhaps it's because he communicates with heads of state, or because of the timeliness of his songs addressing social reform.

During our conversation, the United States Supreme Court was being asked to draft a law banning the burning of the American flag. Cash, not surprisingly, thought there should be a law against it.

"Flag burning?" he said. "I think about the time June [Mrs. Cash] and I went to Vietnam in 1969 and saw the burning flesh. Whether the war was right or not, a lot of people sacrificed their lives. I cherish all the freedoms we have, including the freedom to burn flags. But I also have the freedom to bear arms and if you burn my flag, I'll shoot you.''

I thought of my trip with Cash to the Nixon White House in 1970 when the Vietnam War was raging, and anti-Nixon sentiments were strong.

''If you don't want to stand behind the president, get the hell over so I can,'' he said.

Earlier that day, Cash had denied a presidential request to perform ''Welfare Cadillac'' and ''Okie from Muskogee.'' The former song was about welfare abuse; the latter about a right-wing stance on marijuana smoking and flag waving. Pundits credited Cash with sticking to his beliefs. Cash told me he refused to do the songs because he hadn't made them hits, and he didn't know the words.

Many people who enjoy the rebel in entertainers have made Cash the most successful reformed prisoner in the history of show business. But there is a mistake. This man who has recorded two platinum albums inside federal prisons and who receives hundreds of letters annually from prisoners and their wives has never been incarcerated except for one night in the Starkville, Mississippi, jail. He was detained on a misdemeanor.

Cash's supposed federal imprisonment is one of the most successful, unintentional, and erroneous public relations campaigns in show business. I don't know its origin, and suspect Cash doesn't either. Perhaps it evolved as guilt by association. I guess Cash has sung so many prison songs that people assume he's been in the Big House. He never has. Some people are as destroyed by that news as they would be if they discovered that Walt Disney hated cartoons.

Cash has a history of reaching out to his fans. He has been repeatedly known to call ailing children or senior citizens, deeds for which he sought no publicity.

I asked him about Glen Sherley, who had been incarcerated for fourteen years and was sitting in the front row when Cash gave a prison concert in 1968. The night before, a preacher gave Cash a Sherley composition and Cash surprised him by recording it live the next day on his album. Cash successfully advocated Sherley's pardon, took him on a concert tour with him, and employed him at the House of Cash, Cash's museum in Tennessee.

"But he had spent over half of his life behind bars and he could never cope," Cash said. Sherley, Cash had said earlier, committed suicide.

I've always been intrigued at the high degree of visibility maintained by Johnny Cash. It isn't uncommon to see him strolling inside a Nashville supermarket or shopping center. He attends church alongside everyday people. His commonness is not without its price.

Cash is always receiving unsolicited songs from would-be songwriters who see him disarmed. Ironically, one of the former hopefuls was songwriting master Kris Kristofferson, while he worked as a janitor at Columbia Records where Cash recorded. Label officials told Kristofferson to leave Cash alone.

"So he would slip his songs to June," Cash recalled. Cash confessed that he thought Kristofferson was just another uncommercial songwriter and resented Kristofferson's trying to get to him through June. That's why, he said, he threw Kristofferson's tapes into Old Hickory Lake with other unwanted songs. He listened to none of the tunes.

Kristofferson was a helicopter pilot in the Tennessee Army National Guard.

"Then one day Kristofferson landed a helicopter on my lawn and I said, 'This guy is really determined, so I'm going to see what he's got,' " Cash recalled. Cash said the incident occurred when he had his own prime-time television show. June awakened him. The tourists had formerly tried to get onto their property by climbing the fence and coming in boats across the lake. "Now they're trying from helicopters," Cash thought.

He said he rose from a Sunday afternoon nap and saw Kristofferson emerge from the aircraft with a beer in one hand and a tape recorder in the other.

Cash said Kristofferson was disoriented.

He might have been. In recalling the same incident for my radio show, Kristofferson gave a conflicting account and said he did not see Cash during his infamous landing.

"I don't think he was home," Kristofferson said.

Cash subsequently recorded many Kristofferson songs, including one that Kristofferson brought him via helicopter, entitled "Sunday Morning Coming Down," one of Cash's biggest records.

Cash told me about another ordeal with a songwriter inside a church. He said it was the biggest invasion of privacy he had ever undergone.

He was attending a fundamentalist church whose pastor was the Reverend Jimmy Snow, son of Hank Snow. At the end of each service, it was customary to ask visitors if they wanted to come to the altar and pray. An established member would accompany the newcomer to the prayer rail.

On this particular day, the member who supported the visitor was Johnny Cash.

Cash was kneeling beside the visitor, who noticed, in his peripheral vision, that his prayer partner was Cash. As the two were praying, the man said, "John, John, I've got a song for you."

Cash, just to quiet the man, said he told him he would accept his tape outside the sanctuary. Then, Cash said, he lived up to his word and took the song. I don't recall ever hearing any more about that song.

Merle Haggard would not exaggerate.

It was like hearing Rembrandt say he didn't believe he could continue to paint, or Baryshnikov say he thought his dancing had become wooden. I didn't believe my ears and I didn't agree with Haggard's self-assessment.

The point was that *he* did. In the half fluorescence of the bus, I looked into the eyes of Merle Haggard and saw the face of fatigue. His countenance was etched with too many miles and memories that he feared he could no longer put into melodies. I had felt his greatness for nearly three decades. I was seeing it compacted into the exhaustion of the moment.

"I don't know, Ralph," he continued, "it's just not the same. I know I'm past my prime, and it gets harder and harder."

I gave him the kindest words from my most sincere vocabulary, but was frustrated at my inability to convey my adoration and reassurance. I told him that his art was so perfected, he could have another hit record any time he wanted. He reminded me that only a number-one song was a hit, as far as he was concerned. Number two has never counted with Merle. I knew he really felt that way. No one ever set demands for him higher than those he set for himself.

I felt remiss as his friend. I should have sensed his depletion. Two years earlier, he had all but told me of his mental weariness. But I had been too arrested by his candor. I did not absorb his content.

"I can still sing as good as I ever could," he had said, "but I can't sing as long. When you get older, you can't do anything as long as you once could."

The words began to echo in my mind. I had subconsciously likened him to the iron men. I had never pictured Haggard running down anymore than I had pictured Mike Tyson too spent to spar.

That night, I left Haggard in the bus that left for still another show. On the way home, a library of Haggard recollections popped uncontrollably into my mind. He is the father superior of country music. He is the touching and feeling part of the business that is as integral as musical notes.

I remembered the first time I ever spoke to him via long-distance telephone. He had called in early 1966 from Oklahoma City to play a song over the telephone. He said he didn't like the tune, but had recorded it at the insistence of Fuzzy Owens, his friend and manager. I put another record on the turntable, decreased its studio volume, and listened across the miles to a then-new song entitled "Swinging Doors." In April of that year, the song peaked at number five in the nation. It became the first Haggard standard of all time. But I told Haggard that I did not like the tune, having no idea it would be a hit.

His next release, "The Fugitive," was his first number-one record.

I recalled a battery of transitions, from Haggard the insecure young singer-songwriter, to the artist who was established by the time I left the all-night microphone in 1972.

Haggard's roller coaster life has been the most enigmatic in country music. When he was thirty-three, he was voted "Man of the Year" by the City of Bakersfield, then his home. Twelve years earlier, jurors in that same municipality had sentenced him to prison.

Merle Haggard is trying hard to emulate a male role model he never had for very long. His attempts at masculinity sometimes seem experimental. His father died when Haggard was nine. Haggard told me two years ago that he thinks about the death every day.

"I've missed my father many times," he said. "Just simple things that you miss . . . like smoking Camels with him on the front porch. I was doing that when I was nine. Many times I would have liked to walk up and ask him something. It was real lonely at home (after Dad died). My brother and sister were gone, and I was by myself, and I felt like a real burden to Mom. So I ran away."

He was eleven.

"I think I got into trouble as a teenager on purpose," Haggard continued. "I felt the need to experience the things I'd heard about in Jimmie Rodgers songs. Jesse James was my idol.''

Haggard told me that he had his first felonious trouble after borrowing a car that broke down in the desert, and stealing another at the Barstow, California, railroad station. He did sixty days for car theft. He was thirteen.

Haggard, as his song says, really did spend his twenty-first birthday in prison. He told me that he had gotten drunk and tried to burglarize an all-night restaurant. He said that he and some cronies used a crowbar to try to open the café's back door, whereupon the door was opened by the proprietor.

The restaurant was still open for business.

" 'Why don't you guys use the front door?' the proprietor told us,'' Haggard said. "We jumped in our car and tore off.''

The young hooligans forgot to turn on their car lights and that drew the attention of a state policeman.

"At twenty years old, I went to San Quentin,'' Haggard recalled.

Haggard, at thirty-three, was given a full pardon by then California Governor Ronald Reagan. I asked Haggard how he ever got his pardon application before Reagan and he replied that he used influence through Reagan aide Michael Deaver. Deaver was later implicated for alleged similar activities when he accompanied Reagan to the White House during Reagan's presidency.

Objectivity, regarding Haggard, is difficult for me. I see him as the megastar he is, the only singer-songwriter in the history of country music whose skills arguably surpass Hank Williams's. I also see him, however, as a frightened boy disguised as a macho man. Haggard has always been a psychological accident waiting to happen. His mentality is a mixture of a big ego and little self-esteem. The dangerous combination is the fuel of self-destruction.

He has called me in the middle of the night merely to ask for a telephone number. He would awaken me to arrange to awaken someone else. He wouldn't apologize. I was supposed to know that he would do the same for me.

When the Nashville Network went on the air, a lot of country stars were apprehensive about doing my show. They took a wait-and-see attitude, not wanting to lend their names to anything that was experimental.

Haggard, and Barbara Mandrell, never balked when asked to do my program. He drove from California to Nashville to appear because I needed him. Seven years later, when the show was a television staple and Randy Travis was the hottest act in the nation, Haggard stood me up when he was billed with the young superstar.

I was annoyed, called Haggard at home, and put his voice on the air.

He told North America that he would have come to my show, but he thought he was expected the next night. He didn't know the correct date of his scheduled network appearance. I earlier had made an excuse for him, and said that his visit was scrapped because of his health. That's what I'd been told.

Haggard told me in 1988 that he first entered the California Corrections System at age thirteen for car theft. He said he escaped seventeen times by the time he was eighteen years of age. He was sentenced to new time at San Quentin for escaping from the Kern County jail, although Haggard insists he was released by a jailer who forgot that he turned him loose.

While serving time for escape, Haggard was arrested again for being intoxicated on the prison yard, and spent his twenty-first birthday in a cell adjacent to death row. He acquired resilient self-protectiveness that was tempered by an adolescent life of crime. Ironically, as his wits sharpened, his heart softened. This man with a convict's savvy has a poet's soul.

Haggard can show you how to make a knife from a file. He can also summarize the complex spontaneity with which a broken heart will revive and jot, "Today, I Started Loving You Again."

He will work for days perfecting a new song, then draw press criticism for allegedly being too drunk on stage to remember its lyrics.

He is a man who claims he can still hop a freight train or make homemade beer. He cleans his own fish, often drives his own touring bus, and goes for years without ever donning a necktie. He often dresses like someone employed by a car wash. He chain-smokes unfiltered cigarettes and is not exactly a textbook grammarian when he speaks.

He writes such verse as . . .

Every fool has a rainbow, but he never seems to find
The reward that should be waiting at the end of the
line.
He'll give up a bed of roses for·a hammock filled with
thorns
And go chasing after rainbows, every time a dream is
born.
Every fool has a rainbow that only he can see,
Every fool has a rainbow, and the rule applies to me.

In the middle 1980s, Haggard was literally brought to his knees by the death of his mother, Marty Haggard, his son, said. Marty said it was the blow from which he honestly did not think his father would recover. Merle met me as I disembarked from the airplane in Bakersfield where Buck Owens and a handful of others joined us inside a modest funeral home.

"Mama tried to raise me better, but her pleading I denied, that leaves only me to blame for Mama tried," Haggard had written, about fifteen years earlier. At her funeral, I read aloud for the mama who tried. My text was her diary, written in her own cursive.

Before the service, Haggard and I had walked and spoken quietly while viewing an old railroad boxcar that had been converted into a house. You can imagine the "motif." It had been the late Jàck and Flossie Haggard's home, and birthplace to Merle. As a child, he could hear and feel the rumble of trains passing a hundred yards away. That day, the dwelling was occupied by Marty Haggard, his wife, and two children.

"Hi, Paw-Paw," one of the youngsters said to Merle as we approached.

The grandparental nickname sounded strange when applied to Haggard, once the most handsome and womanizing man in country music. In the 1960s, I was regularly asked by women how they could meet him. Airline stewardesses in particular used to tell me they would come to Nashville if I would fix them up with Merle Haggard.

Haggard and I walked through former grape vineyards where his ancestors had toiled in the desert sun. He told me about poor white people and day laborers who had once worked those fields that are now worked by Mexicans. He recalled the migration of his parents to the west from Oklahoma during the Dust Bowl. To myself, I heard passages from *The Grapes of Wrath*.

Haggard's people had been through John Steinbeck's fictional purgatory. Because of Haggard's empathy, he had too. I didn't wonder how he was inspired to record "They're Tearing the Labor Camps Down," and "Tulare Dust."

We had gone, years earlier, to his house, where a scale-model freight train had the run of the premises. He pressed the levers like a boy while reciting a flawless and spontaneous delivery about American trains that sounded like a pamphlet from the Rock Island Lines.

We went for a ride in the mountains in a 1936 Buick given to him by Bill Harrah, owner of Harrah's Club in Reno. Haggard coddled the antique as if it were gold. Then he literally nearly backed it over a cliff while turning around.

Haggard has the intensity of a maestro, the attention span of a child.

He gets fired up for an idea for two or three weeks, then his enthusiasm wanes. That's why I was indecisive in the late 1960s when he asked me to manage a radio station that he wanted to buy in Bakersfield. Taking the job would have meant quitting WSM. Haggard's intention was to build a broadcast powerhouse that was the West Coast counterpart to WSM. But I suspected that I would quit the best job in

American radio, move my family to California, and hear that Haggard had changed his mind.

So I turned down employment by Merle Haggard.

Haggard is a stickler for showmanship. Yet nothing he does on stage is rehearsed. He told me in 1988 that he sometimes calls out new songs for the band to play that they never have heard.

I was the emcee for a Haggard concert in Michigan. Rain began, and the outdoor audience was getting drenched. Many left. Haggard took his time going on stage, sauntering slowly with a lighted cigarette as if he had all the time in the world.

He was under cover while singing for a crowd that was soggy. He was obstinate and he was late. But he was Haggard, and they went crazy.

Haggard has always had a soft spot for the downtrodden. He has been called the "poet of the common man." I would amend that to "ambassador for the less fortunate." Yet, even in his efforts to help, he is a paradox.

He once decided to do a live album from Nashville's Rescue Mission. He later was unhappy, however, because attendants had had to listen to him sing before they were given a cup of soup. He thought that was patronizing.

Merle Haggard is monitored by other entertainers more than anyone else in country music. When he turned fifty (he's currently fifty-four), he underwent depression and disappeared for a few days. He missed two scheduled shows, and was tracked down by the legendary Johnny Cash. Cash doesn't appoint himself as just anybody's keeper.

"John found me and said 'Haggard, you taking dope?' " Haggard told me. "I told him, 'No John, if dope was my problem, I'd get some better dope.' "

The statement presented an obvious question. In his autobiography, *Sing Me Back Home,* Haggard talked freely about his marijuana consumption. I asked if he'd ever had a narcotics problem. His answer was another example of the confusion he generates.

"No, I never did have a problem," he said. "I got strung out on cocaine for three years when Leona [a former wife] left me and I really thought I was going to die." He reiterated that he never had a drug problem.

There are more stories surrounding Merle Haggard than any other three country stars combined. Amid the tales, I have never heard any star fail to say that he thinks Haggard is country music's ultimate singer and songwriter. He is, in my estimation, the standard toward which the others strive. He is the conscience of country music. I wouldn't want to be in a country music industry that did not include Merle Haggard.

Haggard has been nominated for forty-three Country Music Association awards but has only won six. The figures represent the most lopsided nominations-versus-wins record in the entire country music industry.

There is a certain amount of "politicking" an artist must undergo to garner the prizes. The maverick Haggard refuses to do this. Winning an award sometimes means an increase in an entertainer's performance fee. Haggard doesn't seem to care.

Rather than socialize to attain acclaim for a song, Haggard would rather go off by himself to write a new one.

...25...

THE MOST ASTONISHING, BLOCKBUSTER, LARGER-THAN-LIFE star to explode out of Nashville during my forty years in the entertainment industry is Dolly Parton. She's won more Country Music Association Awards than any other female singer and has had a string of number-one records that were crossovers, including country, rock, and adult contemporary. She wrote many of her own songs, and wrote for other major artists as well. She was the host of her own ABC Television variety show and was reportedly paid $44 million for two seasons, although the show was canceled after one.

She also has one of the most successful motion picture careers of anyone with Nashville ties. She has held starring roles alongside Burt Reynolds, Jane Fonda, and Shirley MacLaine. Not bad for a country girl reared in a shack as one of twelve children.

The first time I met Dolly, in 1965, she had just graduated from high school. She rode a Greyhound bus to Nashville from her native Sevierville, Tennessee, arriving with all her belongings in cardboard boxes. She had visited the Grand Ole Opry as a child, and even got to sing on the Opry show when she was twelve. Jimmy C. Newman, a regular Opry performer, gave up his spot on the broadcast so that the kid from rural Tennessee could get a break.

It didn't take, and Dolly went back to Sevierville. Six years passed before she returned to Music City to stay.

She was befriended by Carl and the late Pearl Butler, who had a big hit in the 1960s called "Don't Let Me Cross Over." They gave her a place to stay and, to this day, Dolly has never forgotten. She gave the Butlers five thousand dollars each Christmas for years, friends say.

The Butlers told me years ago about this young girl singer whom they had heard on the *Cas Walker Show*, a live radio broadcast from Knoxville, Tennessee, near Dolly's mountain home. I was doing my local morning television show, and they asked if I would have her as a guest.

She sang a George Jones song that was uptempo. I've forgotten the title but her high energy devoured the song's beat and lyrics. She bounced onto the set with her girlish giggle and blasted into the tune as if she had been shot out of a cannon. Because the show is done live and signs on before dawn, its mood is informal and low-key out of respect for viewers who are still waking up. While much of the sleepy audience was still yawning, Dolly exploded onto the airwaves with the zest of a high-strung, singing auctioneer.

She was an instant hit.

I asked her back several times to do the predawn broadcast and she always accepted, but there was a hitch. Dolly had no car. I drove to her apartment complex on Murfreesboro Road before 5:00 A.M. to bring her back to my show, then took her home shortly after sunrise. When the city was largely still asleep, except for paper boys and milkmen, Dolly charged out of her apartment. People are disarmed when they meet her, someone who has the appearance of an expensive hooker and the personality of a naive child. There is nothing threatening about her. Linda Ronstadt said that Dolly was the least neurotic person she ever met and I agree with her.

One day after the morning show, in 1966, Dolly asked me to let her off at a laundromat called "Wishy-Washey." I did, and there she met a man. His name was Carl Dean, and she invited him to her house. But she wouldn't let him inside. She thought it would appear improper for the two of them to be alone without a chaperone, so he had to visit her at her uncle's house in Nashville. When Uncle Bill wasn't home, Dolly and Carl sat on the front porch where everyone could see they weren't up to mischief. Dolly was from the country, the real country, and she clung to traditional values.

Before she was ever alone with Carl Dean, she married him. The marriage has lasted twenty-four years—a marriage made in Heaven and a "Wishy-Washey."

Through the years, I've been burned by many celebrities who are unable to keep commitments. They or their agents say they're going to appear on my show. Their appearance is advertised, and then they don't show up. It is unprofessional behavior and maddening to my producers, my fans, and me. Dolly is among that select group of performers who have the dependability of a banker. If she says she'll do something, she will. Given the career demands placed on her today, it's hard to get a commitment from her. But once you do, she keeps it.

I saw her reliability firsthand in 1966 when she recorded for Monument Records and was produced by Fred Foster. She told Foster she wanted to marry Carl Dean and Foster hit the ceiling. He felt that he and Dolly had carefully cultivated her image, and that the image would be damaged if she took a husband. He begged Dolly to wait for one year to get married. During the span, he thought, her career would solidify and not be as vulnerable to the press treatment of her nuptials.

But Dolly, whose priorities are firm, put her man before her career. She wanted him, but not until they were married. So she eloped to nearby Georgia. The couple married in a small town and attracted no press attention. Not even Fred knew. Later, when he told her he thought it was all right for her to get married, she told him she had been for a year! But before running off to the altar, Dolly agreed to do my morning show the day after her secret wedding. And she did it.

She told me that she got up at 3:00 A.M., dressed herself

to the nines, then woke up her husband of just a few hours. She wanted him to take her picture. She got an Instamatic print to record the hallowed day.

Then Dolly Parton came to my morning show and Carl Dean went back to bed.

Dolly, perhaps more than anyone I've ever met, has a capacity to be frank without offending. Her polite directness is refreshing in a business filled with phonies. In that respect, she is a homespun master of social graces. I can testify to the effectiveness of her candor.

I quit smoking cigarettes in 1968 and subsequently became fond of cigars. I probably jumped from the frying pan into the fire, as my penchant for cigars became almost as addictive as the cigarette obsession.

Dolly got me to stop smoking cigars. And she wasn't even trying. Today, I hold cigars as "props," or chew them, but I never light them.

Dolly was a guest on my syndicated radio show and whenever I had a female guest, I asked if she minded if I smoked my cigar. If I had a male guest, I just lit the thing.

No woman before ever complained about the smoking habits of the host of a national show that could be beneficial to her career. No woman did until Dolly.

"Do you mind if I light my cigar?" I asked.

"Well, I been a dreadin' it," Dolly answered.

"What do you mean?" I said.

"Well, I knew I was comin' over here today and knew that you was goin' to light that stinkin' thing, but go ahead if you want to," she retorted.

She wasn't angry. She wasn't hypocritical. She wasn't evasive. She was Dolly.

I later got to thinking about all the important and famous people I probably had offended with the tobacco smoke smoldering inside the small enclosure of a radio studio. Those folks all breathe clean air there today, and they have Dolly to thank.

When I travel, I'm asked about Dolly more than anybody. Dolly is one of my favorite people in show business, and in life. I could not write a book of memoirs without talking about the woman who stole my heart the first time I met her. Since then, I've decided she has the brains of a computer, the heart of an artist, and the spirit of a minister. I'm always amused at people who take Dolly's country girl demeanor too seriously, and think that she's just a hayseed who lucked out in the big city. Those folks are seriously mistaken.

The woman has made a fortune with her manufactured, Mae West aura. She knows exactly what she's doing, including her outrageous attempts at glamour. She takes them for what they're worth, and, as I've indicated, they've been worth millions. Dolly's high-piled wigs and caked, Kewpie doll makeup have been as indigenous to her image as black has been for Johnny Cash. Of course, her mammoth breasts have been invaluable. She's derived millions of dollars' worth of free publicity just from jibes during Johnny Carson monologues.

Reporters—from small-town weeklies right up to ABC's Barbara Walters—have asked Dolly the question, Are your breasts real? She has capitalized on that ridiculous question for years. She has never given a direct answer. Her evasiveness personifies her awareness of the value of mystique. Some famous women will never tell their age, and I bet Dolly never tells whether it was God or a surgeon who bolstered her boobs and her career.

I don't think the woman has an enemy in show business, incredible in an industry filled with insecure and jealous people. During a press conference, Burt Reynolds, promoting *The Best Little Whorehouse in Texas,* was asked what it was like to work with Dolly, and whether he liked her.

"How could you not like her?" Reynolds responded. "The woman is human sunshine."

I don't even think there is bitterness toward Dolly from Porter Wagoner. He made her a featured act on his syndicated television show in 1966 when it was the highest-rated television show produced in Nashville. Porter adopted Dolly as his singing partner. For seven years, the two toured the free world and recorded several number-one duets for RCA Records. He also got her a solo contract with RCA. When the label initially didn't want her, Porter, who had been a hot act on RCA, reportedly pledged his future royalties to the company to compensate for any loss it might sustain by signing Dolly.

There was never a financial loss for RCA. Dolly became the label's highest-selling female country artist ever.

Porter and Dolly went through a bitter feud a few years ago. He supposedly felt entitled to a portion of her earnings after she left his association. After all of that, the two are more than civil to each other, although I'm sure there is some estrangement between them. The point is that many entertainers would be willing to shoot each other after that kind of sustained trauma.

But not Dolly.

In 1988, when she was the hostess of her final network television show, she decided to move production for that one show from New York City to Nashville. Who did she have as a guest on that program? Porter Wagoner. The two sang their old hits for the first time in fourteen years.

Show business is a high-risk, speculative ordeal. There are no guarantees. Many artists, therefore, take the safe route whenever they can. They'll record songs they don't like just because they think the songs are commercial. They'll repeatedly play the same venues where they know they can draw a crowd, rather than reach out for an expanded audience in untested markets.

Whenever I'm asked about brave artists, those inclined to follow the dictates of their dreams even at the expense of risk, I mention Dolly.

Dolly, even as a child, was a dreamer. She dreamed of being a star. The family was too poor to afford cosmetics, and Dolly once told me she put flour on her face as a kid and pretended it was makeup when she played "celebrity."

The woman, to this day, has not outgrown dreaming. Obstacles are things she would see only if she stopped dreaming. But she never does.

When Dolly left the Porter Wagoner show in 1974, she and banjo player Buck Trent departed within two weeks of each other. A lot of people in the music business and a lot of fans were outraged. They felt that country music had given Dolly a stellar career, and she was abandoning the art and the people who patronized it. Some country fans are loyal to the point of being possessive. They wrongly felt betrayed.

Dolly not only left Porter, the man who more than anyone except herself had made her career, she also left Nashville. What's more, she left Nashville for Hollywood, a place where show business practices are far removed from the down-home, familylike fraternity of Nashville artists.

Many Nashville music people were outraged. They implied Dolly was a female Benedict Arnold.

But Dolly told me she had gone about as high in country music as she could go. She wanted to go higher in her career than country could take her. She could have done the "safe" thing and stayed in Nashville; she would have recorded three number-one country hits a year, and toured with Porter, and made her all-but-guaranteed few million dollars annually.

If she failed in Hollywood, where her whole hillbilly persona could become a laughingstock, she might not be able to return to Nashville and the unforgiving country community. I know that was a thought she had, but it was also a thought she ignored.

She quit Porter after they had twice won "Vocal Duo of the Year" from the Country Music Association.

She took the plunge and surfaced a big winner. She would never have made inroads into the movies, nor would she have ever recorded big pop hits, if she hadn't sought West Coast direction to her career. Today, of course, many who criticized her say they knew she was doing the right thing all along.

Dolly does what Dolly wants to do when she wants to do it. Dolly is childlike and like many children, she wants to do whatever she is forbidden to do.

When Dolly was in Los Angeles filming *Nine to Five,* she and her longtime friend and traveling companion somehow got on the subject of nudity. The discussion evolved into a dare. Judy Ogle dared Dolly to walk on the streets of Los Angeles naked. That was a green light for Dolly. When her limousine pulled up to a Beverly Hills stop sign, out leaped Dolly. She told me she was wearing absolutely nothing but a smile. She did a rapid lap around the car and popped back inside.

What would have happened if Judy had locked the doors while Dolly was outside? Imagine those unrestrained breasts hitting her chin as she bounced around the car's perimeter.

Dolly is the most successful, yet most misunderstood, woman in country music, where her roots have remained, despite her endeavors in other entertainment arenas. I get impatient with people who are so taken with her external packaging that they can't see the warm and sensitive artist inside. For years, the only thing some folks wondered about Dolly was whether she was sleeping with Porter Wagoner. I refused to even listen to that kind of talk. But I'm told the question was asked regularly of others, including members of the old Porter Wagoner Wagonmasters Band. Dolly's sleeping habits were the subject of great speculation and debate at many Nashville cocktail parties.

What a waste of time and talk. Who cares anyhow? I get weary of fans and music business personnel who think that because they follow someone's career they're entitled to know all about their private lives. People always seem to want to know the dirt. That's why the supermarket rags sell so well.

I've been told I'm loyal to a fault. Perhaps I am. If so, I'm at fault with Dolly. My experiences with her have been among the most rewarding of all during my career in show business.

...26...

Rusty Wilcoxen, a former producer of *Nashville Now,* told me that something was wrong even before he spoke a word. His bloodless pallor was a mask of urgency.

"Ralph," he said, ". . . there's been an accident. Barbara's been hurt, and they think it's pretty serious."

That was my introduction to the head-on collision between a car driven by Barbara Mandrell and one driven by Mark P. White, a nineteen-year-old college student from Lebanon, Tennessee. He died in the wreckage, so no one ever knew why he chose to propel his car into the wrong lane, and into the path of the Jaguar carrying two children and their mother, the best female friend I have, and the surrogate for the sister I never did.

Six years later to the day, Barbara Mandrell released *Get to the Heart,* her best-selling autobiography. In the book she describes the near-fatal collision and its psychological ramifications, which nearly killed her career.

The text is heady literature that heralds her victorious spirit. Millions were uplifted by her story but there was no such lofty thinking the night of September 11, 1984, when blood oozed from her skull.

People can pick their friends. When they pick a friend to become a "relative," the bonding is a mental weld. She never had a brother, I never had a sister, and neither of us had a friendship like the one we have together.

I have communicated throughout the free world for four decades. But I was speechless—frozen with wordless fear—the night I watched the medical personnel scurry around Barbara's motionless body. Everyone seemed to have so much life. I remember thinking it strangely unfair that the one on whom their lives centered was about to lose her own.

I arrived at the hospital about five minutes before her ambulance. Her sister, Louise, emerged from the vehicle and then attendants eased Barbara's cot down. I was confused. I wanted to do something but didn't want to be in the way. I yearned to go to Louise, who seemed to be going out of her mind with grief.

Funny how the most unorthodox thoughts will uncontrollably race through one's mind at such a time. I thought about Steve, my eldest son, and his injury. That was the last time I had observed a loved one's life held in the balance. I thought about Irby Mandrell, Barbara's father, and Ken Dudney, her husband, both of whom I had dined and socialized with countless times. They would arrive later.

The clamor of hospital personnel and the rattling of equipment was deafening as Barbara's hospital cart was whisked past. The din was only partially diminished as I said a silent prayer.

Barbara was covered with a sheet. Her hair protruded. Its usually radiant blonde tone was changed to a mat of dull, crimson, dried blood. The woman had commanded the most expansive and spectacular stages on the globe. Now she clung to life on a creaky cart not three feet in breadth.

The press was everywhere, flashing cameras into the sweat-stained faces of the doctors. Reporters walked backward, yielding only to the fast approach of Barbara's hospital gurney.

I thought of how many times I had seen this beautiful woman at her best, and now men she'd never seen before were taking her photograph so that the world could see her in her worst hour.

Louise tearfully pleaded for journalists to give the family a break. Her words fell on deaf ears.

Strange, uncontrollable flashbacks continued to fill my head: the first time I met Barbara, in 1968, shortly after she came to Nashville. I remembered the voice of the late Merle Travis, the guitarist and songwriter who wrote "Sixteen Tons" for Tennessee Ernie Ford in the 1950s. Travis asked if I would let a singer from California perform on an afternoon, local television show I was doing. He said she was a real pretty girl who could really sing.

I trusted his judgment, and I said I would.

Then he gave the strangest enticement for me to have her on the show. He said she had pretty skin. I was glad Merle Travis couldn't see the shattered glass embedded that night into her once pretty skin.

I once played an early, 1970s Barbara Mandrell hit on the all-night show titled "Tonight My Baby's Comin' Home." The tune caused scores of American soldiers' wives to call. The women were waiting for their returning men at nearby Fort Bragg, North Carolina.

I thought about 1977 and the first time I learned to ski, with Barbara as my teacher. Midway through the lesson, she was besieged by "Montezuma's Revenge." She had recently returned from Mexico and had unwisely drunk the water. Nature's call forced her to flee down the mountain in rapid and poised pace. But I was left with nothing but the howling wind, swirling snow, and questions about how I would get down that mountain without Barbara's help. Fortunately, she soon came to my rescue.

I thought about Barbara Mandrell's arguably having the biggest career ever to come out of Nashville.

I thought about her grace under pressure, and how her success was rooted in politics as much as talent. She knows exactly what to say, and when. I recalled the time she and I flew with the U.S. Air Force Thunderbirds, and how the pull of G-force left me disoriented. I saw a playback on videotape. She was lucid, coherent, and competent.

I babbled.

During her stormy convalescence from the wreck, Barbara was bedridden for months but her spirit never gave up. She talked freely about the mental changes she was undergoing, how she wouldn't drive a car again, how she didn't want to entertain, how she wanted to sequester herself from the world.

Barbara was regrouping. She was at war with herself. Most wars are won after regrouping.

Barbara, the strongest-spirited person I have ever known, became even stronger in the face of adversity. She had been ambushed. She hadn't been that strong before because she hadn't had to be.

She didn't just rise to adversity. She conquered it.

So it began, the weeks of recovery. We gave updates on her health on *Nashville Now*. The mail piled up in mountains. Extra people were hired to handle letters to Barbara that came to her by way of the show.

We felt obliged to give a nightly report on the recovery of country music's Princess Diana. To her fans, she was royalty.

Barbara astonished the entertainment and medical communities thirty-two days after the tragedy. She appeared, from her home, on national television during the annual Country Music Association awards show. A steel rod held her broken leg straight. There were pins throughout her torso, and pain-killing prescriptions saturating her system. Her broken bones had numbered into double digits. Yet she braced for the cameras, the conduits to her fans, with the composure of a First Lady on the eve of a national election. She was an Iron Lady disguised as a Kewpie doll.

My wife, my sons, and I went with Barbara, her husband, and her children to Colorado in December to take our annual skiing vacation. It was then that I saw firsthand how undone my friend remained from her trauma, and how it distressed her. She told me she had become an introvert for the first time in her life. I knew how out of character that was for a woman who had been a high school beauty queen, had held center stage ever since, and was the hostess of her own prime-time television show for three seasons. On that first trip after her accident, Barbara scarcely wanted to leave her condominium.

She told me that while she had been hospitalized, she tried to play Name That Tune, a game at which she always excelled. But after the wreck, she was unable to identify the melody to one song, she said, and it infuriated her.

A year after the wreck, Barbara was still not her old self. She, like Minnie Pearl, had always enjoyed working. "Stay busy and you'll stay young," they've both often said.

Twelve months after the fact, she was still lethargic.

I thought of how she had driven a dragster while barely out of high school, blasting across a finish line with a four-hundred-horsepower car at 150 miles per hour. She didn't flinch.

She had garnered the most coveted of all the entertainment industry awards—the People's Choice Award. She captured an award above Dolly Parton and Barbra Streisand, and did so by setting a grueling pace of one-night performances twenty years and millions of miles ago. She had been, quite simply, the hardest-working person in show business I'd ever known.

During that ski trip I bought her a book, a history of the Supremes, after she told me she was going to write her autobiography. I thought the book might be helpful. She was indifferent about reading it. Since the wreck, she had difficulty reading, and greater difficulty retaining what she read.

In the winter of 1984, and on through the next year, the Iron Lady was emotionally dented.

Then the spell began to break. She told me she was going to do a comeback show in September 1985 in the Los Angeles Amphitheater. It was a show to star Barbara and Dolly and she wanted me to emcee. I was reminded of the words of the late Stringbean. "I'm the only one on the show I've never heard of," I thought.

There was a party preceding the show. Guests included Morgan Fairchild, Tammy Wynette, Lee Greenwood,

Cesar Romero, John Denver, John Ritter, Steve Allen, and Jayne Meadows.

Then it was showtime. I walked onstage, and realized for the first time how truly national the Nashville Network had become. I received one of the most vigorous rounds of applause in my entire career. I made a few remarks about the importance of the occasion, and brought Dolly on. Her performance marked the only time Dolly Parton ever performed on a show she didn't close. That night, she agreed to be Barbara's opening act.

And Dolly flat out killed them. She did music and comedy and made incessant jokes about her breasts. She said she knew she looked ridiculous, then said she had a brain under her wig, and a heart under her boobs.

The crowd went berserk.

Yet the belle of that ball was Barbara. Only someone coming back from the jaws of death could have followed Dolly successfully. But follow her she did, and won their hearts.

One year earlier, Barbara lay in critical condition in an intensive care unit at Nashville's Baptist Hospital. After twelve months, she rose, and the world fell at her feet, but not before she dropped to her knees.

My "sister" has a deep faith in God. With a Hollywood crowd out front, with international news cameras in the wings, Barbara Mandrell and her band prayed aloud in a backstage dressing room. One more time, she would reach far into herself by reaching out to God. And in reaching for God, she touched the people.

It's part of the private person the public never sees.

There was a party after, but the guest of honor didn't stay long. Barbara and her entourage were antsy because she had booked a live performance in Houston, hundreds of miles and fourteen hours away. She got on an airplane before the deafening applause had became an echo.

She made the plane with ten minutes to spare. Then, she was surely gone. And she was surely back.

... 27 ...

Jimmy Dean was flying from New York to Nashville for a recording session. On the back of an airline pamphlet he wrote a poem. He needed one more song to fill out the session and decided to set the new poem against a background melody while he narrated its verses.

A major music publisher had already turned down the poem, and Dean had no offers for his work when he recorded it, a situation almost unheard of in this business. Pianist extraordinaire Floyd Cramer, who a year earlier had recorded the giant record "Last Date" as one of his numerous hits, and outstanding studio guitarist Grady Martin, who later played with Willie Nelson, owned a small publishing company. They performed with Dean during this recording session and said casually that they could publish his song, a proposition to which Dean agreed.

The song was recorded in a matter of minutes, with few if any revisions, and the attitude at the studio was entirely nonchalant. Five million copies later, "Big Bad John" became the biggest-selling narration in country music history.

Dean did a couple of follow-up songs about the protagonist and then proceeded to record many more hits consisting only of the spoken word with background instrumentation as well as conventional recordings that utilized his singing voice.

Narrations were at their most popular in country music in the 1940s and 1950s. Hank Williams, Sr., when at the height of his career as an artist in America, recorded narrations under another name and had a separate career as "Luke the Drifter." Country singers often include a narration on their albums and in live performances. A vocalist who is unable to express emotional inflections through singing is hard pressed to convey feelings. Dean is a master of the art.

He is also a master of compassion for others, though some people might find that contention astonishing. Dean can be outspoken, windy, and abrasive, traits that make him one of the most misunderstood men in the entertainment industry. People who dislike Dean do themselves a disservice. They're looking too closely at his public personality, and not closely enough at his character.

In a business filled with phony and manipulative people, I find Dean's candor refreshing. Not everyone would agree, including several former guests on Dean's enormous yacht. I witnessed an event there that was very telling of Dean's personality.

The vessel was docked in Kennebunkport, Maine, where Dean had invited Joy and me to join him for dinner. We had gone there on a weekend excursion during which we strolled the shops. When we returned, approximately thirty persons were on board Dean's boat. Cocktails were being served and a full-fledged party was underway. Guests included Neil Bush, who, curiously, introduced himself to me as "the third son of the vice president of the United States."

As the party was approaching its crescendo, Dean rose to ask for everyone's attention. Some people assumed he was going to make an announcement about forthcoming entertainment.

"Do you know what we're going to do now?" he asked.

"No-o-o-o," the crowd said in unison.

"I'm going to dinner," he said, "and you're going to get the hell off my boat!"

And everyone did.

I respect Jimmy Dean for his sheer human willpower. Reared in merciless poverty, he became a self-made man with two distinct careers and a net worth reported at $100 million. He brought country music to his network television variety show as early as the late 1950s. He regularly battled New York executives who did not want what was then called "hillbilly" art on their network. When his entertainment career cooled he could have done what many do, and spent the rest of his life reliving his early days through memories. Instead, Dean rolled up his sleeves and rolled pork into sausage.

The man became a mogul of the American breakfast table.

Jimmy Dean doesn't play the guitar as part of his act. He doesn't dance and he isn't young. But he is an entertainer's entertainer through the sheer mixture of his songs, banter, and jokes. He is a master of timing. He has a feel for showmanship and knows when it's time to do whatever is necessary to entertain. I've never known anyone who could better read an audience. He mixes with them and, of course, insults them. He is a country version of Don Rickles.

One of the ironies about Dean is that he can recall a thousand jokes, literally, but can't recall his social security number.

I met Dean in 1960 when he came to my overnight radio show to plug "Big Bad John." Instead of playing the record, Dean did the song live. The record ends with the words, "big, big man." Dean originally recorded the song to end, "hell of a man." The record label made him do it again so as to sanitize the ending. When he came to the ending of the song on my show, he paused.

"Which ending do you want?" he asked.

I selected the original. Dean said "hell," and that might have been the first time profanity was ever used on WSM. I feared a negative reaction, but not one listener complained.

There is no predicting Dean. He called one day to ask if he could bring George Bush, then vice president, to my television show. I, of course, consented. I would never have gotten such a prestigious guest had it not been for Dean. When I was actually on the air with Bush, Dean dominated the conversation, although the vice president did narrate a "Take Pride in America" video featuring his visit to the Grand Tetons in Wyoming.

I kiddingly chastised Dean on the air about monopolizing the conversation and even asked the vice president to return to the program without his chatty buddy.

Dean will invite you to his yacht, then make you remove your shoes so as not to soil the white carpet. He even did that to the president. He's headstrong, inflexible, tirelessly tenacious, and overly sentimental.

I attended the wedding of the former Connie Dean, Dean's daughter. He tried to sing a special song to her. He broke down, and the bride got up and helped him finish the selection. It was a very moving moment.

Dean fits on my list of people who belong to the live-and-let-live philosophy. I don't understand some of his behavior, but I neither condone nor condemn it.

The tabloid press had a field day in 1990 during his courtship of the Nashville singer Donna Meade. He lived with her, allegedly, although he was married to his wife of decades. He bought Ms. Meade a mammoth diamond ring and was seen with her in Nashville night life. One of the rags published several photographs of Dean and Ms. Meade inside the Bull Pen Lounge at the legendary Stock-Yard Restaurant. Dean's profile in this suspected extramarital dabbling was so high that he became the subject of articles in the legitimate press, and reporters began interviewing his wife. The word "discretion" didn't seem to fit Dean's vocabulary, and I never understood why my friend was so nearly contemptuous of others' perceptions of his activities, except that it was another manifestation of Dean's total disregard for hypocrisy.

People seem to either love or dislike Dean. Those feelings are based on what they see, and what they see is what he is. I like that quality.

Dean has a fetish about punctuality. I remember when he fought to get the young Johnny Cash on his network show, and Cash rewarded Dean by showing up late and high on dope. Dean was angered, and would have nothing to do with Cash for years. Eventually he told Cash about why he had been boycotted. Cash realized that Dean was right and apologized.

Another victim of Dean's insistence on punctuality was Roy Clark, host of *Hee Haw*, the longest-running syndicated television show in country music history. Clark got his first big break as a lead guitar player for Dean when he hosted a local television show in Washington, D.C. Clark was forever tardy for the predawn broadcast and Dean kept warning him about his lateness. One day Clark was late again and scurried to open his guitar case.

"Don't even take it out of the case," Dean told him.

"Let me play a little bit," Clark replied. "You might hear something you like."

"Don't even take it out of the case," Dean insisted, "and I want you to know you're the most talented man I've ever fired." Dean let him go on the spot, knowing he would have to perform live in minutes in a major market without a lead guitarist. Dean is brave.

Dean was the first to put the late puppeteer Jim Henson on television in Washington. Henson had designed just one puppet at the time, a dog named Rowlf. Dean also gave Jerry Reed his first nightclub job in Reno, Nevada, and introduced Roger Miller to the nation on the *Tonight Show* when Dean was a guest host.

Miller was hilarious that night and went on to a stellar recording career. Dean had not met Miller before that show but heard of him through Gordon Stoker of the Jordanaires and took a chance on the zany comedian. Years later, when Miller was a megastar and had his own network show, he sent Dean a gold doorknob on a plaque. Its inscription read, "Thank You for Opening the Door."

Dean, who has appeared in several motion pictures, told

me about the acute anxiety he underwent when he played a character based on Howard Hughes in a James Bond film.

"I was very careful with the part," he said. "At the time I did that film, Hughes was paying me fifty thousand dollars a week to sing in his nightclub. I was scared to death I would offend him, and lose the job."

There isn't a singer in Nashville who hasn't turned down a song that another artist has gone on to make into a hit record. Many singers refuse to talk about these bloopers since this reflects badly on their judgment.

Not Dean.

He freely admits turning down the chance to record "The Battle of New Orleans," a multi-million-copy song for the late Johnny Horton. He also declined "Detroit City," the career-building record written by stuttering Mel Tillis and Danny Dill for Bobby Bare.

Tillis's speech impediment is greatly improved today, and at times is even unnoticeable. But during the 1960s, speech for him was a struggle. Silence went on forever when he fought to get sentences out.

He once came to Dean's hotel to play him songs he had written and Dean passed on every one.

"I'm going to go home and call you back and play a tune called 'Detroit City' over the telephone," Tillis said. "So when you answer, if nobody talks, don't hang up cause it's me."

Once, when Dean was a guest on my syndicated radio show, I asked him how he came up with the idea for "Big Bad John." He said simply that he had worked with a large actor named John Mento during a summer stock production of *Destry Rides Again*. The actor was the only person in the cast larger than Dean, who simply called him "Big John." Then he said, on the air, "You thought you were going to get some big and historical anecdote. Instead, the explanation is as dull as your show."

His assessment of my program was aired to millions.

Dean is an enigma. His lamblike sensitivity is wrapped in a suit of armor. Nothing and nobody intimidates him, at least not outwardly. His caustic sense of humor knows no sacred cows. There is immunity for no one, not even the president of the United States.

Dean, in the 1960s, was the chairperson of an annual Washington fundraiser, the Home Show, to which the best and the brightest were invited. The president attended each year, yet the chairperson was expected to formally invite the chief executive.

Dean contacted President John Kennedy and humbly and graciously asked him to attend. He told the president the gala would be pleased to have him as its guest of honor. He told Kennedy of his admiration for his performance as president and his efforts in international diplomacy.

Then Dean suggested to the president of the United States that it was all right to use Dean's name at the door for admittance, in case the host or hostess had never heard of him.

Minnie Pearl was lying to me in November 1990, and I had no idea. She told me "everything was fine" following her surgery. She had, in fact, undergone removal of eleven lymph nodes, five of which she knew were cancerous.

Later, I would find out that she hadn't wanted me to worry, hence her initial deceit.

"And," she eventually added, "I'm to undergo radiation treatment every day in February."

Minnie Pearl still doesn't talk privately about her infirmity. She does, however, discuss it publicly, addressing women's and civic groups nationwide about the treatability of the cancer that is every woman's nightmare. In early 1991, a treatment center in Nashville was named Sarah Cannon (Minnie's real name).

Until Minnie became ill, I never thought about her mortality. There are some people who everyone thinks will live forever because we all need them so much.

Minnie Pearl is a breathing United States shrine. She is a part of the American way of life, right up there with baseball and Walt Disney and quarter-pounders with cheese.

On November 7, 1990, she celebrated her fiftieth anniversary on the Grand Ole Opry. She had been in show business several years before joining the Opry in 1940. For almost sixty years the primary effect Minnie has had on millions of people was to make them feel better. She has, perhaps, the highest visibility of anyone in country music, and one of the highest in all of show business.

That was driven home to me in February 1991, when I went with Minnie to Los Angeles to appear on the "ACE Awards Show." She entered the backstage area dressed in her civilian clothes. No one noticed her. She walked slowly out of her dressing room in costume to a behind-the-scenes area filled with celebrities, most of whom had little or no interest in country music. However, they instantly recognized, and responded to, the straw hat and price tag above the full cotton dress that is Minnie Pearl's trademark.

Whoopi Goldberg grabbed Minnie as she came offstage. Cicely Tyson bent Minnie's ear for thirty minutes. Muhammad Ali smiled and waved from across the crowded room. Dick Clark, who produced the show, came by to check on her. Lily Tomlin arranged dinner for her.

Another dramatic indication of Minnie's incredible visibility came in 1960 when Joe Allison, cowriter of Jim Reeves's "He'll Have to Go," drew Minnie's straw hat and dangling price tag. He put the sketch on the outside of an envelope with no name or address. He affixed a first-class stamp and deposited the envelope in a mailbox in Los Angeles. It was received by Minnie at the Grand Ole Opry in Nashville.

She once told me how "Minnie" evolved, and the story is fascinating. The former Sarah Colley was an instructor for the Sewell Academy in Atlanta, Georgia. She toured the South teaching dramatic arts to schoolchildren. She was paid a few dollars a week and lodged with families of the administration of the schools where she taught.

That was the plight of career girl Sarah Ophelia Colley in 1936 when she rode a train to a little village near Sand Mountain in northern Alabama. Her job was to teach fine arts to the rough and uneducated farm children struggling along with their parents against a postdepression economy.

She was to meet the school principal at a train station in Cullman, Alabama.

Miss Colley's train arrived in the middle of a blizzard, but the principal never appeared at the station.

The snow was falling so hard the sky was almost black at three o'clock in the afternoon. Miss Colley had her costumes in a large trunk, which someone had unloaded from the train. She saw it sitting alone on the deserted station platform, engulfed in the turbulent snowfall.

Miss Colley had seven dollars in her purse, she told me, and squinted against the blizzard for a sign of human life. There was none.

She trudged into the station, where the stationmaster was preparing to close for the day. He had almost locked her out in the storm, not imagining that anyone would be traveling during such weather. She recalled that he thought her presence implied an emergency.

"No," she told him, "I've come to teach dramatic arts."

There is no telling what he thought about her priorities.

Miss Colley found one man with one old car at the station who could take her to the schoolhouse. He wanted fifteen dollars for the haul. She bartered him down to five, which was two dollars less than every penny she had in the world.

It took the driver an hour to travel fifteen miles up a mountain road. Each time his rickety vehicle almost slid off the mountain path, he shouted to Miss Colley about some unfortunate soul who had plunged off the hill at that very spot.

Miss Colley arrived, wet and exhausted, at the school, where the astonished principal told her he had no idea she would try to negotiate a blizzard just to stage a play. She suspected, in fact, that he had even forgotten about her engagement, since he had booked it during summertime.

The principal told her that he had not provided a place for her to stay. After deliberation, it was suggested that she stay with a mountain family about a mile from the school, and she was put into the elements again.

Miss Colley knocked on the cabin door. She stood in front of a place she'd never been, awaiting people she'd never met, to ask if she could live with them for ten days. She was stranded.

The knock was answered by a seventy-year-old woman. The woman would become the role model for the character that would tickle the free world's funnybone for half a century.

The old woman let Miss Colley live with her and her husband and son for ten days. She told her visitor that she had borne sixteen children and had never failed to make a crop. She called her son "Brother," hence the idea for the fictional "Brother" who is the subject of many Minnie Pearl jokes. Little did anyone know that a national treasure was being born with the creation of "Minnie Pearl." The character is so embedded in everyone's mind that not many people call Mrs. Cannon by her correct name. Everyone calls her Minnie.

The young drama teacher was fascinated with the old and rustic woman and her fierce spirit, which bred a natural wit. Miss Colley began to impersonate her, tried it on stage, and a star was soon born.

I was still a tyke when I first heard Minnie Pearl on the Grand Ole Opry. I worked my first show with her in 1952. It was a benefit affair for the Veterans Administration Hospital. I had been in radio for only one year and wouldn't have thought that Minnie Pearl, then a seasoned performer, would even notice my work as an emcee.

She did, and she told someone I was terrible.

"That boy's got a lot to learn," she said.

She was right. My professional inexperience was exceeded only by my personal naiveté. When I was nineteen, I regarded Minnie Pearl as someone similar to God's daughter, so I was shattered the second time I saw her and she appeared to be drunk. She was probably just feeling a "buzz." She, Eddy Arnold, and Red Foley were having a high ole time during a cocktail party at the disc jockey convention at Nashville's Andrew Jackson Hotel.

That marked my first traumatic realization that some of the people I'd held as heroes were merely human beings. I had never associated Minnie Pearl with drinking any more than I had associated Florence Nightingale with bank robbery. Man, was I green!

I had just heard Foley sing "Peace in the Valley" and "Just a Closer Walk with Thee." I had grown up in the Church of Christ and couldn't fathom that people who sang hymns could swallow whiskey. Again, the problem was not their imbibing. The problem was my exaggerated innocence.

I didn't come to know Minnie as rapidly as I did the other stars. She was not primarily a recording artist, so she didn't visit my all-night radio show to pitch her records. We didn't really become friends until I became a staff announcer on the Opry.

Minnie and I have become especially close since the inception of *Nashville Now*. She performs a Friday night feature on the program called, "Let Minnie Steal Your Joke."

Fans who send her good jokes get the pleasure of hearing them read aloud by Minnie Pearl on national television.

Many of the jokes are unusable because they're dirty. Can you imagine—people send dirty jokes to Minnie Pearl! And many of those dirty jokes are sent by senior citizens.

There is also the odd problem of repetition. If a joke is determined to be the best of the week, that same joke will reappear in the mail hundreds of times the following week. I guess that some viewers think if it was good enough for one week, it will do for another.

One of the great misfortunes in country music is that the public knows Minnie only as a comedienne. She is also a tremendous storyteller of serious lore. She has been around country music long enough to know where all the bodies are buried. I love to hear her tell stories about the mischievous misbehavior of the Opry's old guard.

Some of her recollections, however, aren't so engaging. They're sad because they're true. Minnie was there.

She told me about working a show with Ernest Tubb and Hank Williams in San Diego in 1952. Both Ernest and Hank were late, so Minnie opened the program for the restless crowd. She was talking to the audience but listening for sounds backstage, awaiting the arrival of the stars so she could bring them on stage.

Minnie walked into the wings at one point and saw an emaciated Hank being assisted by a male nurse. The frustrated aide was mistreating him and Minnie said Hank had been harassing him.

Hank's drinking was legendary, and in less than four years, he was dead of an alcohol and drug overdose at the age of twenty-nine.

On this particular day, Minnie said he looked like a walking dead man. She told me how the show's promoter forced Hank to go on, despite his sobbing pleas to be left alone. His bawling and cowering were, she said, pitiable. Minnie told me that she could only think about how dynamic Hank had been in his prime. This day he would stagger on stage and then literally clutch the microphone to maintain his equilibrium.

Minnie felt compelled to see Hank sober up after his humiliating matinee. She was going to get him out of his cups in time for the evening performance.

Minnie and the promoter's wife drove Hank around town just to keep him away from the alcohol and drugs he craved. He began to cramp and appeared to be entering withdrawal.

"It was the longest automobile ride of my life," she said. "But I wanted to be with him rather than leave him at the auditorium. The people there just saw him as a commodity who was supposed to entertain. They didn't love him like I did."

Minnie fought Hank's insistence that they stop the car. He had any number of reasons for wanting to get out, but she feared he would sneak more contraband.

She told me that she is convinced that Hank was a man-possessed by depression and was probably manic-depressive.

She was desperate for anything that would take Hank's mind off his misery and keep him sober.

So the First Lady of country comedy began to sing. In the stillness of a California night, with the Pacific Ocean leaking humidity through the car's open windows, a solitary voice from Tennessee raised into "I Saw the Light," a Hank Williams Gospel standard.

She begged Hank to sing his song with her. He could not.

"I saw the light, I saw the light," Minnie pressed on.

Then a disheveled and drunken Hank Williams, the idol of millions, placed his bony and shaking hand inside the firm grip of the woman next to him. Again, he began to sob.

"That's just it, Minnie," he said, "there ain't no light. It's all dark."

Six months later, he was dead.

There aren't many people left in country music who were around when barn dances were regular performance venues.

Minnie is among the handful, and it's thrilling to hear her tell the stories because she lived them herself.

Minnie Pearl did shows in a different city almost every night for twenty-seven years. She was flown from date to date by her husband, Henry Cannon. In April 1967 the marathon performing came to a screeching halt after the two took off from Baltimore en route to Nashville and home.

The journey was Henry's last flight as a pilot.

At 8,700 feet, not fifty miles from Nashville, one of the airplane's two engines stopped.

Minnie said that for one of the few times in her life she was quiet—largely because she didn't want to upset her concentrating husband, and also because she was frozen with fear.

She insists she never made a sound as he switched from one fuel tank to another, flipped the controls, and made other futile efforts to revive the dormant engine.

Henry calmly put the plane down in a farm field adjacent to Interstate 40 between Knoxville and Nashville. It was a tranquil, but terrifying, descent. Henry and Minnie walked away from the aircraft, and away from the series of one-night shows. That was the beginning of the slowdown of her touring, one-night performances.

The Country Music Association should appoint a committee to select five performers to be inducted into the

Country Music Hall of Fame each year instead of the current practice of inducting only one or two veteran performers annually. The calendar catches up with some worthy entertainers before their dreams of induction come true.

In defense of the CMA, it has been said that to induct so many in one year would dilute the importance of the award. I understand that contention, but I don't agree.

I think immediately of Webb Pierce, who died in March 1991, five months after he was nominated for induction into the Hall of Fame at sixty-four. Tennessee Ernie Ford very deservingly won the honor instead, and now Webb never will, except possibly posthumously.

The Baseball Hall of Fame has an old-timers' committee to select multiple inductees each year. The country music community could take a lesson from that.

Minnie Pearl had been nominated many years in a row before she was admitted to the Hall of Fame on October 13, 1975, at age sixty-three.

The bronze plaque bearing her likeness is displayed inside the Country Music Hall of Fame. The plaque reads: "Humor is the least recorded but certainly one of the most important aspects of live country music. No one exemplifies the endearing values of pure country comedy more than Minnie Pearl. Born Sarah Ophelia Colley in Centerville, Tennessee, educated at fashionable Ward-Belmont College, joined the Grand Ole Opry in 1940. Her trademark—the dime-store hat with the dangling price tag and shrill 'Howdee! I'm just so proud to be here!' made her the first country music humorist to be known and loved worldwide."

Someday, her hilarity will leave this world. It's been speculated that God likes laughter. In His bass voice, I can hear His deep welcome to Minnie Pearl. And I can hear her resounding, "Howdee!"

Following my divorce from Skeeter Davis, I decided to try anything that would get me out of town, and get her out of my mind. I decided I would become a touring entertainer, a new career intended to change my life. This life-changing career was over in a week. Indulge me while I digress.

Touring recording artists must have a single record or album in circulation. I had earlier recorded "I Cry at Ballgames." It was a clever song that we didn't record well. It left no one crying except those who bought the record. I've received heavy kidding about that endeavor. My singing was so bad that Ray Walker of the Jordanaires was asked to sing in unison with me to cover up my bad notes.

I needed an agent and selected Jimmy Key. He booked me and my first-and-only band in Fargo, North Dakota, in the dead of winter to play a dive. On opening night, the temperature was twenty-two below zero. I bought a new Cadillac for the occasion and recall that one of my musicians put his plastic shaving kit in the car's trunk. He dropped the frozen kit, and it shattered like glass on the icy concrete.

As long as I've digressed to this degree, I will tell you about the engagement itself. Glen Davis was playing drums. I'm sure he'll be thrilled about the credit here.

I was paid $1,000 for five days, during which I spent $1,100.

Grand Ole Opry star Billy Walker was booked on the show with me, and was to be backed up by my band, the members of which decided they didn't like him. They thought he was arrogant. It's unwise for any singer to alienate the musicians who play behind him. Billy had that lesson driven home via a difficult route.

Billy had recorded several successful country songs, including "Cross the Brazos at Waco," a cowboy tune that the public thought sounded amazingly like "El Paso," a Marty Robbins song. It used the trumpets and harmony patterns that Marty used.

Billy was defensive about the misconception. The band knew it, and broke into "El Paso" one night as Billy walked on stage.

That miffed Billy, who finished his set, but then had difficulty descending the stage, some five feet off the ground. Davis was already off the platform and pretended to want to assist Billy, as though he were making amends for having annoyed him on stage. Davis extended his arms and suggested that Billy leap into them. Billy astonished everyone by complying.

Davis was standing there with his arms full of Billy as the dazzled crowd roared. But Davis's show of kindness had been a ruse. With everyone watching he kissed Billy squarely on the lips and infuriated the macho Texan.

It's a wonder Billy didn't deck him.

All of this happened on the third night of the disastrous engagement. On the following night, Davis would shout "I love you" to Billy whenever he entered the nightclub, each time reigniting the feud.

I returned to Nashville to tell Key that he needn't bother booking me into such a glorified urinal again. I had had it with life on the road, and couldn't wait to get back to the security of life behind the microphone.

At about the same time, Jimmy Key, for whatever reason, began telling me about a songwriter who he said was the best "song idea" man he'd ever heard.

"Trouble is, he starts a song with a great idea, and then can't finish it," Key said.

Tom T. Hall would agree with that assessment of himself. He would also go on to write more hit records than any other songwriter in Nashville during the 1960s. He was blistering hot. He wrote "The Homecoming," "Harper Valley P.T.A.," and "Ballad of Forty Dollars" in two days.

Tom wrote so many good songs that it was suggested that he sing them himself, just to alleviate his backlog and get them before the public. Tom, therefore, finally agreed to record for Jerry Kennedy at Mercury Records after turning down a number of offers from other major labels.

On the other hand, Ms. Lillian Carter, the mother of the former president, told Tom before a show that his singing was terrible.

"Miss Lillian," Tom said to the First Mother, "I'm going

to break your heart," meaning she was going to love it. I personally like Tom's singing. His style is as close to a "sung narration" as anything I've heard. It forces the listener's attention, much the way Johnny Cash's voice does.

Tom's most successful composition was "Harper Valley P.T.A.," a song that sold five million copies, prompted a network television series, and launched a career that is still underway for vocalist Jeannie C. Riley. Shortly afterward, while recording for Mercury, he recorded some of the most communicative songs to ever emerge from Nashville. Hall's forte was "story songs." And the description is fitting. The narratives contained a beginning, middle, and end and were a wedding of melodies and literature. If Erskine Caldwell ever returns to the world of the living as a singer-songwriter, his name will be Tom T. Hall.

I suspect that I have interviewed Tom more than anyone else in the business, and have played more golf with him too.

During these encounters, I have heard the stories behind the stories of his "story" songs. Most are drawn from real people, such as the one entitled "The Year That Clayton Delaney Died," about a man named Lonnie Easterling, a ne'er-do-well who wanted to do nothing but pluck a guitar around Tom's rural Kentucky home. A defiant woman from Tom's childhood was the inspiration for "Harper Valley P.T.A." As a teenager, Tom was the groundskeeper at a cemetery in his native Olive Hill, Kentucky, which gave him the idea for the "Ballad of Forty Dollars," a tune about a man who is frustrated because he has to dig the grave for a man who owes him forty dollars.

Tom's second-biggest-selling composition bears the title, "Old Dogs, Children, and Watermelon Wine." It too is a true account, drawn from an encounter Tom had with an old black man who was sweeping up a cocktail lounge following a performance Tom had given at the 1972 Democratic National Convention. Tom was frustrated during the show because his sound system wouldn't work. With typical impulsiveness, he angrily gave the entire sound system away to the excited crowd, thereby stopping his show. The gift was of no use to anyone, however, because Tom gave each component to a different person.

He was winding down with a drink when, as the song says, the elderly custodian told Tom, "I turned sixty-two about eleven months ago." Tom interpreted that to mean the guy didn't have to work, as he was now eligible for Social Security benefits.

He visited with the likable codger for an hour, then got up the next morning and caught a flight to Atlanta, Georgia. En route, he wrote the song on the back of an airsick bag. (He and Jimmy Dean should invest in some stationery.) If memory serves correctly, that sack hangs on a wall today in the Country Music Hall of Fame.

Besides the stories about the creation of Tom's songs, there are also stories that have come about *because* of Tom's songs. Tom, for example, had a hit entitled "Ravishing Ruby." He has a tremendous following among children, due largely to the kids' albums he's recorded. One little girl misunderstood Tom's enunciation of "Ravishing Ruby" and insisted to her mother that Tom was singing "Radish and root beer."

The mother told this story to Tom before a show and asked him to straighten out the child, then promptly took her seat beside her youngster in the front row.

Tom ambled on stage, struck a chord, and broke into his first song, the lyrics of which went like this: "Radish and root beer." He said he could see the girl nudging her mother.

Tom, in the 1980s, became a successful writer of fiction and developed a following among other established authors, including Herman Wouk.

Once, Burl Ives was singing "Old Dogs" in performance and forgot the words in midshow. Wouk, whom no one knew was in the crowd, stood on his feet and finished the song with the band accompanying from the stage.

Hall, part of a ten-member family, came to Nashville on January 2, 1964, in a rose-colored old Cadillac and had forty-six dollars to his name. He approached his craft professionally. He reserved three hours daily for songwriting.

No matter how he felt, no matter what he had to do, no matter what he had done the night before, he would sit before a blank piece of paper and stare. Sometimes, he said, it seemed to stare back at him.

But despite his disciplined approach, he can be as mischievous as an errant child.

He told me about attending a banquet sponsored by Broadcast Music Incorporated, where he met his wife-to-be, the former Dixie Dean. He was sitting across the table from the legendary Mother Maybelle Carter, and next to her sat Dixie.

Tom had no idea then that Dixie would become his wife. But an intelligent man like Tom knew the unretractable value of a first impression. That didn't stop him.

Tom noticed Dixie was eating a baked potato.

"Is that why you are so fat?" he said to his wife-to-be. Maybelle, Tom recalled, was furious.

Tom noticed Dixie was wearing a mink stole, and a while after that, he asked her to wear it again.

"That stole was Helen Carter's," Dixie responded.

"Well, that's a helluva note," Tom snapped. "You marry somebody thinking they own a mink, and you find out they borrowed it from someone. Are those your teeth?"

To prove her teeth were real, she bit him.

The Grand Ole Opry began in 1925, and country music's popularity has been growing ever since, although at a staggered pace. I think country music got its greatest infusion of talent in the 1960s through creative men like Tom T. Hall. Tom took his craft more seriously than himself.

Tom's songs will be sung, indeed celebrated, long after the glorious life behind them is gone.

Chet Atkins once said, "If there is a genius in Nashville, it's Ray Stevens."

I agree, and will go further and say that Ray demonstrates that brilliance can be wrapped in chicanery. Ray is one of the most regimented but unpredictable people I know, if that is possible. He is a cross between General Norman Schwarzkopf and Clarabelle the Clown.

He raised the novelty song to an art form, then nurtured the art with such giant records as "The Streak," "Ahab the Arab," and "The Shriners' Convention."

As a reward for sales of "The Streak," he was given a glass replica of a nude runner. He told me he broke it when he rolled over on it in his sleep.

Ray was fuel to the flame of the "streaking" sensation that swept America in 1974. Sixteen streaking songs were recorded and went nowhere until Ray did his, which went to number one. He heard it on a Nashville radio station just one hour after he recorded it. It became a fad that at least one fan run naked through each of Ray's shows. Because the spotlight was in his eyes, Ray couldn't see the sprinters, although the practice brought great joy to members of his band, standing out of the light.

Ray has amused millions with his falsetto shrieks and unorthodox emissions on his comedy records. Often, his sounds are satiric, and people listening think the choir of voices is his band being intentionally silly. What they don't know is that almost all of the voices heard on Ray's records are his. He overdubs his own voice in several different harmonies.

Ray is also a very considerate comedian. He made a record about a Shriners' convention that was inspired by a night he spent in a hotel during a Shriners' confab. After writing and recording the song, he wouldn't release it until he was able to play it for the national president of the Shriners. He wanted to be sure the satire wouldn't offend them.

Ray came to Nashville in 1962 with a beat-up Plymouth and a U-Haul trailer. He didn't own enough, he said, to fill the trailer.

He hit the charts with "Ahab the Arab" within two months and recorded the song again years later. Because of the song's immense popularity, Ray adopted a camel as his logo. Fans from everywhere send him camels. He was going through a family album and found a photograph of himself when he was just a year old. He was holding a ball, and on the ball was a camel. Make of that what you will.

While promoting "Ahab the Arab," Ray played the Buddy Dean Show in Baltimore, Maryland. A real camel was brought onto the set. It made the exact sound that Ray had impersonated on his record. Ray said he'd never heard a camel before he made his recording and was astounded at how accurately he had mimicked the beast.

Ray is a songwriter who writes when he's inspired and when he isn't. He did the *Andy Williams Summer Show* and decided he needed a hit song to precede his weekly network television exposure. He secluded himself for three days, and emerged with "Everything Is Beautiful."

He is also among those few Nashville vocalists who will admit to having turned down a hit song. "Raindrops Keep Falling on My Head" was pitched to Ray before B. J. Thomas, who was to have a monster record with it.

"I didn't like that song because of the line about the feet being too big for the bed," he said. "Needless to say, I made a mistake there."

Another reason he declined "Raindrops" was that he had a new song, "Sunday Morning Coming Down," the Kris Kristofferson classic. Ray's version was superb, but only went to number 55 on the popularity survey. A year later, the same song would go to number one for Johnny Cash.

Ray, perhaps more than any artist I know, laughs at his foibles—even if they're serious.

He was doing a show at the Kennedy Center in Washington, where he followed Roger Williams's act. Williams had placed plywood under the piano bench. Ray couldn't see it in the dark. As he endeavored to sit down before the black-tie crowd, he tripped headlong into the piano bench and microphone. The noise sounded like a twenty-one-gun salute. He cleared his throat, readjusted himself before dignitaries, and turned to conceal his torn coat.

He created a hard act to follow for himself.

During that same engagement, he was told that Vice President Agnew might have to leave the concert early. A secret serviceman told Ray that he would signal him from the wings if Mr. Agnew decided to depart, and that Ray should stop his program. It wasn't intended that Ray should leave.

When Ray got the sign, he said, "Ladies and gentlemen, I've just been told that the vice president has to leave and I don't want him to walk out on my show."

Ray got up and left during the middle of "Everything Is Beautiful," not knowing he was expected to return. So he never did.

...28...

KEITH WHITLEY SAID HE HAD UNDERGONE A PROBLEM with drugs and alcohol, and the tone of his voice rang with understatement.

He elaborated with restraint about his afflictions on my syndicated radio show on January 11, 1989. Keith's latest song, "Don't Close Your Eyes," had just reached number one on the country charts, preceded by several in the Top Ten lists. Four months earlier, he had won the Country Music Association's Horizon Award, given for the most "promising" career in country music.

Keith was critically and commercially successful, acclaimed by publications as varied as *People* and *Rolling Stone* magazines. His act was "safe," loved by daughters and unthreatening to mothers. Yet on this day, he was risking his family image to confess to millions his former problem with controlled substances.

"I know there are people within the sound of my voice who are going through what I went through, and I want to help them," he said.

He said he had been helped, and others could be too. He was reformed and was celebrating his new life one day at a time.

Keith's physique wasn't large and yet I so admired his

candor, he seemed like a tower when he rose from his chair at the program's end. When I saw him four months later, he was horizontal, dead of an alcohol and drug overdose. An autopsy showed twenty-two ounces of alcohol and an undetermined quantity of cocaine inhabiting his lifeless frame. Death was caused by the excessive amount—and rapid ingestion—of the lethal mixture. Keith was the father of two and husband of the RCA recording star Lorrie Morgan. He was indisputably superstardom waiting to happen. He was the flesh-and-blood embodiment of a dream of a lifetime—a lifetime that ended at thirty-three.

I'm often asked about the behavior of celebrities, their finances, romantic affairs, and debaucheries. I am frequently asked about the addictions that have haunted performers throughout the history of show business.

Many people think alcohol and drug abuse is no more widespread in the entertainment business than in any other industry. It just gets more attention, they say, because of the concentrated media attention. Show business, I think, gets a bad "rap" from the press. We have no way of knowing about drug abuse outside of show business.

I don't have an answer to why substance abuse plagues our business the way drought plagues agriculture.

To this day, I think of Keith, and the senselessness of his death. His widow told me that she blamed herself. She had been on a concert tour and felt that if she hadn't been on the road, she could have prevented Keith from swallowing the fatal blend.

I told her she couldn't always be there to protect him, but she said she always had been. Then she related a story that made my blood chill. Keith, despite his boy-next-door image, had been a closet binge drinker of immense proportions.

There were folks in Nashville who knew he once had a problem. But, as the singer T. Graham Brown said through tears during a news interview the day Keith's body was found, "We all thought he had put his problems behind him."

Lorrie Morgan shivered as she told me of her endless battle to keep her husband sober.

Perhaps retelling his story here will lend the help that Keith said he wanted others to draw from his travails.

"Nobody knew how bad his drinking and drugging was," Lorrie said, "not even his closest friends. He had the entire record-buying world fooled. He was nervous, and he couldn't sleep, and I'd tell him that I would do anything to help him rest, hold him, have sex with him, or just talk to him all night, but that I wouldn't let him have a drink. And he'd fight me for it, and I wouldn't give in, and sometimes he got hostile. Real hostile.

"I found out he was hiding it around the house. I'd go to sleep, and after I did, he'd get up and sneak into the kitchen or wherever he had put his whiskey. He wouldn't want me to catch him, so he would just chug a whole bottle real quickly. I'd wake up the next morning and he would be there in bed with me, dog drunk and violently ill."

Lorrie came up with an ingenious idea. Each night, before she and Keith retired, she tied a rope from her ankle to his. She literally bound him to her. If Keith even tried to turn over, the tug on her leg woke her up.

There they lay in the late winter of 1988, both of them holders of national number-one records, held together by a knotted and braided cord that held drunkenness at bay. Many times, Lorrie said, she would be awakened in the wee hours by Keith's shaking hand fumbling under the covers with her cumbersome knots. He was trying to go from the bondage of a rope to the bondage of a bottle. The addiction of this meteoric star, not yet in midlife, was desperately advanced.

Lorrie was at her wits' end—wanting to help the man she loved but wanting to keep his secret from a trusting and admiring public. It was a quandary that nearly broke her down before it killed Keith.

There is always mass mourning among the country music community whenever one of its members dies. Keith's funeral was held a few days before Memorial Day, 1989. The tribute continued two weeks later when Larry Gatlin performed a Whitley song on my national television show. The applause had hardly subsided when I was told by a production crew member that Lorrie Morgan was on the telephone.

I put her live on the air.

She thanked Larry, and then the set grew silent. I realized that millions of viewers were waiting for me to say something profound to the grieving widow but the only thing I could think of was that I could think of nothing to say.

I had been to the funeral home, and had vicariously visited death's edge many times with friends in the business— a business peopled by the reckless. I was simultaneously sad for, and furious at, Keith Whitley. I told Lorrie and the listeners that I had no more comments, and we went to a commercial break. It was one of the few times in forty years of broadcasting that I was speechless.

Addiction within the ranks of country music has made hilarious stories. There have been countless times I've had to laugh, to keep from crying—or cussing—over men and women whose talents have been honed inside lives in disarray.

I think of Johnny Paycheck. In the late 1970s he had an enormous hit, a blue-collar anthem titled "Take This Job and Shove It."

In October, 1978, Paycheck, whose real name is Donald Lytle, was recording an interview for my syndicated radio show. I don't know if he was high, or if it was just that he had spent so much of his life that way. He couldn't sit still. His restlessness was clearly unnatural. He never left his chair, but he kept weaving nervously from right to left. His upper torso swung like an inverted pendulum. I fully expected him to swing himself out of his seat. I was using a directional microphone, and each time Paycheck's sway took him two or three feet from it, his voice faded on the air.

Listeners could hear my questions, then hear his response in a volume that—to them—seemed to rise and fall mysteriously.

The engineer had a terrible time trying to maintain voice level. He had to turn the microphone setting up and down in coordination with Paycheck's movements. In engineers' terms, he had to "ride the gain."

During commercials, the engineer would run out of his booth, tell me his problems, and ask me to keep Paycheck steady in his chair.

I put up with that all during the session. I'm sure Johnny doesn't remember his behavior. I'd be surprised if he even remembers the show.

As long as I'm discussing chemical abuse, let me recall an incident that happened years earlier.

I had played a new Johnny Cash record and commented on the air that I thought the song was unworthy of John's talents. That's all I said.

Cash had been riding around town listening to my show on his car radio. Within minutes, he came crashing through my studio door while I was on the air. His clothes were wrinkled, his odor was foul, his eyes were glazed, and one foot was bare. This was the man who would eventually be the host of his own prime-time variety show on ABC from 1968 through 1972.

I was staring at him, this unorthodox persona, and that's why I didn't see his flying boot. He had removed it before entering the studio, intending to throw it at me for panning his new record. And he did.

The thing hit the wall with the thud of a muffled cannon. Listeners thought there had been gunfire in the studio.

Johnny's mind might have been altered, but his throwing arm was not. He missed, barely, with two pounds of sharp-toed footwear. Soon afterward, he was arrested trying to cross the border from Mexico with hundreds of amphetamines.

Johnny has made no secret of his recurring problem with chemical dependency. He voluntarily checked himself into a rehabilitation center as recently as 1990, then came onto my show to announce that he had done it.

*   *   *

I have been privy to the goofy self-humiliation of booze-swilling, pill-taking, cocaine-sniffing entertainers for years.

I was the emcee on a 1966 tour with an up-and-coming singer, Waylon Jennings, Bob Luman, and the hottest country star of the day, Faron Young.

Country stars had more mystique then than they do today. They usually could not be seen on television programming, as there were only a handful of syndicated shows. Most country music fans could only imagine what their musical heroes looked like. It was a big deal when their favorite singers came to town for live concerts. They put the faces together with the voices.

On Easter Sunday in 1966, I was on the road with the Hank Williams, Jr., show in Asheville, North Carolina.

Faron Young, with a string of hit records spanning two decades, was so popular that, despite limited television exposure, people began to buzz when, shortly after noon, we walked into a restaurant. They recognized him from photographs they had ordered by the ton from radio stations. We had driven all night from Charleston, South Carolina, and had gone directly to the restaurant from the bus. We were unshaven, wrinkled, smelly—and Faron was drunk.

Imagine a travel-weary troupe of hillbilly entertainers walking into a midwestern restaurant where people were wearing their Easter Sunday finery. A lot of folks were staring but I don't think it was entirely due to our popularity.

Faron has a reputation for behaving "peculiarly" when drinking. His mouth gets as foul as his voice is loud. I could see the buildup of an alcohol-induced rage beneath his reddening face. In the crowded restaurant, he no doubt sensed his nonconformity. About that time, an incredibly beautiful woman floated across the room. She had a radiance that preceded her, as she endeavored to leave the restaurant. Her six-foot-two-inch husband was in tow.

In a show of mock chivalry, Faron began to tease.

"Let me open the door for you, pretty lady!" Faron said,

and he did a bow from the waist worthy of a Shakespearean actor.

The woman gulped. The man told Faron to get lost.

"I'll whip your ass!" Faron told the towering man. Faron is only five feet nine inches tall, so his words were spoken into the underside of the man's chin.

The woman took her husband's arm and quietly said, "Let's go."

The two left the restaurant, and what could have been an unpleasant disruption of an Easter Sunday was tactfully averted. (I've always thought that, for whatever reason, God protects children and Faron Young.)

Not all the misbehavior I've seen is caused by addiction. We work in a very high-pressure business and sometimes have to blow off steam willfully, with no booze to blame the tantrum on. Not everyone in show business who occasionally gets drunk is an alcoholic. Not everyone has a sad tale to tell.

Red Foley's story, on the other hand, was one of the most tragic. In these pages I've related tales dealing with outrageous behavior, much of it self-destructive. I can think of none, however, more sad than that of the man called the "Bing Crosby of country music."

Foley had been host to ABC Television's successful *Ozark Jubilee* from Springfield, Missouri. Giants such as Patti Page and Rosemary Clooney were his guests in the 1950s. He had been a brilliant star on the Grand Ole Opry stage. His recording of "Peace in the Valley" became a Gospel music standard and he had a string of hits—"Chattanooga Shoe Shine Boy" and others that were household words as 1950s America shifted its broadcast priorities from radio to television. Red was a bona fide, international star.

No one in show business, however, stays on top forever. Even the tenured giants, such as Sinatra, the remaining Beatles, and the late Elvis, who retain their colossal popularity, now induce only a fraction of the frenzy they inspired at their peaks.

Red Foley had a harder time handling his diminished stardom than anyone I've ever met. The fact that he could no longer pack them in got into his mind—and he got into a bottle.

The hardest thing for me to observe isn't the pain-filled struggle of young entertainers coming up, but the unavoidable tumble of veteran showmen going down.

Red Foley hit bottom with the force of the one-man empire he was. He went in and out of several Nashville detoxification centers.

I had been doing the all-night show for five years when Red popped into the studio. He was drunk.

I considered not putting him on the air but was concerned that I might offend a legend. I was also afraid he might make a fool of himself. Besides, there were only a handful of major country stars in 1959, and there certainly wasn't a surplus of network television stars who visited my show.

I tried an interview. It was a disaster.

Red, at the time, was being considered for the lead in a television adaptation of *Mr. Smith Goes to Washington*. I asked him about the upcoming series, thinking he would plug his show. Red was melting into his seat. His every word was slurred. I suddenly felt guilty, as if I were a co-conspirator in a legend's self-destruction.

But I pressed on. One of my interview techniques is, whenever an interviewee begins to fall flat, to talk about something with which he is intimately familiar. I decided I could save the situation by bringing up Red's longtime performing partner on the *Ozark Jubilee*, his comic sidekick Uncle Sipe Brasfield, brother to legendary Grand Ole Opry comic Rod Brasfield.

"Well Red, how's Uncle Sipe?" I said cheerfully.

There was a long pause.

Red's eyes began to film over.

"You know," he said, "when *Mr. Smith Goes to Washington* came up, they didn't want Uncle Sipe to be a part of it. They only wanted Red Foley!"

He shouted his own name, and even the most inattentive of listeners could tell Red was furious and out of it.

The remark was clearly disparaging, and totally out of

character. Remember, this is an industry whose members didn't talk negatively about each other then. I thought to myself that Uncle Sipe would be brokenhearted.

Red Foley was making an ass of himself on my show.

"Red, it's good to see you," I said, and I turned off his microphone. He was still babbling when I went to a thirty-minute side of Hank Thompson's "Live at the Golden Nugget."

I gave Red's road manager the sign to get him out of my studio, and I sat there in the dark listening to the festive sounds of partygoers on a live album recorded half a nation away.

I thought long and hard—for days—about what I had done. I wondered to myself about my apparent insolence.

I got my chance to make amends, but that too turned into disaster.

I didn't see Red Foley again until shortly after President John F. Kennedy was assassinated. On a flight layover in Washington, I visited Kennedy's grave and had just returned to the airport when I ran into Red.

It was midmorning, Red's road manager was trying to read, and Red was trying to stand, visibly drunk.

As I approached the legend reduced to a disheveled man, I noticed that Red's trouser fly was open. His white shirt was protruding from the zipper. He looked like a standup comedian playing a drunk. I didn't laugh. Neither did the hurrying Washingtonians who paused to stare in disbelief.

I stuck my hand well in front of me as I approached Red. I walked right up to his face, put my mouth against his ear, and said, "Red, your fly is open."

Red, who had one of the most powerful baritone voices I've ever heard, said, "It is? My fly is open? You say my fly is open?! I'll fix that right now!"

Standing in the middle of an aisle, Red made a conspicuous production of adjusting himself. For an instant, I wondered if he was going to drop his trousers. He attracted a great deal of attention, and people began to laugh, not with him, but at him, and he was too out of it to even know.

I asked Red to join me for a cup of coffee. I sure thought

he could use one. A waitress recognized him, and he couldn't do enough for her. He was that flattered. Someone later said he thought Red was ready to blow off his show just to stay in the presence of someone who supplied the admiration he craved so strongly.

Red was perhaps the most suave emcee in the history of country music. He could bring entertainers on and offstage with a grace that surpassed many of their talents. In 1963, Red was the master of ceremonies on a package show in South Carolina starring the young singer Bobby Bare, whose career was smoking hot because of "Detroit City" and "Miller's Cave." Bobby was scheduled to close the show, and it was hard on Red not to be the headliner. It was hard on Bare, getting top billing over a true musical legend. He was obsessed with impressing Red Foley, who had sung only a few songs in-between bringing other acts on and off the platform.

Foley gave a riveting introduction to Bare, who walked into the spotlight as the house shook with deafening applause.

As Bare approached the microphone, he later told me, Red spoke into his ear.

"Bobby," he said, "they used to applaud for me like that."

Staggered by what Red had just said to him, Bare did two encores, though he paid little attention to his own lyrics. At the show's end, he hurried backstage, searching for the one-time master. Bare told me he was looking for something to say to Red, and couldn't wait to hear what Red had to say about him and his singing. But by this time Red had long since left the auditorium.

He hadn't heard Bare sing a note.

... 29 ...

THERE ARE FEW BEINGS ON THIS EARTH MORE LOYAL THAN some country music fans.

More than twenty-four thousand people attended the 1991 Fan Fair, an annual, week-long mixer of fans and celebrities held in Nashville each July. People drive thousands of miles, wait in long lines to dine in the restaurants, and stand in even longer lines in the sweltering southern summer to get the autographs of the singers they enjoy.

Two fans stood on a concrete floor for nine hours to get Randy Travis's signature. Country music fans feel strongly that they are a part of the star's family. Rock fans write letters and buy souvenirs and recordings, and country fans obviously do so as well. But country fans take this devotion a step further and make it more personal. Some write to their idols reciting personal problems and seeking intimate advice. Others send gifts and get-well cards. Still others name their children after the stars. Many involve themselves in their favorite singers' private lives.

Shortly after Reba McEntire's separation from her first husband, she was inundated with letters tendering advice for the lovelorn. After her divorce was granted, she received bundles of letters from women telling her she had done the wrong thing and that they were disappointed in her for not sticking by her man. They had regarded her as an example of marital fidelity and loyalty, they said, and she had sorely disappointed them. One woman even told Reba she had no right to get a divorce.

Ronnie Milsap said the most measurable input he ever received during his early career came at the autograph table after his concerts. Fans told him in no uncertain terms what they liked, and didn't like, about his show.

Obviously, not everyone who listens to country music is so straightforward. But there are people who seem to feel no remorse for frankness because, in their minds, family talks frankly to family.

Some fans ask stars for money. I suspect there is not a successful singer in Nashville whose mail doesn't include stories of need and pleas for help. When Loretta Lynn was just beginning to hit it big, recollections of her own past poverty were still vivid in her mind. Her managers caught her slipping hundred-dollar bills to people who approached her after concerts with hard-luck stories.

This is unusual on the surface and even more so in motivation. These fans ask for personal attention and help, not because they are irresponsible but because in their minds they are convinced they would help the star if the needs were reversed and they had the means. There isn't much that country fans wouldn't do for the luminaries they admire.

Tom T. Hall has remarked upon the speed with which some country fans will shift from courtesy to verbal abusiveness. The fan wants to buy a star a drink one minute, then scolds him the next, the way brothers or sisters will spontaneously change the tone of their conversations.

One of the worst examples I ever saw of this was in Las Vegas in 1968. Buck Owens was recording a live album at the Mint Hotel and had asked me to be the record's emcee. We were taking a break and a woman noticed Owens easing toward the backstage door.

As Owens tried to walk past her en route to some fresh air, she approached him. "Oh, Buck," she exclaimed, "I've got all of your records. I think you're wonderful.

You're the best entertainer I've ever seen and I can't tell you how much you mean to me.''

Owens thanked her politely and walked past.

The producer, Ken Nelson, runs a tight production ship and told the cast we had five minutes for a break. We knew he meant it. In Las Vegas, many high-paid unions are used in shows and schedules are taken very seriously.

As Owens and I headed back toward the stage and the resumption of recording, we again encountered his admirer.

''Oh, Buck, I want your autograph, will you please sign this for me?''

''I'll be glad to,'' said Buck, ''but I can't until after I finish this recording. I have to get back to the stage right now so we don't run overtime.''

''Why you son of a bitch! I wouldn't have your damn autograph!'' she yelled and bolted out, turning off as quickly as she had turned on her alleged love.

Some fans also take quite literally the songs that stars sing. They don't realize that the singer is merely trying to entertain and think he or she is confessing through music.

Ronnie Milsap has been married to his only wife, Joyce, for twenty-six years. He doesn't drink but he is a major music publisher who encounters what he thinks are good songs about infidelity or drinking.

''I can't record those tunes,'' he said, ''because some of the fans think you really mean it when you sing about that stuff.''

Barbara Mandrell had the same experience years ago when she recorded ''Married, but Not to Each Other,'' ''If Loving You Is Wrong, I Don't Want to Be Right,'' and other songs about adultery.

This doesn't mean that country fans are simpleminded. It just means that some of them are incredibly trusting, the way, again, that family is of family.

Family is often possessive of family, and once again, country fans are no exception. There has been a proliferation of publications covering country music because fans have an insatiable desire to know everything about the stars. The supermarket tabloids have expanded their country music coverage to rival Hollywood's. Some fans will ask the most personal questions, and sometimes expect me to do the same thing during interviews. I believe in candid interviews, but there are places where I draw the line.

I refuse to ask anyone about his or her sexual persuasion and I won't ask about divorce.

I think sexuality is totally personal and none of anyone else's business. There have always been rumors in show business about people who may be homosexual but I refuse to pass them along, even in private conversations.

Such information could ruin a career in country music with its emphasis on conservative, traditional values.

I won't discuss divorce because it's often simply too painful. I speak from personal experience.

Jeannie C. Riley once did my radio show a few hours after her longtime marriage ended. I could tell she was uneasy, to put it mildly, and I thought that her discomfort was more than just fatigue or stress.

I didn't know about the divorce until the program's end and insisted that she should have told me, and we would have postponed the interview. I can report, happily, that Jeannie and Mickey Riley have since remarried.

Buck Owens appeared on one of my shows the day after his three-day marriage to fiddle-player Jana Jay ended.

He walked into the studio, sat down, and said, "Hi Ralph, I just got a divorce. Want to talk about it?"

I said we could if he wanted to, and he went on about it for some time over the radio airwaves as nonchalantly as he would discuss a haircut.

Roy Nichols is a legendary country guitarist who played for years for Merle Haggard. Many Decembers, Nichols got a divorce. By January, his life would be back in repair.

Haggard wrote a number-one song entitled, "If We Make It Through December." The song is about the economic stress on an unemployed father at Christmas. I thought it was inspired by the gasoline crunch in 1973 and 1974 but it was actually inspired by Nichols one December when he got through the Christmas season without getting a divorce.

The curiosity some country fans express about the personal lives of singers has bred press coverage that is nothing less than meddlesome. When George Jones was unsuccessfully fighting alcoholism, the press wouldn't get off his back. I remember an incident wherein a policeman tailed Jones as he left a bar, and a television camera crew tailed the cop.

The officer nailed Jones on Franklin Road and of course asked him to step out of his car. He ordered Jones to throw his head back and put his finger on his nose. Meanwhile, a television camera recorded the whole thing. The tape showed up as news footage and the images were lifted for photographs that hit the newswire services. Jones was fighting a life-threatening problem and the press showed him no mercy.

I think it was wrong the way the press swarmed over Waylon Jennings when he was busted for cocaine in the late 1970s. Such things are public record, and the public has a First Amendment right to know. But it's too often taken too far.

Who among us hasn't had financial difficulties at some time inside an inflationary United States economy? The stress of that is sufficient unto itself. The press compounded the misery in the last year for Tammy Wynette, Dottie West, and Willie Nelson. Personal finances, especially, aren't matters for public discussion. Imagine having your financial statements and bank balances published for all the world to see. I suppose it is the price we pay for being in show business.

The media pursue these issues because some of the fans want it. I think it's an invasion of privacy and just plain old-fashioned rudeness. On the other hand, nothing can jerk away a pedestal of arrogance faster than a country fan. The fans provide a check and balance to the egos of stars. It's a service most country personalities, including me, occasionally need.

MEMORIES

I'll never forget being an emcee for a package show in Indianapolis with Dave Dudley, Webb Pierce, Mel Tillis, and Faron Young.

I walked offstage and into a men's room in the lobby. I was standing before a urinal and a guy next to me had a hot dog in one hand and his manhood in the other. He was chewing with his mouth open, and looked my way. I don't know what the moral is of that story, except that I was too revolted to talk to him.

In the hallway, a little boy approached me. He held his autograph book behind his back and said, "Hey, can I have your autograph? Ain't you somebody?"

I told him I wasn't famous, but there were a lot of famous people on the show who would sign their names for him.

The lowest example of a fan's boldness I ever heard involves Anne Murray. She was seated in a public restroom and a faceless voice in the next stall suddenly said, "What is Mac Davis really like?"

I don't know if she answered. Then a hand bearing a blank sheet of paper extended from the adjacent stall, under the wall, and into Anne's area, near her feet.

"May I have your autograph?" the fan said. Anne never saw the woman's face. She told me she refused to sign. Today, Anne blows the story off as a lark and is amused by it.

There is something else about this phenomenal and paradoxical personality called "the country music fan" that many entertainers often forget. Many fans want to be entertainers. Some live their lives vicariously through their musical heroes.

Before Keith Whitley died of an alcohol and drug overdose, he told me that he began his abuse as a teenager. In his immature, adolescent mind, he thought he had to do that to become a country star.

One could go to a Dolly Parton concert in the 1970s and see women in the audience with big blonde wigs and sequins on their clothes.

Elvis Presley was an indisputable factor in the sale of black leather jackets in the 1950s.

There are other examples of fans wanting to be stars to the point of obvious emulation.

Country celebrities sometimes have to be protective of the fans to whom they are unwilling role models. They forget how many people are fascinated with celebrities and show business, and would do anything to be a part of it. Show business is more business than show for most of us in it. It's a hard, pressure-filled job, but many fans, falsely, see it as perpetual excitement.

I had a firsthand lesson in this aspect in 1968 when a fellow who played the spoons appeared on my local television show. I thought the appearance was a lighthearted affair that would give everyone, including the performer, a kick. The spoons, after all, are a fun instrument whose mastery isn't exactly comparable to playing a harpsichord.

I didn't know the spoons player thought being on my show was an enormous deal. In his mind, I later learned, it represented his big career break. He had come to town from Atlanta to appear on television in Nashville, Tennessee, and hopefully get a recording contract from an entertainment executive.

Before coming on the program he had quit his job. He thought he would no longer need conventional employment in the wake of his "discovery." He had been given a farewell party by friends who gave him congratulatory gifts for having made it in show business. He was, they cheered, going all the way to the *Ralph Emery Show*.

To me, he was another act on still another show.

The man did his thing, I told him I enjoyed it, he signed the necessary paperwork to be paid, left the studio, and I never saw him again. The accounting department contacted me several months later to tell me the check that had been sent to the spoons player had come back via return mail several times.

The man returned home from the big break that never happened to live among friends he was too embarrassed to face. Had I known he quit his job to come to Nashville, I would have suggested that he take another job in Music City and hang around waiting for a break. I would have used him on my show a few more times to augment his income and increase his exposure. I had no idea how serious he was about show business and I would never hear it from him. A few days after his disappointing debut, he committed suicide.

...30...

THERE IS SOMETHING MAGICAL ABOUT THE SOUTH WHEN it snows.

A White Christmas seals the sentiment of the season wherever it happens, but especially below the Mason-Dixon Line, where it's a rarity. Snowfall during the last week of December will transform the holiday mood from frantic to spiritual. The mineral-rich earth that drinks in sunshine most of the year is given a rest. There is peace under the snow for the dirt of Dixie. Similarly, the people rest.

On the last Friday before Christmas, 1990, Joy and I drove through spitting snow en route to the Fannie Battle Day Home in Nashville. Accumulations of up to three inches, a veritable blizzard in Nashville, were forecast. Travelers on Nashville's crowded interstates hoped the traffic-clogging precipitation would never fall and couldn't wait until it did. For the hurried and overworked, snowfall is December's favorite dread.

We pulled into the home and the newspaper and television reporters awaited us as they had for nineteen years, the length of time we've been entertaining the children, ages eleven and under. They can attend Fannie Battle if their mothers are employed or in school. The minimal tuition is based on income. The majority of those who attend the school are from economically modest backgrounds. Some are hardship cases.

I am accompanied on my annual sojourn to the school by entertainers, including singers, magicians, clowns, and other headliners. Tom T. Hall, after recording a children's album for Mercury Records, once took his entire band to the school. Joy and I give each child presents and cash. The afternoon is fun for them, fulfilling for us.

I'll be returning with a special program in December 1991, date of the school's hundredth Christmastime.

As a child, I never attended Fannie Battle, but I grew up in its neighborhood. I might have gone to it, but my mother couldn't afford day care, not even when it was pro-rated according to parental income. I empathize with those kids.

Success in the country music world after a childhood of poverty is not a unique situation. There are few in my industry from an Ivy League background. The childhood poverty of legends such as Johnny Cash and Dolly Parton is common knowledge. It's as if childhood deprivation is a prerequisite to becoming a country star, as is evident in the new crop of budding superstars, such as heartthrob Clint Black, a former construction worker and high school drop-out from Texas; Ricky Van Shelton, a former common laborer from rural Virginia, and Alan Jackson, who, for three years, worked in the mailroom at the Nashville Network before hitting celebrity pay dirt.

There is always a background near the soil among those who sing from the soul. Compacting a life of fifty-eight years into a few hundred paragraphs has been difficult. I've tried to guess who and what you would have me talk about. There were times, no doubt, when my guesses were wrong. It is hard to summarize a life and career when neither is over. Although this is my first book, I hope it won't be my last. Someday perhaps we'll meet again in new pages that are the pulp and paper milestones of my life.

The expected snowfall didn't materialize during that last, pre-Christmas weekday. Joy and I joined a bevy of country music luminaries that night at a regal holiday festivity attended by, among others, Minnie Pearl, Eddy Arnold, renowned record producer Billy Sherill, Marty Robbins, Jr., and country music publisher Buddy Killen, at whose estate the party was held.

The collective wealth of the approximately one hundred guests measured in the millions of dollars. Most of those people had spent many comfortable Christmases and yet each guest, I'd venture, could recall a leaner Yuletide. That recollection, next to country music itself, might be our greatest bond.

It was an hour's drive, largely along darkened, two-lane roads, from the gala to my house. Cruising the frozen countryside, listening to the soft buzz of the car heater, I pondered my weekday, morning television show, how much I loved it, and how much I loved getting to sleep in Saturday morning.

I crawled into bed, turned out the light, and thought about my wonderful friends who might still be at the party—and about the special children of Fannie Battle, whose Christmas shebang had been over for hours. I suspected it was still underway in their minds, during the first night of dreams that will recur for the rest of their lives—or until they come true—as mine did for me.

* * *

"Mr. Whitehurst, let's go home!"

Epilogue

After the hardcover publication of MEMORIES, I asked Barbara Mandrell to give me her honest opinion of my book, since I knew that she was incapable of false flattery.

She praised the work and pointed out two mistakes. I wish to correct them now.

I had written that Barbara returned to work one year after her near-fatal automobile wreck. It actually took her seventeen months and seventeen days to recover. I also wrote that Henry Cannon and his wife, Sarah Cannon (Minnie Pearl), nearly crashed in a twin-engine airplane. It was a single-engine aircraft.

I also mistakenly reported that the plane crash that killed Patsy Cline occurred in 1964. It happened in 1963.

Don Imus, a morning radio host at WFAN in New York City, pointed out mistakes concerning the Bobby Thompson home run that decided the early 1950s pennant race between the Brooklyn Dodgers and New York Giants. The game was played on a Wednesday, the bases were not loaded, and there were not two outs.

So my autobiography contained those errors, not so terrible considering the book covers 58 years recorded in about 90,000 words.

* * *

A lot happened in 1991 that I was unable to address in my autobiography because the manuscript had gone into production, so I'd like to share some updates with the reader.

In June, one month after I finished writing the entry on Minnie Pearl, she suffered a debilitating stroke. Reading the newspaper account, I wondered how much Minnie, then 79, could endure. She had already undergone breast removal, chemotherapy and radiation treatments.

Against all admonitions, she went on a performance tour in the spring to celebrate her fiftieth year as a member of the Grand Ole Opry. She had just played Detroit with Willard Scott from NBC's *Today Show* and told me later how thrilled she was to have worked with him. Her previous show had been in Houston at the invitation of President Bush.

She returned to Nashville to collapse.

The left side of her body was paralyzed.

I am hard pressed to count the number of times I've visited Minnie Pearl. In the past few years, I saw her most frequently when she was a Friday night performer on *Nashville Now*. I, along with millions of fans, miss her appearances tremendously.

I wasn't able to see Minnie after her stroke until she left the hospital; the doctors had ordered tight security at the medical center and I didn't want to violate any rules.

When I was finally able to visit Minnie at her home, I was shaken. I've seen Minnie hold thousands of admirers in the palm of her hand. The day I visited her, she couldn't hold her head upright and she couldn't walk at all.

The stroke left her throat muscles paralyzed and she became dehydrated because she could barely swallow. On Christmas Day, she was readmitted to the hospital, suffering dehydration and low blood pressure.

The woman who had looked into blinding spotlights around the world now lay on her back looking into Nashville's gray and brooding sky on New Year's Day. She could not move her head from the pillow.

Minnie tells me she feels imprisoned, that her room is a cell; her bars, the window frame.

When Minnie is in her wheelchair, her head sags downward and to the right, and her chin rests on her chest. The therapists tell her to hold her head upright and she tries, but she says the effort gives her a headache.

"But I've got to do it!" she asserts, a sign of determination that pleases me considerably.

I took Jimmy Dean to see Minnie in August of 1991. He was accompanied by Donna Meade, his fiance. Dean teased and baited Minnie, and she hoisted a glass of Maker's Mark bourbon with him.

Dean and Ms. Meade sang an a cappella and impromptu version of "Have I Told You Lately That I Love You?" Minnie smiled, but her husband was overcome by emotion and had to leave the room. I just felt warm inside.

Minnie's doctor tells me that Minnie's greatest wish is to go onstage one more time. She would like to make her comeback on *Nashville Now*. She said to me, "But you don't have anybody on in wheelchairs, do you?" The question broke my heart.

I told her that we could pick her up and seat her in a regular chair, if she liked. For that matter, she could have my host's chair; it doesn't matter where she sits, Minnie Pearl is the all-time queen of country comedy. A queen sits where she wants.

A joyous occasion in 1991 was the fall wedding of Donna Meade and Jimmy Dean. I was best man.

I have seen Dean perform live in Las Vegas. I've seen him do live, network television before millions of people. I've seen him under all kinds of stressful situations, but I've never seen him as nervous as he was thirty minutes before his marriage to Donna.

We were walking down a brick pathway approaching the guests. Dean looked like he had swallowed vinegar. His demeanor was entirely somber, and I felt it was my job to lift his spirits for what was supposed to be a festive occasion. But nothing I said worked.

His reluctant footsteps echoed on the bricks as if he were walking to his execution, not his nuptials. I didn't know what else to say to prompt a smile so I gave it one last shot.

"Dean," I said, "you look great, but you have a hard-on and I think it's showing."

Bingo!

Dean's countenance cracked just as the guests turned to see the groom. Everyone thought he was smiling so broadly at the thought of matrimony.

The country music world lost three good friends in 1991. The first was Dottie West.

Dottie had been hospitalized in July, after she drove her car into a rock wall on her way to an appearance on the Grand Ole Opry. It was to have been her first appearance on the Opry since her much publicized financial woes.

We all felt so sorry for Dottie in her final years. Due to bad investments, she lost everything she had, including a six-bedroom, 18,000-square-foot mansion, and wound up in an apartment after sleeping a couple of nights in a used car.

Federal officials got wind that Dottie was hiding some of her personal property from a bankruptcy court, and raided a storage locker. Virtually everything they found was sold at an auction held during the Country Music Association's annual Fan Fair. Furs, furniture, career souvenirs, tubes of lipstick, and irreplaceable items of sentimentality, such as Crayola drawings done by her children when they were young, were all up for bidding.

The trophies of almost six decades of life were gone in the slam of an auctioneer's gavel. Dottie had played Dallas the night before, but oddly wanted to be in Nashville to see her most personal possessions fall into the hands of bidding strangers. Some bought her artifacts and then selfishly asked her to autograph them. She complied.

A lot of folks thought Dottie's presence was an exercise in masochism. I wanted to ask her why she chose to be present during her blackest hour, but never got the chance.

Dottie had asked me to send a Nashville Network film crew to the auction to record the injustice. I later found out that a crew from *Crook and Chase* was going, so I let them cover the ordeal.

During the auction, Dottie occasionally retired to a car parked in the 100-degree heat, and she couldn't run the air conditioner while she tried to sleep, for fear of asphyxiation. She'd toss and turn on the front seat, then re-enter the auction house with her mascara streaked from the combination of sweat and tears.

The fans kept bidding for her things and physically pulled at her. Outside the building, balloons and hamburgers were sold amid the distorted sound of recorded country music. Conspicuously absent from the repertoire were her own songs with Jimmy Dean, Jim Reeves, and Kenny Rogers. No Dottie West solos were played either.

Everyone at the auction was there to prey on a woman whose music had entertained and soothed much of the record-buying world. Dottie's "fans" that day were largely people she had never previously met. Some, between casting lots for her property, would tell her how much they had always loved her. They nearly "loved" her into a nervous breakdown.

The black cloud that hung over Dottie West in the last years of her life finally settled on August 30, 1991, when she was running late for an Opry appearance. Her car stalled on a Nashville thoroughfare, and she must have felt she had no time to call a taxi.

She accepted a ride with a stranger. Reports later indicated that the eighty-one-year-old driver suffered from impaired night vision. His car veered off an interstate exit ramp and a Nashville newspaper reported that the vehicle was airborne for seventy-two feet.

After the accident, Dottie fought for life for five days, during which she was given thirty-five pints of blood.

I went to her funeral with Larry Gatlin and his wife, Janis. Sitting nearby were June and Johnny Cash. The church was dotted with other celebrities. Steve Wariner, who began his recording career through the efforts of Dottie West, sang "Amazing Grace."

The casket was closed, and the sanctuary dripped with lavish floral wreaths. The minister gave a eulogy that was laced with cliches, saying precious little about Dottie except that she had come into the world as Dorothy Marie Marsh.

Then her body was taken perhaps a hundred miles to her home of McMinneville, Tennessee, where she was given a modest graveside ceremony attended only by members of her family.

The federal government and other creditors who had hounded Dottie West—the first female country singer ever to win a Grammy Award—never got their bounty.

Dottie West had been born in a shack and reached her mansion. She earned millions of dollars giving thirty years of priceless entertainment. She died broke—and not even a tombstone adorns her grave.

Tennessee Ernie Ford died on October 17, 1991. He had become ill after a visit to the White House to see President Bush. Ernie's son had said that his father was recovering nicely in a Washington hospital, but two days later he died. It took me by surprise.

I played an old Ernie Ford radio interview in the wake of his death. Ernie told me on that show that the handle "Tennessee" was merely ad-libbed as a farewell to a radio audience. "This is old Tennessee Ernie Ford," he had said, and signed off. The name stuck forever.

I had forgotten that he had recorded "Sixteen Tons" just as a filler song for an album and the "B" side of a single. He chose the tune after performing it on his network television show in the 1950s. It went over well with the studio audience, so he thought it would do okay for a record.

It sold a million copies within the week, and became by far the biggest record he ever had.

I recalled how he joined that seventy-five-member cast in February 1990, for the *All-Star Salute to Ralph Emery*. Ernie decided he would sing "Sixteen Tons" on the show, but modify the lyrics. He wrote the new words on the plane en route to the rehearsal.

He was so proud of his revisions that he called Barbara Mandrell from the lounge telephone of the aircraft, flying at 30,000 feet, and sang the new lyrics to her.

When he finished, passengers around him erupted into applause.

People like Johnny Cash and Merle Haggard are called country music crusaders because they took the music to a wider audience in the 1960s. But the late Red Foley and Tennessee Ernie Ford are one ahead of them. They took the music to network television in the 1950s.

And they took an irreplaceable part of country music with them when they passed away.

The veteran Grand Ole Opry announcer and my former WSM associate, Grant Turner, died two days after Ernie Ford. Grant's death on October 19th came during his forty-seventh year on the Opry. Grant worked the *Friday Night Opry* until midnight and passed away before daylight Saturday.

Shortly after I went to work at WSM thirty-five years ago, I began to affectionately call Grant the "pack rat." It was a nickname given to him by T. Tommy Cutrer and me because Grant came in every morning with a thermos bottle, mail, a box of cookies, three or four long-play albums, and four or five 45-rpm single records.

He looked like an attic with legs.

I never heard Grant Turner say an unkind word about anybody. I never heard him utter a profanity. He was everybody's grandfather, and every day was a family reunion.

And, just as in the cases involving the passing of my other friends, I was surprised at what I recalled about Grant.

He practiced tunnel vision more than any announcer I've ever known. He would focus on the copy before him, and read into the microphone with unfaltering concentration. It was impossible to distract him—until one day.

Grant was reading the 4 A.M. headlines as usual. There

was a girl in the studio who made her rounds regularly, so I asked if she would help me play a joke on Grant and, after hearing what I had in mind, she complied.

"Grant is going to be here in a minute," I told her. "He is going to sit right there with his head down and read the news. I want you to sit right here."

I positioned her strategically, wanting Grant to be able to see only her knees as he scrutinized the text in front of him.

Grant came into the studio, laid aside all of his baggage, and then methodically began to read the news. It was so routine for him, I doubt he even listened to himself.

Suddenly, I cleared my throat loudly and it leaked into his microphone. Grant's eyes jolted upward and as they did, I jerked the woman's dress up to her waist. The legendary Grant Turner, dean of WSM and Opry announcers, was speechless and couldn't resume reading the headlines.

Instead he fumbled, cleared his throat, and played a record.

Grant Turner was responsible for the radio popularity of a couple of major recording artists. He introduced me to the comedy of Jerry Clower and I began to play it on my all-night show. This first air play established Clower's career.

Grant also turned me onto Brother Windy Bagwell, a gospel artist who recorded some novelty tunes that did well.

When Grant turned sixty-five he faced compulsory retirement from the Opry by its owner, then the National Life and Accident Insurance Company. But the Board of Directors voted to make an exception for Grant, and allowed him to remain at the Opry.

I was glad about that. I think it allowed him to live fourteen more years.

I want to acknowledge Norm Frazier, more popularly known to viewers of *Nashville Now* as "The Killer."

"The Killer" has been a part of *Nashville Now* since it

went on the air in March 1982. He rarely speaks a line of dialogue. Mostly he stands behind me when I go into the studio audience and hands out gifts to the people I've interviewed.

He rarely smiles, shows little expression, and reminds me of a mannequin. But he is a fixture of the set, and if he misses a single night, the fans want to know where he is.

He is country music's answer to the mute guy on the Bartles and Jaymes commercials. He looks so quietly comical, dressed in his impeccable finery, while handing out flamboyant tee-shirts, the likes of which I'll bet he's never worn in his life.

In the first edition of this book I discussed my morning television show, which I did intermittently in Nashville for twenty-eight years. There won't be a twenty-ninth. I quit the program the day after Thanksgiving Day, 1991.

My departure was unceremonious. Chet Atkins and Lorrie Morgan joined me on the pre-dawn broadcast. So did my wife and a bevy of loyal sponsors and regular studio attendants.

Conspicuously absent were the scores of celebrities whose careers were launched by that show, visible for the first time to international music industry executives.

On the final program, video clips from earlier shows were run. I gave a few heartfelt "thank yous," and the show signed off at 7 A.M. as it had most of the time since 1963.

Joy and I didn't talk much about this ending of my career on Nashville's Channel 4. Two days later, on Sunday night, I just didn't set my clock for 4:30 A.M.

Today, I usually rise at about 9 A.M. I'm awakened by sunshine leaking into the room, not a bell ringing in my ear. I have new energy. I was more tired than I knew from all those years of burning the candle at both ends. I realize now that I was about to burn out. The quality of my life has improved immeasurably.

*   *   *

On the day before Thanksgiving, 1991, I was told that my autobiography would appear on the *New York Times* best-seller list.

I never imagined my book would be on that prestigious list, no less stay on it as long as it did.

Three years ago, I was adamant about not even wanting to write a book, insisting that no one was interested in what I had done, or with whom I had done it.

Country music fans proved me wrong and I shall be eternally grateful.

INDEX

ABC Radio Network, 61, 76
ABC Television Network, 59, 198, 240, 258
"ACE Awards Show," 219
Acuff, Roy, 13, 54, 56, 77, 93, 119, 123–124, 130, 169
Ali, Muhammad, 123–130, 219
Allen, Steve, 171, 211
Alley, Elmer, 113, 156, 166–167, 177
Allison, Joe, 219
All-Star Salute to Ralph Emery (1990 TV program), 141, 260
Ameche, Jim, 149
American Bandstand (TV program), 83
America's Town Meeting of the Air (radio program), 61–62
Anka, Paul, 81
Arnold, Eddy, 221, 254

Astaire, Fred, 34
Atkins, Chet, 230, 263
Axton, Hoyt, 169

Bagwell, Brother Windy, 262
Bare, Bobby, 217, 243
Beatles, The, 181, 240
Benkoil, Maury, 148
Benny, Jack, 12
Bess, Tootsie, 121–122
Big Bopper, The, 81
Black, Clint, 170, 253
Blackwood Brothers, 53
Boone, Pat, 62, 67
Brasfield, Rod, 241
Brasfield, Uncle Sipe, 241–242
Brimley, Wilford, 171
Brothers, Dr. Joyce, 170
Brown, Billy, 82
Brown, T. Graham, 235
Bryant, Felice and Boudleaux, 108

Bush, George, 115, 169–170, 215, 256
Butler, Carl and Pearl, 199

Calloway, Joe, 62–63
Cannon, Henry, 224, 255
Carson, Johnny, 160, 202
Carter, Mother Maybelle, 230
Carter Family, 55
Cash, Johnny, 55, 65, 147, 181–188, 196, 202, 216, 228, 232, 238, 253, 259, 261
Cash, June Carter, 55, 185, 187, 259
Cas Walker Show (radio program), 199
Cavett, Dick, 175
CBS Evening News, 160
CBS Morning News, 173
CBS Records, 83
CBS Television Network, 75, 160, 173
Clark, Dick, 83, 219
Clark, Roy, 216
Cline, Patsy, 81, 92; death of, 123, 255
Clooney, Rosemary, 240
Clower, Jerry, 262
Cobb, David, 70–76, 90
Cochran, Hank, 121
Colter, Jessi, 109, 155
Columbia Records, 83, 150, 181, 187
Copas, Cowboy, 85, 111, 123
Corbin, Paul, 165
Country Music Association, 78, 113, 130, 197, 198, 204, 209, 224–225, 234
Country Music Hall of Fame, 224–225, 229
Cramer, Floyd, 212
Cronkite, Walter, 160
Crosby, Norm, 171
Cutrer, T. Tommy, 72, 261

Damone, Vic, 171
Dancey, John, 71
Darin, Bobby, 81
Davis, Betty Jack, 96
Davis, Glen, 226, 227
Davis, Mac, 249
Davis, Skeeter, 95; marriage to Emery, 95–103, 104, 105, 107, 225
Davis Sisters, 96
Dean, Buddy, 232
Dean, Carl, 199–200, 201
Dean, Dixie, 230
Dean, Jimmy, 169–170, 212–218, 257–258
Denny, Bill, 78
Denny, Jim, 77–78
Denver, John, 210
Devine, Ott, 87
Dick, Charlie, 92
Dick Clark Show (TV program), 154
Dickens, Jimmy, 78, 93–94
Dill, Danny, 217
Dion, 81
Domino, Fats, 81
Dowden, Jane, 149
Draughon, Louis, 63–64
Driftwood, Jimmy, 82
Dudley, Dave, 249

INDEX

Dudney, Ken, 207
Duvall, Robert, 171, 182
Dylan, Bob, 182

Eden, Barbara, 171
Emery, Betty Fillmore, 38–43, 68, 96
Emery, Joy, 105, 134–146, 158–160, 189, 252, 253, 263
Emery, Kit, 137–141, 144–145
Emery, Michael, 138, 140–144
Emery, Steve, 41–43, 68, 99, 138, 139, 140–141, 207
Everly Brothers, 80

Fairchild, Morgan, 210
Farr, Jamie, 171
Federal Communications Commission, 122
Flatt, Lester, 90
Flatt and Scruggs, 65, 90
Foley, Red, 54, 62, 88, 118, 132, 221, 222, 240–243, 261
Foley, Shirley, 62–63
Fonda, Jane, 198
Ford, Tennessee Ernie, 172, 208, 225, 260–261
Foster, Fred, 55, 152, 200
Frazier, Norm "The Killer," 262–263
Friday Night Frolic, 80, 104

Garland, Judy, 34
Garner, James, 171
Garroway, Dave, 173
Gatlin, Larry, 236–237, 259
Gayle, Crystal, 92

Gibson, Don, 123
Gilley, Mickey, 154
Glaser, Tompall, 109, 155
Godfrey, Arthur, 173
Goldberg, Whoopi, 219
Gosdin, Vern, 173
Goulet, Robert, 171
Graham, Billy, 181, 182, 185
Grammy Awards, 113, 260
Grand Ole Opry, 12, 13, 55, 65, 73, 75–76, 77–80, 101, 104, 114, 117–124, 162, 165, 198, 219, 221, 222, 230, 240, 256, 258, 261
Greenwood, Lee, 210
Griscom, Tom, 170
Gulas, Nick, 61

Haggard, Marty, 194
Haggard, Merle, 92, 170, 181, 189–197, 247, 261
Hall, David, 167, 170
Hall, Steve, 177–180
Hall, Tom T., 132, 156, 162, 227–230, 245, 253
Hannah, Wayne, 71–73
Harrah, Bill, 195
Harris, Emmylou, 169
Hart, Gary, 170
Hawkins, Hawkshaw, 123
Hee-Haw (TV program), 92, 155, 216
Hensley, Hairl, 163–164
Henson, Jim, 216
Herman, Woody, 161
Hershiser, Orel, 171
Hill, Eddie, 66, 72–73
Hines, Ed, 69–70
Holland, Bob, 55

Holly, Buddy, 78
Horton, Johnny, 65, 81, 82–84, 217
Hostettler, Joe, 167
Hughes, Howard, 217
Hughes, Randy, 123
Hunley, Con, 169
Husky, Ferlin, 66, 76, 81

Ives, Burl, 229

Jackson, Alan, 253
James, Sonny, 119
Jay, Jana, 247
Jennings, Waylon, 109, 110, 121, 153, 155, 184, 239, 248
Jimmy Dean Show (TV program), 88
Jolson, Al, 34
Jones, George, 65, 86, 171, 184, 199, 248
Jones, Grandpa, 97
Jones, Shirley, 171
Jones, Tommy Lee, 171
Joplin, Janis, 152
Jordanaires, 78, 216, 226
Judds, The, 110, 112–113

Kaye, Sammy, 53
Kelly, Gene, 34
Kennedy, Jerry, 227
Kennedy, John F., 218, 242
Kent, Jimmy, 59
Key, Jimmy, 226, 227
Kilgore, Merle, 147
Killen, Buddy, 254
King, Larry, 175
King, Pee-Wee, 161

Kristofferson, Kris, 150–152, 182, 187–188, 232

Lasorda, Tommy, 171
Lawrence, Carol, 171
Lawrence Welk Show (TV program), 61
Lee, Johnny, 154
Leno, Jay, 171
Lewis, Jerry Lee, 62, 154
Lombardo, Guy, 53
Long, Hubert, 56
Lord, Bobby, 147
Louis, Joe, 12
Louvin, Charlie, 80
Louvin, Ira, 80
Luman, Bob, 239
Lynn, Loretta, 65, 92, 110, 114, 171, 245

McEntire, Reba, 171, 244–245
MacLaine, Shirley, 198
Mandrell, Barbara, 66, 154, 170–171, 179, 193, 206–211, 246, 255, 261
Mandrell, Louise, 207, 208
Martin, Grady, 212
Meade, Donna, 215, 257
Meadows, Jane, 171, 211
Mercury Records, 101, 227, 253
Miller, Roger, 106–107, 110, 216
Milsap, Ronnie, 153, 170, 245, 246
Monument Records, 152, 200
Mooney, Ralph, 87
Morgan, Bill, 72

INDEX

Morgan, George, 73, 78
Morgan, Lorrie, 73, 112, 235–237, 263
Morrow, Buddy, 53
Murray, Anne, 154, 249

Nashville Network, The (TNN), 71, 112, 157, 165–180, 193, 211, 253
Nashville Now (TV program), 112, 113–116, 137, 157, 165–180, 206, 209, 222, 256, 262
NBC Television Network, 60, 71, 76, 78, 110
Neal, Patricia, 171
Nelson, Ken, 246
Nelson, Rocky, 62
Nelson, Willie, 97, 109, 110, 152–153, 155, 171, 248
Newman, Jimmy C., 198
Newton, Wayne, 171
Nichols, Roy, 247–248
Nixon, Richard, 186
North, Ira, 18

Oak Ridge Boys, 154
Opry Almanac (TV program), 113
Opryland Productions, 165
Opryland U.S.A., 170, 178
Opry Star Spotlight (all-night radio program), 78, 83, 87–88, 90, 96, 101, 105, 107, 109, 117, 120, 125–130, 135, 147, 148, 149, 152, 159–163, 185, 208, 241
Orbison, Roy, 55
Orkin, Dick, 148

Ormes, Bill, 55
Overton, Dave, 104
Owens, Buck, 82, 83–84, 87–88, 194, 245–246, 247
Owens, Fuzzy, 191
Ozark Jubilee (TV program), 88, 240, 241

Page, Patti, 85, 169, 240
Parker, Colonel Tom, 69–70
Parton, Dolly, 55, 110, 170, 198–205, 210, 211, 249, 253
Paul Sisters, 115–116
Paycheck, Johnny, 237–238
Pearl, Minnie, 77, 119, 123, 127, 210, 218–225, 254, 255, 257
People's Choice Awards, 210
Pierce, Webb, 56, 78, 225, 249
Platters, The, 81
Pointer Sisters, 170
Pop Goes the Country (TV program), 153–157
Presley, Elvis, 54, 62, 69–70, 80, 181, 240, 250
Price, Ray, 65, 82, 87–88
Pride, Charley, 121, 154
Pruett, Jeannie, 162

Ralph Emery Show: radio program, 149–153; TV program, 110–115, 250
RCA Records, 69, 70, 82, 96, 101, 103, 153, 180, 203
Reagan, Ronald, 192
Reed, Jerry, 216
Reese, Della, 171

Reeves, Jim, 65, 76, 81, 82, 90–91, 103, 219

Reynolds, Burt, 198, 202

Rich, Charlie, 173

Richburg, John, 43–44, 55, 80

Riley, Jeannie C., 228, 247

Ritter, Dorothy, 130–131, 133

Ritter, John, 131, 211

Ritter, Tex, 109, 125–133

Robbins, Marty, 65–66, 76, 81, 86, 88–89, 90–91, 163, 226, 254

Rogers, Ginger, 34

Rogers, Kenny, 154, 170

Romero, Caesar, 211

Ronstadt, Linda, 199

"Roof the Goof" (radio program), 65

Rooney, Mickey, 170

Roosevelt, Franklin D., 8, 12–13

Rose, Fred, 55–56

Russell, Johnny, 41, 86

Ruth, Babe, 149–50

Samples, Junior, 92–94

Scott, Willard, 256

Scruggs, Earl, 90

Scully, Vin, 171

Shepherd, Cybill, 171

Sheppard, T. G., 169

Sherill, Billy, 254

Sherley, Glen, 186–187

Simpson, Jack, 60

Sinatra, Frank, 152, 240

Smith, Carl, 78

Smith, Connie, 162–163

Smith, Red, 49–50

Snow, Hank, 119–120, 188

Snow, Jimmy, 188

Stamps Quartet, 53

Stapp, Jack, 148

Stern, Bill, 45

Stevens, Ray, 230–233

Stewart, Jimmy, 171

Stoker, Gordon, 216

Stoneman Family, 122

Strait, George, 171

Streisand, Barbra, 151–152, 210

Stringbean, 97, 132, 210

Sullivan, Ed, 177

Tennessee School of Broadcasting, 43–44

Texas Playboys, 111–112

Thomas, B. J., 232

Thompson, Hank, 242

Tillis, Mel, 217, 249

Today Show (TV program), 110, 113, 256

Tomlin, Lily, 170, 219

Tonight Show (TV program), 160, 216

Tootsie's Orchid Lounge, Nashville, 121–122

Travis, Merle, 208

Travis, Randy, 110, 113, 171, 193, 244

Trent, Buck, 203

Truman, Harry, 8

Tubb, Ernest, 54, 77, 93, 96, 222

Turner, Bill, 165

Turner, Grant, 104, 127, 261–262

INDEX

Turner, Ted, 156, 157

Twitty, Conway, 65, 86–87

Tyson, Cicely, 219

U.S. Navy Recruiting Show, 143

Van Shelton, Ricky, 253

WAGG Radio (Franklin, Tenn.), 55–57

Wagoner, Porter, 127, 179, 202–204

Walker, Billy, 226–227

Walker, Ray, 226

Walters, Barbara, 202

Ward, Jackie, 162

Waugh, Irving, 114

Weaver, Dennis, 171

Welk, Lawrence, 61

West, Dottie, 154, 248, 258–260

Whitehurst, Jerry, 165

Whitley, Keith, 234–237, 249

Wilburn Brothers, 56, 92, 122

Wilcoxen, Rusty, 206

Williams, Andy, 232

Williams, Anson, 171

Williams, Don, 169

Williams, Hank, Jr., 117–118, 147, 155, 156, 239

Williams, Hank, Sr., 45–46, 54, 56, 65, 85, 117–118, 192, 213, 222–224

Williams, Roger, 232

Wills, Bob, 111–112

Wise, Chubbie, 119–120

Wiseman, Mack, 153

Wismer, Harry, 45

WLAC Radio (Nashville), 43–44, 59

WLCS Radio (Baton Rouge), 67–70

WMAK Radio (Nashville), 69–73

WNAH Radio (Nashville), 40, 48–55

Wood, Del, 55

WSIX Radio (Nashville), 59–67, 69

WSIX-TV (Nashville), 60–61

WSM Radio (Nashville), 48, 59, 66, 181, 195, 214; Emery as overnight disc jockey on, 71–159; Emery retires from, 159–163, 261

WSMV-TV (Nashville), 110–116, 147, 166

WTBS-TV (Atlanta), 156

WTPR Radio (Paris, Tenn.), 44–48, 55

Wynette, Tammy, 155, 156, 210, 248

Young, Faron, 65, 239–240, 249

Youth Incorporated, 32

Youth on Parade (radio program), 62